EVENINGS & WEEKENDS

Andrew Baulcomb

EVENINGS&
WEEKENDS

Five Years In Hamilton Music, 2006–2011

James Street North Books is an imprint of Wolsak and Wynn Publishers, Ltd.

Cover image: Mike DeAngelis
Cover and interior design: Marijke Friesen
Author's photograph: Jon Fairclough
Typeset in Sentinel
Printed by Ball Media, Brantford, Canada

The publisher gratefully acknowledges the support of the Canada Council for the Arts, the Ontario Arts Council and the Canada Book Fund.

James Street North Books
280 James Street North
Hamilton, ON
Canada L8R 2L3

Library and Archives Canada Cataloguing in Publication

Baulcomb, Andrew, author
    Evenings and weekends : five years in Hamilton music, 2006-2011 / Andrew Baulcomb.

ISBN 978-1-928088-24-0 (paperback)

1. Musicians—Ontario—Hamilton—Biography. 2. Music trade—Ontario—Hamilton—History and criticism. 3. Hamilton (Ont.)—Biography. 4. Baulcomb, Andrew. I. Title.

ML205.8.H22B38 2016   780.971352'05   C2016-904664-8

For Ciara and my family

I'm so lost, and I live just around the corner.

ARKELLS
"John Lennon," *Jackson Square* (2008)

CONTENTS

PROLOGUE

HAMILTON, ONTARIO, CANADA is a blue-collar town of five hundred thousand souls living in the shadow of the country's largest and most affluent metropolis, Toronto. It's where I was born, and I've called it home for all of my thirty-two years. For more than half those years I've wanted to be a writer, and writers in Hamilton have never starved for new material. It's a wild burg with a colourful, tumultuous, tragic history that's often stranger than fiction. As a storyteller, it's the perfect place to cut your teeth and get a little grime under your fingernails.

Hamilton smells bad in the summer and sparkles in the winter. We have steel factories in the east and a university in the west, suburbs to the south and one of the country's largest freshwater lakes to the north. We have cascading waterfalls and industrial wastelands, bright young students and desperate vagabonds. The city has maintained a long, sordid relationship with hard drugs, motorcycle gangs and organized crime, but it's also known as a haven for artists, innovators and entrepreneurs.

In the lower city, the part that lies beneath the Niagara Escarpment, the houses are tall and narrow, and built with solid red bricks and vinyl siding. They're tight-knit, like the people who occupy them. On top of the Escarpment, an area we refer to as "the Mountain," the lots are a little wider and the people a little more well to do. For older generations, enemy territory in

1

Hamilton extends east or west beyond James Street – a major thoroughfare that slices through the heart of the city. For younger Hamiltonians, this cultural divide can also involve the upper and lower city.

Downtown Hamilton was a wonderful place to live and work during the middle of the twentieth century. It was full of department stores, office towers, transit lines and movie theatres with thousand-seat auditoriums running up and down King Street. Gore Park, a beautiful pedestrian promenade flanked by shops and restaurants, was the envy of the country.

But by the time my generation inherited the downtown core in the early 2000s, Eaton's, Kresge's and other department stores had skipped town. The grand old theatres had been shuttered or condemned. The streetcar tracks had been ripped out of the ground. There were few pedestrians and fewer concerts, and none of the hip art galleries and boutiques that now pepper the core. There was no money and no plan. Traffic flowed in one direction and all roads led to the city limits. Some locals never left – those who'd built a life in the core; they still remembered better times. They loved their fish markets and their hockey rinks and their corner delis and their lovely old neighbours with faded Portuguese and Italian flags draped over concrete stoops, swaying in the breeze. They weren't going anywhere.

• • •

During the dawn of the Jazz Age in the late 1910s and early 1920s, temperance movements in Canada and the United States created a black market bootlegging ring around the Great Lakes. The north end of the city, the docklands, became a rowdy stopover for budding criminals ferrying homemade booze throughout the region. Rocco Perri, a Hamilton-based gangster

2

and rum-runner originally from Calabria, Italy, became known as "King of the Bootleggers" and "Canada's Al Capone." Hamilton's penchant for illegal activity, coupled with the emergence of large steel mills and other factories farther east along the lakeshore, helped fuel our long-standing love affair with hard-driving music for hard-living, hard-drinking people. Rock and roll may as well have been forged on the waterfront.

By the middle of the century, Hamilton had earned a reputation as a thriving musical hub. Ronnie Hawkins, a swagger-filled singer from rural Arkansas, came to Hamilton in 1958 and used the Grange Tavern as one of his early proving grounds. Long before filming *The Last Waltz*, the Band tested their mettle as one of Hawkins's early backing bands, performing regularly in Hamilton's saloons and ballrooms before winning the affection of Bob Dylan. Richard Newell, a local harmonica player better known as King Biscuit Boy, shared stages with the likes of Muddy Waters and Janis Joplin. John Ellison, a West Virginia blues-rocker famous for the hit "Some Kind of Wonderful," moved here in 1974 and never left. British bluesman Long John Baldry also made a home in the area for many years. Area groups such as Lighthouse, which featured Hamilton-born Skip Prokop, and Crowbar, with their 1971 monster hit "Oh What A Feeling," carried the city's reputation for anthemic, blues-driven rock and roll well into the 1970s.

By the end of the 1970s, punk rock had taken over. In fact, Canadian authors Sam Sutherland and Liz Worth argue the genre owes as much to Hamilton as it does New York, London or Los Angeles. "The members of Teenage Head are real-life rock soldiers," Sutherland writes in *Perfect Youth*, his fantastic retrospective of early Canadian punk. "They formed in Hamilton, Ontario, in 1975. They drew from the same set of proto-punk influences as the Ramones. They started to play short, atavistic rock and roll in 1976, before they ever heard the word 'punk' or a note played by the Sex Pistols." Along with Teenage Head, bands such as Simply Saucer and Forgotten Rebels cemented Hamilton's punk reputation during the late-1970s and early 1980s. Frankie "Venom" Kerr, lead singer of Teenage Head, died in 2008 following a lifetime of substance abuse and hard living. But his shadow looms large over Hamilton's music community to this day.

During the mid-1990s, Hamilton rock groups Junkhouse and the Killjoys joined Sloan, the Tragically Hip, Change of Heart, Our Lady Peace and Alanis Morissette in Canada's alternative music boom. Daniel Lanois, who had already produced landmark records from U2, Peter Gabriel and Robbie Robertson, launched a music career of his own on the strength of the albums *Acadie* and *For the Beauty of Wynona*. Sonic Unyon, an upstart indie label based in the downtown core, helped launch or revive the careers of Treble Charger, Hayden and Thrush Hermit, and issued records from local bands such as SIANspheric and Tristan Psionic. It was all fun to watch and listen to and absorb, but it never really belonged to my crew.

• • •

My generation was asked to get comfortable with less, and to do it in a hurry. We had gone off to university in record numbers, with the promise of careers and comfort at the other end, only to graduate and enter the workforce just as the bottom fell out of the global economy. Many of us were tens of thousands of dollars in debt before we even had a full-time job. Young people with engineering and commerce degrees from prestigious Canadian universities began working as bartenders and stock clerks. Student loans became impossible to pay back. Home ownership slipped out of reach – not just in Hamilton but major Canadian cities from Halifax to Vancouver. For many of us, the prospect of taking on a mortgage, driving two cars, having two kids, collecting a pension and retiring at sixty – the dream and the legacy of the baby boom – was suddenly more fantasy than reality. We were a generation of renters and boomerang basement-dwellers. We were underemployed, single and running around the city much longer than we should have been. We had more free time and restless energy than we knew what to do with.

In the midst of this economic turmoil, music and culture in Hamilton began to flourish. People looked inward – not to Toronto or Montréal or New York – to create something special that reflected our unique time and place in the world. The music was still tough and tenacious, but in many cases, also defiantly original. People started going downtown again. New independent businesses opened on long-abandoned street corners. Concert halls and underground clubs suddenly had lines snaking around full city blocks. I was fortunate to witness the birth of a whole new cultural movement first-hand.

I began writing the book that became *Evenings & Weekends* in 2011, while working as a newspaper reporter at *Niagara This Week*. During that period, I spent my evenings and weekends interviewing bands and hammering out copy, driven by the sheer knowledge that something special had taken place in my own backyard during the previous five years. More than anything, I wanted to capture the tempo of the times – the highs and the lows, the ugly, unfiltered truth. Young Rival drummer Noah Fralick gave the first interview for this book on August 3, 2011. Max Kerman, lead singer of Arkells and a former classmate at McMaster University, sat down with me for the second and third interviews in October. That's when I knew it was really going to work.

More than anything, this is a book about being in the right place at the right time. Sharing a common experience. Meeting like-minded people. Experimenting and taking chances. Feeling the need to create and consume and binge and purge with no need for external validation or fear of making a mistake. Like Manchester in the late 1980s or Seattle in the early 1990s, the Hamilton of my twenties was one of those unique and powerful scenes that appear in the unlikeliest of places. Those who are lucky enough to experience those times for themselves never forget them.

These are the stories of Juno Award winners and after-hours downtown DJs; of folk-rock troubadours and electronic music pioneers; of idealistic punks and gritty hip-hop heads; of venue owners, reporters, radio hosts, students, burnouts, girlfriends, boyfriends and downright weirdos – all bound by a desire to escape the mundane and devote their lives to the pursuit of music and art in Hamilton, at a time when everyone else was saying the city was dead. And every single word of it is true.

2009

I BEGAN 2006 AS THE SENIOR EDITOR at a magazine called *andy*, the arts section of the *Silhouette*, McMaster's student newspaper. I had been hired the previous year to replace an outgoing staffer. I had to drop a class in order to take on the extra workload, but the *Silhouette* was worth it. The office was alive and teeming with energy. It felt like a real newsroom, even though none of us had ever set foot in one. It was exactly what I'd been looking for in a university experience. I was twenty-one years old.

I immediately fell in love with the late nights, long production runs and free records that came with the position. Before long, I spent more time at the *Silhouette* than in my own home. Every Wednesday, our staff of fifteen would assemble to begin work on Thursday's edition. Our office was little more than a glorified garage in the basement of McMaster's Student Centre. It had white brick walls, garish fluorescent lighting, no windows and only one entrance in and out. We had a break room in the back corner with lumpy couches and an old fridge, and a tiny photo-editing suite located beside it. Officially, we were paid for fifteen hours of work per week. Off the books, half the newsroom practically lived in that office. At any given hour of the day, the *Silhouette* was a functioning clubhouse, lunchroom, pub, library and youth hostel – and occasionally, a bedroom for two.

We'd sip student union coffee, eat chips and candy bars, and chat about movies and records while laying out and proofing our Thursday edition. Editors would fight over the office stereo. Someone would take a pizza order. Senior staff would argue over headlines and ledes. Photo editors would argue over crops and colour levels. Cigarette smokers would visit the arts quad for a break, and the pot smokers would follow soon afterward. Every once in a while, if the office was quiet and our work was nearly finished, someone would crack open a warm beer or pour an ounce of whisky. I was living the dream.

• • •

When I started writing for the paper as a volunteer several years prior, Tim Robinson – an old family friend and older-brother figure who initially brought me into the fold – was senior editor of *andy*. A local musician and budding DJ named Simon Toye served as music editor. I had a buzz cut, Simon had a shaggy mop of brown hair; I wore plain wool sweaters and blue jeans, Simon wore Who T-shirts and skinny black trousers; I collected CDs, Simon collected vinyl records. We should have functioned like oil and water, but it was a perfect fit from the start. Both of us were born and raised in Hamilton – Simon in the east, myself in the west. We both played guitar, and we both had a fondness for Canadian indie rock and outsider art.

2006

During my first semester at McMaster in the fall of 2003, I saw an advertisement for Sloan on the back of the *Silhouette* on a Friday afternoon and nearly dropped the paper. One of my favourite bands from high school was booked to play at the largest bar on campus. I had only completed a handful of CD reviews up to that point, but I was determined to land the story. The only problem was that Simon already had the interview.

I jogged over to meet Tim at a pub in nearby Westdale Village and plead my case. Tim told me he'd speak to Simon, but there was no guarantee. I walked home dejected. I opened my email later that night and had a new message from Simon: "hey andrew, spoke to timmer. the sloan interview is yours. have fun."

One week later, I was seated on a leather couch in the McMaster Student Centre opposite Sloan guitarist Patrick Pentland. The very same Patrick Pentland I had grown up watching on Much-Music. Lead singer of "Money City Maniacs," "Losing California" and "The Good in Everyone." He was wearing a sun-kissed AC/DC baseball cap; his blue jeans were ratty and road-worn. He watched me from behind a pair of thin, round glasses and smiled politely.

I pushed "record" on a borrowed cassette player and ran a detailed list of questions. The interview went well and I was feeling confident. We talked about the band's early days in Halifax and their gradual move to Toronto. We talked about old records and dissected their latest offering, the streamlined and polarizing *Action Pact*. We had a good rapport going. I could see Pentland begin to relax and really open up. He invited me to watch the band's soundcheck after the interview was finished. I was in.

Then I committed a cardinal sin. A rookie mistake I still cringe over. I pulled their latest record from my backpack and asked Pentland for his autograph. He paused, smiled and obliged. I was instantly mortified. Reporters don't ask for autographs.

EVENINGS & WEEKENDS

It was a huge lapse in judgment, but I'm glad I did it. In music journalism, the line between fandom and professionalism has always been somewhat blurry, and I've crossed it many times. When I look at my copy of *Action Pact*, with Pentland's signature scrawled across the cover, I always grin. I was still invited to soundcheck.

Over time, Simon assigned me more music features. I interviewed Death From Above 1979, the Stills, Bedouin Soundclash, Joel Plaskett, Peter Elkas, controller.controller and Sam Roberts, as well as many local bands with a connection to McMaster. I filed carefully typed eight-hundred-word features for the arts section after each interview. It was a powerful addiction – seeing my byline in the paper sent a shot of adrenaline racing up my spine.

It was Simon who first introduced me to Max Kerman – a gangly political science student and aspiring singer-songwriter. He was a regular visitor to the paper's cramped basement office – promoting shows and handing out flyers, or talking excitedly to anyone who'd listen about his latest batch of songs. Two years my junior, Kerman was only a few years away from winning his first Juno Award as the lead singer of one of Canada's most successful rock bands, Arkells. But at the time, we were both still navigating the ups and downs of life on campus. Kerman soon introduced me to his band, Charlemagne. He brought me a copy of their brand new demo, *The Broken Tapes*, later that year.

• • •

Not long after the start of the 2006 winter semester, three friends from the *Silhouette* and I decided to rent a car and drive to New York City. The trip was a last-minute impulse. Among other things, we wanted to see CBGB, the legendary Bowery punk rock institution, before it closed forever. Only Terris Taylor, a fellow arts editor at the paper, had been to New York before and he was eager to return. Chris Arnett – another *Silhouette* staffer, and a future roommate and groomsman at my wedding – was also along for the ride. Pat Moore, a friend and stringer at the paper who seemingly never removed his old newsboy cap, rounded out our crew.

I was tingling with excitement. We all were. Brooklyn hip-hop. Bowery punk rock. Chinatown takeout. Greenwich Village guitar shops. All-night clubs in the East Village. All-night drinking in our hotel room. Unpredictable madness. We were set to leave on the Tuesday morning of our annual reading week vacation. I couldn't wait.

At the US border, we stopped for American money, warm beer and tiny foil bags filled with salty chips or sugar-coated berries. Terris loaded a case of Miller High Life into the trunk and peeled the cellophane wrapping on a carton of Camel cigarettes. We all took a single pack. I tucked mine into the breast pocket of my black winter jacket. We sailed over the Peace Bridge into downtown Buffalo and rocketed eastward. I was in the driver's seat, Pat to my right, Terris and Chris in the back.

By nightfall, as we approached the Lincoln Tunnel from New Jersey, I saw the Manhattan skyline for the first time. Terris was driving now. I craned my neck from the back seat to get a better view. Towering columns of glass and steel stretched across the horizon from north to south. Midtown and the Financial District twinkled against the black, cloudless sky. I couldn't see the beginning or the end of the island. A dozen lanes of traffic slowly merged into one tiny stream, and suddenly we were in the tunnel and crossing under the Hudson River. Overhead lights whizzed past as we zipped through the narrow tube, ready to explode into the city. The stereo was silent. Everyone was tense.

Suddenly, we were in the belly of the beast. It was pure chaos – horns blaring and traffic rushing in all directions. Huge swarms of pedestrians at every corner. Nowhere to stop and no time to think. Terris guided the car onto West 30th Street. Everyone remained quiet and focused. We swung north onto Sixth Avenue and nearly ploughed the car into a row of parked taxis while gawking at passing landmarks. We pushed north toward our hotel on West 48th.

Two days later, on a darkened avenue near Washington Square Park, we tiptoed around NYU students and Chinese tourists while searching for weed. Everyone was on high alert during the hunt. Foreign city. Foreign laws. Unfamiliar territory. A year earlier, Broken Social Scene producer David Newfeld had been arrested by four undercover police officers after buying weed on Lexington Avenue. Toronto music journalist Stuart Berman revisited the scene in his history of the band, *This Book Is Broken*: "Thinking they were muggers, Newfeld pushed one of the officers away; in return, he received several bruised ribs, two black eyes, a bloodied face…and a charge of resisting arrest."

Just after ten p.m., we passed a lone figure on the sidewalk wearing a Yankees baseball cap and a thick black hoodie. His hands were stuffed into a navy blue down-filled jacket, zipped up to his neck. I caught his eyes as we were passing.

"Whatchu need?"

"Weed," Pat coughed out. We kept walking. I glanced back at Terris. He was smirking.

"Follow me," the dealer offered.

Pat pivoted and started jogging in the opposite direction. He caught up to the dealer and kept pace with strong, even steps. Pat pulled his newsboy cap low over his eyes. Our group followed from half a block away. Hands were shaken. Money and product were exchanged. I held my breath and braced for a police

14

takedown. I pictured drugs and money falling into the gutter, heads slammed up against the hood of an unmarked police car. Passports seized. Car impounded. Lives ruined. Reputations enhanced. With a quick nod, the dealer crossed the street and disappeared behind a brick apartment building. He never once broke stride and didn't look back.

We bar-hopped around the East Village and the Lower East Side for the rest of the night. At 2A on Avenue A, Terris convinced a pair of middle-aged women that we were in a garage rock band from Montréal. The women, clad in black leather jackets and animal-print leggings, proceeded to call him "Tennis" for the rest of the night, cackling each time he corrected them. At Max Fish on Orchard Street, we sipped from tall cans of Pabst Blue Ribbon and watched locals shoot pool at the back of the crowded bar, trying to blend in and failing miserably. Chris bought a bottle of sake at a corner bodega and we took turns hauling from the paper bag in a darkened alcove. We took a taxi uptown well after last call and got off at 48th and 8th, where a man showed us Polaroid photos of a young woman's chest covered in semen and asked if we wanted to buy them. We politely declined.

Back in the hotel room, we stripped down to our underwear and stuffed towels under the bathroom door before turning on the shower. Terris leaned against the sink and sparked a pair of tight, fat joints. We passed the weed and giggled, letting the pink-tiled room fill with steam and smoke.

On our last day in the city, during an afternoon walk along the Bowery, we finally came upon our destination, CBGB – its unmistakable red and white awning hovering over the doorway, the number "315" still the most famous address on the strip. In decades past, the club served as a home base for the likes of the Ramones, Television, Blondie, the Dead Boys, Cro-Mags, Agnostic Front and Madball. It was a proving ground for multiple generations of NYC punk and hardcore. Teenage Head played on this notoriously decrepit stage during the late 1970s. So did the Viletones, the Diodes and other first-wave Canadian punk bands from our own backyard. We had arrived less than a year before the original bar was to be shuttered forever and we were eager to take a peek inside.

After touring the dim venue – caked in three decades of graffiti, vomit, spit, blood and Bowery grime – we stepped back into the chilly afternoon and flagged down a pedestrian for a photo. We needed a group shot in front of CBGB before it closed forever. I handed my camera to the photographer, a young woman in her early twenties, and everyone smiled. The young woman paused and scrunched up her face.

"Why do you want a photo in front of this shithole?"

"Uhh, well, during the 1970s there was a pivotal scene here that…"

Click.

The young woman took three quick steps and placed the camera back in my hand. The resulting photo is a perfect representation of her confounded expression – slightly crooked, slightly out of focus. Half of us looking down at the sidewalk, the other half forcing awkward grins. The photographer was off as quickly as she'd arrived, walking down the block at a rapid clip, leather boots clapping on the concrete. I stuffed the camera inside my jacket pocket and we took off in the opposite direction. Patti Smith closed the club for good later that year. John Varvatos, a high-end menswear purveyor, now occupies the tiny space at 315 Bowery, surrounded by a Chase Bank outlet and several independent shops. The red and white awning is long gone.

• • •

The *Silhouette* was my gateway into everything. I gained confidence as a writer and built a small portfolio. I interviewed every band on campus and many more that travelled to Hamilton for shows. My collection of albums began to grow and my tastes expanded with it, and I started going to more local concerts and became a regular at downtown clubs such as the Casbah and the Underground.

It was at the latter where I met Brodie Schwendiman – a former teacher turned entrepreneur and talent buyer. We had first crossed paths in the fall of 2002, during my last year at Westdale Secondary School. At the time, I was playing in a strange math-punk-garage band known as the Langston Heights. Schwendiman was booking us to play regular gigs at his brand new venue, the Underground, at 41 Catharine Street North. Every member of our group was underage. Schwendiman used to stuff us into a stall in the men's washroom when cops on the neighbourhood beat would swing into the basement club for an unexpected visit. We would perform alongside local bands such as the Ride Theory, Keyser Soze, the Marble Index and Red Echo – featuring future Juno Award–winner Tomi Swick – and occasionally earn a coveted opening slot when a touring band came to town.

The Langston Heights recorded one album that was lost to a computer crash, save a few rough demos. We officially called it quits in 2003, when university pulled us in different directions. But the Underground, a venue that gave many local musicians their start, would stand as one of Hamilton's most crucial live music hubs during the mid to late 2000s.

Born June 7, 1974, William "Brodie" Schwendiman spent the first few years of his life playing sports and attending school in east Hamilton, before his family relocated to the sleepy community of Dundas on the west side of the city.

"I wasn't a music person so much in my youth. I liked music, and I was conscious of what to put on our basketball team warm-up tape, but that was about it," says Schwendiman. He speaks slowly and softly, carefully considering each word. It's late 2012, and I've been invited into the Casbah – Schwendiman's current base of operations – to chat privately with the quiet and unassuming thirty-eight-year-old. The bar is dark and calm, illuminated only by a handful of tea lights and small decorative lamps. This is his home turf. His kingdom. He's comfortable here and it shows.

"It was a lot of AC/DC, but it got weird near the end. That was around the time that Lollapalooza was breaking as a festival, and Nirvana was entering the mainstream consciousness. A little bit of that kind of stuff ended up on our tape as well. I remember I had a Ministry song, an industrial band, and I think it scared the teachers. They weren't really sure what to make of it."

After graduating from Parkside High School, he entered McMaster University and pursued a bachelor's degree in kinesiology. He later earned a master's degree in education from D'Youville College in Buffalo. At that point, the ambitious twentysomething had dreams of becoming an elementary school teacher with the Hamilton public school board, and spent his first eighteen months after graduation on the supply list while searching for full-time work at area schools. All the while, Schwendiman was gaining more and more experience booking local concerts on the side. It wasn't long before he switched focus.

"I had turned down a few supply teaching jobs in a row, and that kind of bumps you down to the bottom of the list. I wasn't really thinking about supply teaching anymore . . . I took some part-time jobs here and there, but living by myself in a downtown bachelor apartment wasn't too expensive at the time." In the months leading up to the Underground's grand opening in

September 2002, Schwendiman was living in a modest apartment on Park Street, behind city hall.

As live music became more of a full-time focus, Schwendiman gained a reputation around Hamilton for booking interesting, slightly off-kilter talent into sputtering downtown clubs such as the Raven and the Hudson – recruiting groups such as Russian Futurists, Holding Pattern, the Dinner is Ruined and a wide selection of punk, hardcore and math rock bands from across Southern Ontario, New York and New England.

"The Underground didn't happen because I pursued it. It happened because it was put in my lap," he admits. "The Raven had closed in May of that year, and it was a closure that was abrupt. I had a dozen shows or so that were sort of committed to happening, and I no longer had a room to do them in."

Throughout the summer of 2002, pre-booked shows were hastily transferred to alternative venues such as the Corktown Tavern on Young Street, the short-lived Home nightclub on Ferguson Avenue North, Sonic Unyon on Wilson Street and even Schwendiman's tiny apartment on Park Street. He struggled to rebook several months' worth of concerts and follow through on commitments, and never dropped a gig.

As connections with area booking agents solidified – thanks in large part to his successful summer scramble – word began circulating that the old Texas Border nightclub on King William Street was looking to open a new rock venue in their basement. Ian Wallace, a former advertising representative with *View* magazine, referred the young talent buyer to the club's owners and facilitated their first introduction. Schwendiman's initial impressions of the dingy basement were mixed, but he knew right away the space had potential.

"I came in to meet the owners, and there was this gutted, empty basement. I started to envision in my mind how it needed to change to become a functional rock club," he recalls. "It was just a brownish-grey cement slab. There was no stage. There was a dance floor where they used to have a dance club. There was a whole bunch of debris and garbage and tossed-off equipment in the back corner, but there was a bar already built and a fridge in place."

Schwendiman asked for thirty thousand dollars from the upstairs Texas Border to turn the basement into a revitalized rock club, with three-quarters of the money going into a brand new PA system. The remaining funds were used to build a large plywood stage and DJ booth. By September 2002, the Underground was just about ready to crack open the front doors for the first time. Schwendiman was hired as the Underground's talent buyer and was paid relative to the success of his new enterprise. There was no salary and no health benefits, and his wage stemmed from "consulting percentages based on success" – the same system he had operated under at the Raven. Still, he was young, excited and highly motivated.

Popular local groups such as the Marble Index, Keyser Soze, Red Echo, warsawpack, Flux AD, Hoosier Poet and the Ride Theory soon became regular performers at the new venue.

"The Underground became big fast, because Brodie did a great job of making it. I mean, it was an underground space, so it always kind of had that cavern-y thing to it," says James Tennant, long-time program director at McMaster University's 93.3 CFMU radio. "And there were some great bands at the time. That, actually, was when warsawpack and Flux [featuring a young Julie Fader] were both still around, and both big bands. They were the two bands you could count on to fill a room. No question."

"Brodie was the first guy on the block, and he was always the king. He's always felt, a little bit, like everybody's out to *get him,*" adds *Hamilton Spectator* music editor Graham Rocking-ham, lowering his voice for the last two words before laughing. "He was the only live venue getting original music seven nights a week. That's what he was doing, and it was remarkable. But that was it. I mean, you had cover bands in the suburbs, you had cover bands in some other places, you had some country and western, and you had some dive action going on. It was not great."

Without the Underground, Young Rival – one of the most in-fluential and popular groups in Hamilton during the late 2000s – would not have become a true working band. Guitarist and singer Aron D'Alesio and drummer Noah Fralick followed a path together to Young Rival that started with a garage rock outfit called the Ride Theory. During the early 2000s, the Underground was their office, their factory floor. It was a comfortable setting to test new ideas or simply punch the clock and blast through old standards. The club, and Schwendiman, instilled an early blue-collar ethos that has guided the band for more than a decade. Show up. Shut up. Go to work and go hard. It's served them well over the years.

. . .

I've seen Young Rival in one form or another more times than any other band, and they still blow my hair back each and every time. They are the greatest local rock and roll band of my gen-eration. They are my Teenage Head. The three longest serving members – D'Alesio, Fralick and bassist John Smith – are some of the most influential, creative and genuinely enthusiastic members of Hamilton's local music scene.

Back in high school, D'Alesio was far and away the best lead guitarist I had ever met. He could rip lightning-fast blues solos drenched in reverb all over the neck while I was still mastering the pentatonic scale. He had a vintage goldtop Gibson Les Paul that was the envy of all our guitar-playing peers, and sang with a rich voice that landed somewhere between the Kinks' Ray Davies and John Lennon on codeine. D'Alesio was effortlessly cool in a manner that can't be faked.

Fralick, a gifted drummer, was smart, charming and funny, and at eighteen displayed a passion for live music that far exceeded any of our shaky teenage ambitions. Fralick was also driven. He wanted the Ride Theory to become a hardcore touring band – to embrace the lifestyle and embody the myth. He desperately wanted a record contract and longed to play bigger shows in hallowed halls all over the continent. He wanted it all.

A promising student with an interest in music, history and political science, Fralick was finishing off his last year at Westdale Secondary School when he was approached by D'Alesio – an old friend from his east-end neighbourhood – about playing together. D'Alesio wanted to start a new band that paid homage to the likes of Led Zeppelin, the Kinks, the Zombies and the Everly Brothers.

During the spring of 2002, the band evolved to include Chris "Sauce" Jankus on bass and D'Alesio's cousin Kyle Kuchmey on rhythm guitar. That summer, Fralick and his bandmates devoted their full energies toward perfecting a brash mixture of Detroit garage rock, British blues and California surf.

Together in the Ride Theory, they looked unstoppable. The first time I saw the band perform live, during a student-run concert in the Westdale Secondary School cafeteria, I couldn't wrap my head around what was happening on stage. *How could anyone our age be this good?* As a guitarist and budding songwriter, I wasn't even in the same league. It was around this time that abandoning music for writing began to look attractive.

I recall sitting in a west-end basement with the other members of my own band, the Langston Heights, when the Ride Theory came over with a copy of their brand new CD, *Hamilton*. We were slated to play a show with them at the Underground in December, and both bands were eager to swap recordings and gauge each other's new sounds prior to the concert. We played our demo first – a rough recording captured in our drummer's garage, featuring five of our best tracks performed at the outer limits of our capabilities.

Then D'Alesio switched CDs and hit play on his band's latest offering. I was immediately embarrassed and sunk into the couch, staring at the floor. If we were decent, they were untouchable. Everyone in the room knew it, especially the members of the Ride Theory. It was only a matter of time before the rest of the city found out, too. Remarkably, they almost didn't even exist.

"It is almost a fluke that Aron and I met," says Fralick, reflecting on his earliest days behind the drum kit with the Ride Theory. "It's almost a fluke that Aron and I started a band."

It's pouring rain out, but we're comfortable inside his apartment on Stanley Avenue. Two chairs sit opposite a slim coffee table, flanked by a turntable, piles of records and books and old music equipment. There isn't a television in sight.

"Ice?"

Fralick is peering out from the kitchen and shaking a small glass tumbler, which he promptly fills with three lopsided cubes. A copy of Doug Carter's *Cool Fool: Blues Rockin' in the Hammer* sits unopened on the coffee table. Nearly a decade after starting his own artistic journey, he looks back on those early days with great fondness.

"You come storming out of the gates," says Fralick, discussing the band's attitude during the pre–Young Rival days. "You're a young band, and you just want to play these fast songs where you feel like you're just blowing people away. If you see some band that plays before you and you're slightly intimidated, you get cocky about it and you're like, 'we're going to fucking destroy them'...we were so confident, and I think we still are."

Kuchmey offers no hesitation when discussing the same subject.

"It wasn't really 'us better than them,' it was more, 'we know exactly what we're doing here, and let's just do it.' We had a couple of experiences under our belt where we did just that, and those nights were a lot of fun and we got tons of good feedback," says Kuchmey. "We were still really young at that point, and really hadn't seen too much of what was out there. As far as we knew, we hadn't seen anything better than what we were able to do yet, except if we went to a huge concert."

Not everyone shared the band's enthusiasm. Brodie Schwendiman was on the judging panel at an early showcase at the Casbah, and while dazzled with the band's technical skill, he was not immediately won over by the mod-rock revivalism.

"I did feel that they were the best band, as far as what they were executing. But I made a choice based on originality. Even to this day, there are components of what they play that's not original-sounding music. It's retro-style music that's been done before," says Schwendiman.

Even though Schwendiman voted for a different band that night, the gig provided him with a solid first look at the Ride Theory – a band that would help solidify the Underground's musical reputation in the months and years ahead. "How young they were, executing the music as well as they did, was really eye opening. You wouldn't be able to forget them once you saw them for the first time."

"Going to see the Ride Theory, they were so young. I told them, 'your ties are too wide for the music you're playing,'" says

24

Graham Rockingham. "Then you saw them opening for the Yardbirds at the Corktown. Then you saw the tour schedule and the music videos. It all started happening."

In 2005, with Smith having replaced Jankus on bass, the Ride Theory released their second full-length record, *In This City*, on Toronto's Sunny Lane Records. The disc represented a big step forward in sound and scope. D'Alesio never sounded better as lead guitarist, but the band's days of wild soloing and snappy riffs were already beginning to wane.

Uptempo songs such as "Motel Woman" and "I'm on Board" carried the garage rock torch forward, but it was a much more delicate tune called "My Girl June" that tapped into a different side of the 1960s. The song's acoustic guitars, light brushes on the drums and soft vocal harmonies produced a sound much closer to the Carpenters than the Kinks. Long-time fans could already sense the band moving in this direction. At live shows, towering stacks and thundering drums were slowly replaced with a more pared-down backline. D'Alesio began swapping his roaring Les Paul for single-coil guitars that were more bright and sparkly – first a cherry-red Telecaster and a sunburst Stratocaster, then a black-and-white Danelectro with lipstick pickups he still plays to this day.

In February 2006, Fralick told the Queen's University *Journal* the band felt they had matured as songwriters and performers: "Over the last year or so, [D'Alesio and Kuchmey] have undertaken new forms of songwriting," Fralick explained. "It's ... more of a crafting than just a sort of 'jamming and coming up with an idea.' We found [our time constraints] really beneficial for making well-crafted songs, as opposed to just hook-based songs that just sound good as we play them."

• • •

Alexisonfire's *Crisis* was released in August 2006 on Distort Records. It was a revelation in Canadian punk: brutal and unforgiving, yet restrained and introspective.

I would blast *Crisis* in the *Silhouette*'s basement office during late-night writing sessions fuelled by stale doughnuts and black coffee, banking stories for upcoming issues. I would stare at the grim album cover, featuring a pair of frostbitten hands photographed after the devastating winter storm of 1977, and pore over the black-and-white map of Southern Ontario in the album's inset – St. Catharines and Buffalo on the eastern edge of the map, Hamilton on the west – mystified by the band's interest in local history. I was captivated by their ability to merge these local stories with those from around the world, weaving in complex themes of isolation, frustration, despair, angst and fear. The music was relatable on so many levels. Top to bottom, it was my favourite album of the year.

On warm summer nights, my friend Mike Tufts and I would cruise out to Gage Park on the east side of the city in his mother's sedan with the windows rolled down. If we hit the lights at the right time, we could ride the "green wave" for eight kilometres, from our homes in Westdale Village all the way down to the Delta without stopping. Mike would slide *Crisis* into the car's CD player and light a cigarette as we rounded onto Main Street, in front of Westdale Secondary School. The opening blast of "Drunks, Lovers, Sinners and Saints" would echo down Longwood Road as he hit the gas coming out of the turn.

By the time *Crisis* was released, George Pettit, lead singer of Alexisonfire, had become my favourite frontman in Canadian music. Pettit had a few tattoos peeking out from under his sleeves, but often dressed in a plain T-shirt, high-top Chuck Taylors and blue jeans. He lacked the bold style and loud affectations that so often define our understanding of "punk," which I found refreshing. Still, he was cut from the same cloth. His stage presence was menacing. He often sported fresh stitches, bruises or chipped front teeth. He spat water and beer into the crowd and made a habit of diving over security and straight into the pit. His voice was guttural. It was *pained*. In contrast to bandmate and co-lead vocalist Dallas Green (now of City and Colour fame), Pettit could never win over critics and casual fans simply by stepping up to a microphone and projecting with angelic clarity. It took a lot more convincing. It took a lot more muscle. In some strange way, Pettit represented everything I loved about Hamilton. The classic underdog, he was the neighbourhood boxer fighting for recognition while everyone else is busy saying the kid next door is the greatest of all time. He was that kind of contender.

It wasn't until years later that I learned he had been living in Hamilton all along. Not only living here, but quietly producing some of his band's biggest albums on a plot of land on the rural outskirts of the city. If St. Catharines gave Alexis a crucial early foothold in the Canadian music industry, Hamilton pulled them one step closer to the top of the mountain.

At the Mulberry Coffeehouse in May 2012, Pettit is much more subdued than his onstage persona would suggest. As we settle into a booth near the back of the café, I watch as the twenty-nine-year-old stares into a cup of black coffee from underneath a brand new Toronto Blue Jays cap pulled low over his eyes. Alexisonfire has been dead for nearly a year, and his future in music remains uncertain. Pettit is a family man now, with a wife and young son, living in an orderly home on a quiet residential street on the Mountain. I agree not to discuss the band's breakup, and the conversation quickly shifts into our shared interests – punk rock, the *Crisis* record, CFL football and the strange appeal of our city.

EVENINGS & WEEKENDS

In 2003, Pettit moved from the rural beach town of Grimsby, Ontario, into a two-bedroom apartment on Emerald Street South, just east of downtown Hamilton. His melody-driven posthardcore band had gained a surprising number of fans, and Alexisonfire's 2002 self-titled debut became a staple on MuchMusic thanks to a string of humorous and visually arresting videos for "Pulmonary Archery," "Waterwings" and "Counterparts and Number Them." Yet even as the band's career took off, Pettit resisted the urge to pack up and move to Toronto.

"Toronto was where the big pull was. Everybody was going to move there anyway, and it would have made a lot more sense to live there. But I think I was on some sort of weird Queen Street–hating vibe," recalls Pettit. "And I always genuinely loved Hamilton. I had been coming here since I was a little kid, and coming to shows here since I was thirteen or something like that. It just made sense."

When the time came to record the sophomore Alexis record, the band enlisted the help of Stoney Creek producer Julius "Juice" Butty, who managed Silo Studios on a piece of land not far from the Hamilton Gun Club, near the city's southeastern edge. The sessions for what became the band's second record, 2004's *Watch Out!*, took place there, in a cramped, blacked-out studio with Butty at the helm.

"He had recorded two Grimsby bands that we knew, and he was just this under-the-radar kind of guy," says Pettit. "He's got this little dark room where he's basically boarded off the windows and it has this zany pattern on the walls ... it was always very tight. I remember opening the doors and the sunlight would hit you right in the eyes on this farm."

During the Silo sessions in Hamilton, Butty expanded the band's sound beyond its punk and math rock roots, showcased on *Alexisonfire*, to include more atmospheric sounds, intricate

28

compositions and heavier tones – the latter becoming a crucial component of both *Watch Out!* and *Crisis*. According to Pettit, working at Silo instead of a big-budget Toronto studio was a revelation for the band. Most importantly, it provided the necessary factors for artistic reinvention – time and space. Sonically complex, high-concept songs such as "No Transitory," "Control," "It Was Fear of Myself That Made Me Odd" and "Happiness By The Kilowatt" were all fine-tuned under these ideal conditions.

"[Julius] really produced the songs," recalls Pettit. "We would write a song and have it all recorded, and then he'd just cut and paste something and was like, 'I want you to hear this.' He'd shift stuff around, move a chorus, add a second chorus, and then we'd listen to it and be like, 'yeah, that's the song.' We'd end up re-recording it the way it was supposed to be. He was very, very smart and had a great ear for it."

Following a huge world tour in support of *Watch Out!*, and despite mounting pressure to record abroad, the band returned to Silo in Hamilton in 2006 to record parts of *Crisis*, with new drummer Jordan Hastings behind the kit. *Crisis* was punishing, in both volume and subject matter. Heavier tracks such as "Mailbox Arson" and "This Could Be Anywhere in the World" painted a bleak picture of modern western civilization, while singles such as the streamlined, uptempo "Boiled Frogs" examined the crushing woes that stem from devoting one's life to an unfulfilling career. While not necessarily a concept record, *Crisis* was the most fully realized, carefully constructed album the band had ever produced.

"I think we wanted to take another step further away from our contemporaries," Wade MacNeil explained in a 2014 Dine Alone Records documentary about the band. "We focused more on songwriting at this point. It's okay if a part repeats itself. That's a good thing to do. So we kind of started writing choruses, and Dallas and I started singing together. We started looking at the songs as, 'this is what's best for the song.'"

"We knew what worked with a crowd," Pettit continues. "You could see how stuff we had done on our last records really resonated with the crowd, and then with *Crisis* I feel like we just flexed that." Much of the power in the band's "flex" came from Butty and a new collaborator, Nick Blagona, who was brought in for the *Crisis* sessions to help track drums and attain the biggest sound possible in the studio. Where *Watch Out!* was intricate, literary and experimental, *Crisis* was decidedly more clear and present. The band maintained this approach throughout the remainder of their career.

For *Old Crows/Young Cardinals* – which was ultimately the band's final full-length album – Alexis once again recruited Butty and travelled to the world-famous Armoury Studios in Vancouver to lay down the tracks, with additional recording completed back in Hamilton at Silo. The song "Emerald Street" was a bittersweet love letter to Pettit's old stomping ground – a dark and ominous tale about "pregnant teens on the Barton Street bus" and "homeless people living off crusts" on the east side of downtown.

"Before *OC/YC*, we were actually courting a bunch of different guys and big-name people. These were American guys who had done big metal records, and some people we were really interested in working with," Pettit tells me. At the last minute, everyone pulled the plug and decided to stay in Canada to work with Butty once more. "We were all poised and ready. We were going to go out to Los Angeles and do a record, and we totally chickened out. We were like, 'nope, we're going to do it with Juice and Blagona.'"

• • •

30

In September, I resumed my editorial duties at the *Silhouette*. I filed stories and edited volunteer copy, attended concerts and movie premieres, sipped terrible coffee and smoked the occasional cigarette in the arts quad with Chris and Terris during late-night production runs. I made plans with other staffers to attend the national student newspaper conference in Vancouver in January, and debated a return trip to New York City. A group of us took a taxi to the Underground on a Wednesday night, in the middle of editing the newspaper, to catch Sloan on their fall Canadian tour for the album *Never Hear the End of It*. Max Kerman floated in and out of the office and kept me informed about upcoming shows. Other local musicians were also becoming frequent guests.

Producing a weekly broadsheet newspaper while attending class and maintaining a social life was still fulfilling and exciting, but some of the sheen had worn off. Production runs became less of a challenge and more of a chore. We started filing the arts section earlier in the night, and spent less time loitering in the basement office. Chris and I began reading classic novels and handmade punk zines in a desperate attempt to find inspiration. When that didn't work, we simply hit the pubs.

Six weeks into the school year, I met her.

It was a cool day in October. The campus was littered with red and orange leaves that crinkled under my Converse sneakers as I walked to and from class. It was the height of mid-term season and the newspaper office was quiet. We had scheduled a volunteer writers' meeting on a Thursday afternoon and I didn't expect many to attend. I slumped down beside one of the sports editors and stared at the large, blank whiteboard hanging on the wall in front of us. Another editor plucked an acoustic guitar and swivelled back and forth in a computer chair. Volunteer writers slowly trickled in. I pulled a marker from my desk and began sketching out next week's storyboard.

She was last to arrive – dressed in a slim black peacoat and black beret. Her pink cheeks and slight nose were sprinkled with brown and orange and ochre freckles. She smiled at Chris and took a seat on the far side of the table, producing a small black notebook from her leather handbag. I had never seen her at a newspaper meeting before. None of us had.

"Hi everyone," she offered, bright green eyes dancing around the table. "I'm Ciara."

• • •

Throughout the fall of 2006, Schwendiman's Underground – along with a handful of other venues in the downtown core – functioned as a proving ground for up-and-coming musicians, and a reliable stopover for homegrown rock and roll acts on cross-country tours. Constantines, the Weakerthans, Joel Plaskett, Sloan, Peter Elkas, Death From Above 1979, Stars, Metric, the Stills and the Organ all began making regular visits to Hamilton. If they weren't playing at the Casbah or out west at McMaster, they were most likely playing at the Underground.

The club also served as a meeting place for musicians and writers from all corners of the city. Simon Toye and Max Kerman were regulars, along with future members of Young Rival, the Dinner Belles, Monster Truck, Cities in Dust, San Sebastian and other area bands. One such musician was Aaron Goldstein – a guitar prodigy and budding producer originally from Toronto. With a long, curly ponytail, a beige peacoat and thin wire-rimmed glasses, Goldstein didn't exactly stand out as an avant-garde underground rocker on campus. But what he lacked in style he made up for in character and raw talent. Universally well liked and respected, Goldstein could shred, compose, play multiple instruments and hang with just about anyone in the Hamilton scene.

"I first came to Hamilton in 2004," recalls Goldstein, who enrolled at McMaster as a mature student after "fucking around" and dropping out of a liberal arts program at Humber College after just one year. We're seated across from one another at the Ship on Augusta Street, tearing into a pair of loaded club sandwiches with a basket of sizzling fries between us. It's a few weeks before Christmas 2011, and the pub's bay window has been brushed with a light dusting of snow. Goldstein's hair is trimmed into a tight, curly afro. The peacoat is gone, but the glasses remain.

It was older friend from high school, living in a house on King Street West near the Highway 403 overpass, who invited the somewhat directionless guitarist to give his education another go. "I came here basically because I knew my friend. I lived with him and his pals, and they were all great dudes. They started to expose me to all kinds of music I had never heard...we started to go see a lot of shows, and we had an attic on the third floor of this house where I was able to set up my drums and amps and all kinds of stuff...it was great, 'cause it was huge and cheap."

As a mature student, Goldstein was only allowed to take one course at McMaster during his first term – a factor that gave him more time for experimentation with multi-track recording in the attic of his new home. With more free time to write and record music, he began to hammer out and develop new guitar riffs, many of which would be later plucked for his band Huron's self-titled record.

While studying, Goldstein hosted a show on the campus radio station, 93.3 CFMU. *The Reverend's Attic* offered him a direct line to some of the city's newest musicians, many of whom would go on to achieve great success. But for most of his first and second years in Hamilton, Goldstein was hanging out almost exclusively with his roommates. Music was still very much a personal hobby; of course, that was about to change in a big way. Partway through his time at McMaster, Goldstein started hanging around a student house at the foot of Carling Street known to locals as "Rocky Saugeen." It quickly became a hot spot for self-booked, semi-legal concerts in the west end of the city. House shows at Rocky Saugeen and similar spaces in the downtown core introduced the city's next wave of musicians to each other for the first time.

"On a popular night, the wood-panelled walls would sweat and the gig posters that lined them would begin to curl at their edges," recalls Nicole Nicolson, a local music writer and long-time merch-seller and door-worker in Hamilton's indie music scene. "Here, you'd meet Hamilton's finest musicians in their truest form, before they had been realized. In fact, some are still working on it all these years later. I think back to the audience then, and of their place now: a surprising number finishing law school, some in wildly successful bands on European tours, some school teachers and married. But this came before that. This was our time at Rocky Saugeen."

"I remember some great house shows around this city. Rocky Saugeen obviously had some great ones," says local roots rock singer Terra Lightfoot, who attended McMaster with Goldstein and many other musicians.

"There was no room to move if the night was popular, but it was full of people you didn't mind touching," adds Nicolson. "Unlike other venues in the city, if you were there it was because you knew someone and were welcome to enjoy the space. So many bands, local or otherwise, played on that spot on the floor it's hard to pick a favourite. A combination of Max Kerman, Aaron Goldstein, Adam Melnick, Mike DeAngelis, Cam Malcolm, etc., always produced a good sound, and now a good memory, considering the well-earned success those guys have found."

34

• • •

Meanwhile, Max Kerman was all too eager to begin his career as a musician. Together with guitarist Mike DeAngelis, bassist Nick Dika and the band's original drummer, a fellow student named Everett Rooke, he formed Charlemagne – an upbeat roots rock outfit born in the concrete corridors of the Brandon Hall student residence at McMaster. Still completely green, the four-piece wasted little time booking shows at west-end house parties and on-campus venues such as Quarters and the Phoenix, a popular graduate student pub. The fact that Charlemagne even existed at all was another happy accident. Dika, a native of quiet college town London, Ontario, describes the band's formation as somewhat random.

"From my perspective, I really kind of walked into it," he begins. "The first week of university, you have complete license to talk to whoever you want and nobody thinks it's weird. Everybody's just trying to meet everybody. [The band] ended up meeting, and I didn't even have my stuff, my bass or my amp, in Hamilton. I was just hanging out with Max. He liked baseball, and he liked all the other things I did besides music…I wasn't a player who was really serious and committed to being in a band, but [Max] knew Mike and was talking to him in the same way. We ended up just starting to play together in the basement of Mike's residence. It came together fairly randomly."

"Max was just the kind of guy in residence who'd be, like, 'hey I wrote some songs, you wanna check 'em out?' It didn't matter if it was me or some random girl," Mike DeAngelis recalls. "Usually, it was super innocent. Max, especially in first year, was just the most rambunctious guy and a very social person."

"Max was the first guy to really pick my brain about music. He wanted to know everything about the business, and had no problem asking questions," offers the Rest's Adam Bentley, a fellow undergraduate student at McMaster during the mid-2000s.

"Before I had even seen his band, I felt like I had heard them. He was so enthusiastic. We ended up playing with Charlemagne quite a bit. In the early days, the band wasn't quite what they became.... I thought they had the potential to be a big, crossover type band. From day one, it seemed Max could be the same guy off and on stage. It made the band hugely relatable. They seemed like the obvious choice to take the next step."

Many of Charlemagne's earliest songs were derived from the kind of hard-driving, soul-infused rock music that trickled down from their parents' 1960s-era record collections. Kerman's father, born and raised in New York City and an alumnus of Wayne State University in Detroit, was known for spinning classic Motown and Beatles records while young Max was coming of age. "I brought in *Abbey Road* to play for my kindergarten class," Kerman tells me, laughing. This childhood influence, combined with a newfound love for the likes of Joel Plaskett, the Weakerthans, Constantines, Sam Roberts, Sloan and Cuff the Duke, helped shape the band's early sound. Though Kerman was far from a confident songwriter. Not at first, anyway. During his formative years at Harbord Collegiate Institute in downtown Toronto, he spent more time on a basketball court than on stage. He also preferred smooth hip-hop and Top 40 R&B over Canadian indie rock, and didn't truly hit his stride until linking up with his future bandmates at McMaster.

"I didn't go to school with many suburban white kids that would be interested in playing in a band," says Kerman, who ironically grew up on Major Street, not far from the rock and roll hotbed surrounding College and Spadina in downtown Toronto, and a few blocks from the legendary El Mocambo nightclub. "It wasn't like there were a bunch of kids whose parents had listened to the Beatles."

Hamilton may have been their newfound home, but it was during a trip to Toronto that the members of Charlemagne first crossed paths with Goldstein. Although the band was little more than a struggling collection of dorm-room strummers, they were eager to expand their sound and reach. Goldstein, who by then had begun recording music in earnest, would soon play a crucial role in taking the band to another level.

"I met Max Kerman and Mike DeAngelis on the GO bus. We were all waiting at the stop at Dundurn and King, and it was super packed because it was North By Northeast [NXNE]," Goldstein recalls. "We started talking about Matt Mays, Joel Plaskett and a lot of mutual interests we had...they may have thought I was a little bit crazy. I was wearing a peacoat and still had long hair in a ponytail. But at the end of the bus ride, we crossed the road over to [Union Station] and somebody asked somebody for their number. It was enough of an interesting conversation that we decided to keep it going."

DeAngelis – originally from Guelph, Ontario, about an hour west of Toronto – remembers the meeting well. "He was definitely in rock-and-roll mode, and we just struck up a conversation with him. He said, 'I run this radio show if you guys want to come in,' and we ended up going to his house and recording some music with him."

Throughout 2006, as Charlemagne picked up more gigs around town and gained confidence on stage, the band's twenty-year-old singer eventually passed along a rough demo CD for his new pal Goldstein to dissect and critique. "I was like, 'you know what? This is great, and the songs are great. But if you want to know the truth, the drums sound like shit in this part' and whatever else I said," laughs Goldstein. "I don't know if he liked it or not, but it didn't turn him off of me somehow." DeAngelis also recalls the band's playing at the time as being a long way off from technically proficient.

"I was super bad. Like, really bad," he offers with a smile. "I remember when I first started playing with Max, he was teaching me open chords and stuff like that. I had only ever really played barre chords before, and that's where I was at. Between me, Max and Nick, we were all starting with a relatively low level of musicianship. But there was a 'sum is greater than its parts' kind of mentality."

As the members of Charlemagne prepared to enter another fall term at McMaster, Goldstein and mutual friend Adam Melnick moved into a tiny bungalow on Broadway Avenue, near the west side of campus. The duo positioned all of their gear in the home's unfinished basement and Goldstein set to work building his very own ad hoc recording studio – a self-described "primitive" operation comprised of a pair of speakers, an old receiver, a sluggish computer with ancient software and several used microphones. After listening to the early Charlemagne demos and noticing a spark in the group's songwriting, Goldstein offered to re-record some of the songs in his new basement studio.

"At first they were like, 'nah, I don't know.' They were kind of weird about it," recalls Goldstein. "But we finally decided they would come and at least record, and I could offer some opinions."

According to DeAngelis, the ensuing sessions on Broadway Avenue were far from perfect, but the band emerged with their first proper demo, *The Broken Tapes*. "We took to Aaron right away, because he was super enthusiastic about music, and he also just wanted to help us record. We had no luck recording music before then, and as it turns out, we didn't have a lot of luck

38

with Aaron either. His computer crashed and it was definitely a learning process for everyone involved."

The nine-song offering – featuring two "bonus" tracks, including a cover of the Band's "Tears of Rage" and a live take of the song "Zoe" from a gig at the Casbah – was certainly rough. Guitars barely in tune, warbling vocals, long compositions and little self-editing. Still, it was light years ahead of most basement bands' debut recordings. The compositions were strong, and the band already had a clear grasp of balancing melody and power. Even then, Kerman was showing signs of being a fearless bandleader in the tradition of 1960s soul and R&B revues. Halfway into the song "Portrayal of Our Leader," Kerman leans into the microphone and yells, "Introducing...Mike D!" before DeAngelis fumbles through a clumsy blues solo. It's a technique he employs to this day on stages from Burlington to Berlin – introducing one of his bandmates by name right before they dive into a solo or the song's main hook.

That same fall, Charlemagne set out on their first proper "tour" of Southern Ontario – a two-day journey to Peterborough and Kingston, partially organized by Cam Malcolm. During a weekend home from his studies at Trent University, Malcolm read about Charlemagne in the *Silhouette*. Intrigued, he contacted the band via email and began discussing a shared bill with his Peterborough-based rock and roll band, the Sweet Homewreckers.

It was Charlemagne's first taste of life on the road, and the first spark of a deep friendship with Malcolm. Within a few years, they'd all be traversing the Canadian Prairies, and planting black and gold flags all over the continent.

• • •

Throughout the fall of 2006, Charlemagne wasn't the only band making waves at McMaster. Toronto rapper and multimedia student Miles Jones had released his debut full-length album, *One Chance*, as his graduate thesis and was making inroads in the notoriously fickle downtown TO music scene. Folk singer Robyn Dell'Unto, who would later pen the catchy *CBC Radio 2* favourite "Sidecar," was gigging regularly at west-end pubs and other student haunts. In addition to all this, the Rest, a self-described "pop, noise, heart, wonder, space" collective fronted by charismatic lead singer Adam Bentley, released *Atlantis, Oh Our Saviour* in November. Full of rich, meandering compositions and a healthy dose of experimentation, the band's debut record offered a beautiful and intricate counterpoint to some of the more brash and violent sounds coming from the west end of the city.

Simon Toye fell into the latter category. That fall, my former colleague at the *Silhouette* was riding high off the unexpected success of his band Cities in Dust and their debut record, *Night Creatures*. Released in April on Toronto's Paper Bag Records, it's a perfect snapshot of the mid-2000s punk, new wave and dance fusion that dominated college rock radio at the time – including bands such as Franz Ferdinand, the Bravery, Arctic Monkeys, Kaiser Chiefs and the Killers – with stylistic nods to everything from Germs and Black Flag to the Who and the Kinks.

I received a copy of the new Cities in Dust record at the *Silhouette* and cracked open the plastic jewel case as fast as possible. I was in awe of my friend's rise to success. One year prior, we had been sitting shoulder to shoulder in the newspaper office, scribbling notes for record reviews and eating junk food late into the night. Now, I was about to review Simon's record. It was bizarre and thrilling.

This was still two years before Arkells would release *Jackson Square*. At the time, the only other touring band I knew on a personal level was local garage rock upstarts the Ride Theory. In hindsight, Cities in Dust may have been my first connection to the Canadian music industry on a much larger scale. It broke down an invisible barrier of some kind – opening up a whole new world of possibilities when it came to documenting and pitching stories about local music. All of a sudden, people from other places started tuning in to what was happening in Hamilton: industry insiders from Toronto, reporters and promoters from rural college towns, curious fans from across Canada and over the Atlantic Ocean. Our secret was about to be revealed.

• • •

"When we were in high school, [Zach Frank and I] both worked at Sunrise Records. Him in Kitchener-Waterloo, and me at Centre Mall in Hamilton. So our paths may have crossed in one form or another," says Toye, enjoying an afternoon pint at Democracy on Locke Street South in April 2014. He's wearing a tight black leather jacket and a deep V-neck T-shirt, his long and lean frame towering over the table. Toye speaks slowly and evenly.

As we chat, he recalls an evening at Burlington's Kingdom nightclub as the pair's first official meeting. The duo shared a fondness for late nights, loud guitars and limited-edition records from day one. The details are somewhat fuzzy, but Toye recalls how soon afterward Frank masterminded a gathering with bassist Craig Nordemann and drummer Matt Winters – all mutual friends in one form or another through McMaster's thriving music and art scene. The meeting took place at Nordemann's student house in Westdale Village. One of the city's most exciting new punk bands was born out of a random basement meet-and-greet between semi-familiar art-punk fanboys.

"We didn't have any songs, and Zach had no idea of what he wanted to do. He just knew he wanted to do it," Toye recalls. "I had been a guitar player at that point for the better part of ten years, and I never had any aspirations to join a band. I did probably want to DJ at that point, though."

For many casual fans of Cities in Dust, *Night Creatures* was the band's high-water mark. The album, recorded at Signal to Noise in downtown Toronto with Uncut drummer and budding producer Jon Drew, is a fresh and fun statement delivered at the apex of an entirely new punk global movement. It's also just a very cool record. Tightly wound and jittery with just the right amount of vintage punk snarl, it became a go-to at local house parties and that fall received a heavy rotation on our newsroom stereo. Toye's controlled but manic guitar playing perfectly complimented Frank's tortured howls on tracks such as "Save the Last Dance," "All the Girls" and "Chop, Chop, You're Dead!"

"I was pretty close with Craig from Cities in Dust. We both had shows on CFMU and were taking communications [at McMaster]," says Adam Bentley. "They were the first local band we played with that I felt were on to something. We played with them in Waterdown, at a venue called Moe's Tavern. The place was huge and they must have played to about twenty people, but that didn't stop Zach from rolling all over the floor and dancing on the bar like a demented version of *Coyote Ugly*."

"They were very in-your-face, as far as their music went. They were a tight unit," says Jamie "Gunner" Smith, a legendary radio host and long-time producer at Mohawk College's 101.5 FM. "I thought they were a great band, and I thought they should have done a little better than they did. That happens. Just because you love a sound doesn't mean it's going to resonate with everyone. But I think that if they'd come out a little bit earlier their music would have gone over down in the States."

Unfortunately, Cities in Dust never had much luck on the road. A one-off showcase in England in 2005 failed to make a dent in the already heavily saturated UK indie rock scene. Even with the success of *Night Creatures,* a large-scale domestic tour never materialized. The farthest the group made it in Canada was Lennoxville, Québec – a college town roughly 150 kilometres east of Montréal – for a rowdy show at Bishop's University alongside the Mark Inside. As the months wore on and momentum slowed, the members of the band began losing interest. The idea of recording a follow-up to *Night Creatures* was quickly scrapped.

"The was zero acrimony over it. There was no finger pointing, and there wasn't a fight about it," Toye recalls. "Part of it, I think, was just us becoming different people with different priorities. Zach put his body on the line for us, and I think it started to take a toll on him, you know? For me, I kind of wanted to do different things."

For many local fans, the band's lasting legacy stemmed from their on- and offstage relationship with local outsiders, best friends and musical nemeses Sailboats Are White. "Sailboats were important for us," Toye admits. "They were pretty well established before us. They were one of those bands we would see a lot at the Underground and the Casbah. They certainly inspired Zach a lot. He took a lot of what Kevin was doing as a singer and kind of channelled it into – not his persona, necessarily – but songwriting, and maybe his stage presence a little bit, too.

"The style that I think Sailboats Are White were really good at was kind of fast, punchy, choppy, and we took some of that," he continues. "We did definitely play a lot with them. Looking back at it, I kind of forget a lot of what that was like. We kind of got swept up in the whole Toronto thing really quickly."

• • •

Featuring a core lineup of Kevin Douglas on lead vocals, Matt Bourassa on bass and Kevyn Wright on guitar and keyboards – with "literally a dozen other members" rotating through at various times, Douglas offers – Sailboats Are White crawled out of Hamilton at the turn of the millennium and earned a reputation as the wildest, most unpredictable and most self-destructive band in the city. It was frenetic buzz-saw punk rock backed by an electronic drum machine; a wall of noise produced by a shambolic collective of outcasts, maniacs, dreamers and drunkards. Too wild to tame. Too bizarre to categorize. The best and the worst at any given moment. Fucking incredible.

"Sailboats were just insane," says Graham Rockingham, who caught some of the band's earliest shows at the Underground. "I remember with Kevin, it was like seeing a young Jim Morrison. It seems like a ridiculous thing to say, but it was like, 'I'm in the Whisky a Go Go'…where Jim Morrison was doing the murdering his parents thing live on stage, refusing to even acknowledge that there was an audience, gripping poles and weeping. That's what Kevin was like. You never knew what he was going to do."

"Kevin just fed off the moment a lot of the time," adds Boxcar Sound Recording producer Sean Pearson, who mixed and mastered the band's debut record, *Turbo!*, and also captured Douglas's wailing vocals during the recording process. "It was so sporadic that sometimes I bet he didn't even know what was going to happen until it happened. That's how off the cuff it felt to me, anyway…and likewise, I don't think the band knew, either. The rest of the guys didn't have a clue what he was going to do. That just brought the level of performance up, for me, every time."

From Douglas's perspective, the entire gritty mess that was Sailboats Are White played out like some kind of disorienting Bertolt Brecht theatre piece. The aim of any interaction – be it a live performance or a casual meet-and-greet – was to confuse and alienate; to push buttons and antagonize. If the audience or the reporter or the label head or the venue owner felt uncomfortable, Douglas was doing his job.

"My onstage persona was very reckless and offensive. It was a natural way for me to act," says the band's frontman, fielding questions via Facebook messenger from his home in Toronto. "I definitely craved attention and unfortunately did not care if it was positive or negative. From my actions, it seems like I actually preferred negative. I enjoyed getting a rise and making people uncomfortable."

If the band had any chance at achieving success outside of Hamilton, it came in late 2005 with the release of their first full-length record, *Turbo!* Bizarre and brutal, rambunctious and rollicking, the twelve-song offering had real potential to elevate Sailboats Are White to the crest of the new dance-punk wave that had been building throughout the previous year. *Perfect Youth* author Sam Sutherland reviewed the album for *Exclaim!* in fall 2005 and offered one of the best descriptions of the group's unconventional mishmash of sounds: "Like a (more) drunk MC5 with no drummer, Hamilton's Sailboats Are White kick out the jams, drum machine-style, knocking over every table in the room during a scramble for the bar, dragging their instruments with them.... The vocals of Kevin Douglas are strained to the point of exhaustion, and by the end of the record's fourth track, he sounds ready to pass out due to lack of oxygen. Thankfully he doesn't, and the band blast through eight more tracks of electro-punk fury, pausing only occasionally to take a big swig from their respective bottles."

By 2006, with *Turbo!* gaining steam in the alternative music press and the band's anarchistic reputation growing steadily, Sailboats had become Cities in Dust's chief counterpoints in the budding Hamilton punk scene. Equal parts friends and adversaries – especially Douglas and CiD lead singer Zachary Frank – the two groups constantly pushed each other to new extremes, both on and off stage. Who can play the fastest and loudest? Who can be the most abrasive? Who can cause the most damage? Who can drink the most beer and still complete a full set? But in Douglas's own words, one key factor always stood as an invisible barrier between the two camps. While Cities in Dust strived for mainstream acceptance – or at the very least, longed to put out well-produced music, build a core fanbase, make key connections and mingle with industry insiders in Toronto – Sailboats favoured total annihilation. They always found a way to "blow it" when the chips were high, Douglas tells me. Former Sonic Unyon staffer and principal backer Oliver Knutton often took the brunt of it.

"[Cities in Dust] worked hard for opportunities and shook the right hands, while opportunities fell in our lap and I pissed them all away by being crass and unbelievably hard to work with," Douglas begins, somewhat remorsefully. "I regret letting down the people that went to bat for us. I regret the countless hours, dollars and late-night phone calls we made to bail us out of situations. Oliver Knutton being the biggest one. I wish there could have been more of a return on his investment than a legend that he funded and gets no credit for. That dude seriously put his neck out there for us over and over again because he believed in us, and I did everything in my power to let him down."

"We had a lot of opportunities to take the band to the next level. Oliver really helped us by putting our record out, generating press and buzz, and getting us a booking agent and shows," Bourassa tells me via email. "I think the party lifestyle, which Kevin gravitated to the most, at the time made us lazy, and no one had the money to pay for flights or anything or wanted to take that leap and take risks, financially, that so many bands do. We blew it by getting into fights, kicked out of shows … people thought we were fucked and wouldn't book us. We got this rep, and in the end it didn't prevail or work for us. We let Oliver down because we didn't capitalize on the things he helped provide for us. We were snotty kids who didn't see these awesome opportunities."

"At the same time," Douglas concedes, "I can guarantee that any amount of fame and money I would have received would have contributed to my demise. I honestly think not 'making it' is the best thing to happen to me. I was overindulgent and self-destructive. I didn't know it at the time, but was later diagnosed with super-duper ADHD and was self-medicating and seeking attention."

Sailboats Are White dropped *Turbo II* in August 2008 – a nine-track offering initially released online and via cassette. They entered a long-term hiatus just two months later, leaving a deep chasm in the local punk scene. More than a decade after first working with them, Sean Pearson still credits the band as one of the city's best and most uncompromising musical exports of the mid-2000s.

"They were probably one of the first groups that were really trying to push that DIY aesthetic, and not feel like they had to have a drummer," says Pearson. "The drums had this very dance-y, almost 1980s kind of vibe. Then you had this harsh guitar and a really driving band playing overtop. There's just so much to those guys. You can just keep getting further into it."

"Sailboats Are White was very raw and, as I said earlier, a therapeutic outlet. We were, as I am, very polarizing," offers

Douglas, reflecting on his own mixed legacy. "I've never been happy not leaving an impression. People are either all-in with us or they hate us. And I'm more than fine with that. I actually think it's what I was going after. So, in thirty years if a kid finds our record, I hope their minds are either blown in amazement or their eardrums are blown in disgust."

• • •

Soon after Max Kerman released *The Broken Tapes* with Charlemagne, the twenty-year-old was ready to take his basement rock aspirations to an entirely new level. Still operating as a four-piece and playing relatively small shows around Southern Ontario, the band was on the cusp of major changes in the weeks and months ahead – beginning with the addition of two new members and the birth of a supercharged, keyboard-driven sound. But not before a side project known as the Surly Young Bucks and an almost-love triangle nearly derailed the whole thing.

Guitarist and songwriter Dan Griffin – originally from the sprawling suburbs of Mississauga, Ontario, just west of Toronto – had been slowly making a name for himself in Hamilton's music scene. It wasn't long before he caught Kerman's attention during a string of shared gigs in campus pubs. In the months before Griffin officially joined forces with Charlemagne, the two frontmen developed a competitive and, at times, bitter rivalry within the McMaster music scene.

"Aaron Goldstein ended up at the Boston Pizza on Main Street West, and it was an open mic night," recalls Kerman, sipping a Tim Hortons coffee in my downtown apartment during the fall of 2011. He's slumped on the couch, keeping one eye on game one of the World Series as it flickers on the television with the volume off. "Dan Griffin was there, and I kind of knew him.

He was a year ahead of me in school, but his ex-girlfriend was a friend of mine. We laugh about it now, but at the time Dan didn't like me very much because I was the other 'songwriter guy' who was allegedly hitting on his girlfriend."

"It was never super contentious," Mike DeAngelis assures me. "I remember in the early days of Dan being in the band, we all had a laugh in the van when everything came out and we got down to brass tacks about the past. It was just funny, in the end."

Griffin's girlfriend knew the founding members of Charlemagne from living in Brandon Hall at McMaster and had been talking up Kerman for quite some time. Griffin wasn't outwardly impressed, but that changed in a hurry when he saw the band live for the first time. "I was so jealous. She dragged me out to go see him play at some point – this was an early version of Charlemagne. I begrudgingly went to see them at a battle of the bands and I thought they were really good."

As the trees in Westdale Village turned from orange to brown, Kerman and Goldstein became more involved with the Surly Young Bucks. They eventually decided to invite Griffin to a practice. The goal was to have a loose collective of musicians rotate in and out of the lineup, like some kind of country- and folk-infused Broken Social Scene. Griffin was the perfect fit for the band's blend of roots rock, soul and folk music. He joined the group one summer evening at Goldstein's Rocky Saugeen jam house on Carling Street, and the connection was instantaneous.

"He picked up the guitar and of course was killer. Then we sat him behind the drum kit and he was killer. He just added so much to the band…he could sing, he could harmonize, all these things. He was way ahead of everybody," offers Kerman.

With Griffin officially in the band, the Bucks continued to pick up gigs around Hamilton, playing the Casbah, the Underground and the Pepper Jack Café on King William Street. As the band expanded its repertoire, Charlemagne became less and less of a musical priority for Kerman and his new bandmates. "Mike was really involved [with Charlemagne], but Nick was pretty focused on school so he took the band somewhat seriously. And our old drummer didn't take it seriously at all. He left his drum set at my place all the time and never practiced," says Kerman.

Even still, the troubled four-piece soldiered forward and continued booking gigs in and around the Hamilton area, with Griffin filling in on drums for the occasional show. A fall gig at the Casbah with Tokyo Police Club was particularly memorable for keyboardist Graham Wright. Years later, the two bands would become labelmates on Dine Alone Records and tour America together. But at the time, their introduction was somewhat awkward.

"We had never met them before, but they were on the show. They did a cover of our song 'Nature of the Experiment' as part of their set, which is a little cheesy," jokes Wright. "But I always remembered it, because it was funny."

When Oshawa's Cuff the Duke rolled into town in mid-October, Charlemagne was hired as the opening act for a show at the Casbah. Griffin, a huge fan of the headliners, asked if he could sit in with Charlemagne for the night and play keyboards. The band obliged, and despite only one rehearsal as a five-piece, the show was a moderate success. "I went to Long & McQuade and just rented a keyboard," recalls Griffin. "I grew up taking lessons, but I had forgotten about piano for years. We rehearsed for the Cuff show and that was really the turning point. It was the first time that I was playing keyboard in that role, and the first time it became clear that it could be a possible element in the band."

Griffin was asked to join on a permanent basis, but the addition of one new member soon led to the ousting of another. The band parted ways with their founding drummer not long after the gig with Cuff the Duke and began searching for a new player to anchor the rhythm section. Within a matter of weeks, twenty-one-year-old Tim Oxford was brought into the fold – a Newmarket, Ontario, native and friend of Griffin's from the Queen Street West music scene in Toronto. Not long afterward, the new five-piece began working hard on material that would comprise the *Deadlines* EP. It was an exciting time for the young band, as well as those who were witnessing their evolution first-hand.

"I went to the first show where the Arkells had Tim playing drums," says local singer-songwriter Terra Lightfoot. "I think they were Charlemagne then and Aaron Goldstein was playing pedal steel with them. Cute."

"They were always eager to get any airtime," says Jamie Smith. "They would just be like, 'you want us to come on and play and sing?' I'd be like, 'yeah, sure!' They got it. They had the songs, they had the talent. I could see that band only getting bigger and bigger."

By year's end, a five-piece version of Charlemagne was solidified. The new lineup played their first show in January, at the legendary El Mocambo on Spadina Avenue in Toronto, and continued rehearsing throughout the following winter and spring. Their next major goals involved securing a record deal, writing and recording a full-length record and touring the entire country. But first they needed a new name.

• • •

Hamilton has always been home to a wide range of female talent and the mid-2000s were no exception. Ottawa folk singer Kathleen Edwards lived here during the peak of her career – a period that gave birth to her strongest record to date, the beautiful and brutally honest *Asking for Flowers*. Melissa McClelland, born in Chicago and raised in nearby Burlington, settled in Hamilton with her husband and musical collaborator, Luke Doucet. The pair currently performs under the handle Whitehorse. Former jazz singer Jessy Lanza settled back in her hometown of Hamilton after a few years in Montréal to write and record her critically acclaimed debut album, *Pull My Hair Back*. The list goes on.

Still, nothing came close to the fury, tragedy and sheer mayhem that enveloped one all-female punk band from the east end of the city – Pantychrist. Type the group's name into an online search engine and you're likely to recoil. Inner-city tales of heroin addiction, robbery, murder and incarceration leap from the screen. The stories are grim and the subject matter highly disturbing. But they're also a part of the band's history and legacy that lead singer Danielle Delottinville wants to move on from. She needs to.

When I interviewed Delottinville over the phone on a warm and rainy July evening in 2014, our conversation focused on none of the above. The Pantychrist I first encountered as a young music writer with the *Silhouette* was a brash, unapologetic, frightening and deliciously snotty four-piece hardcore outfit with roots in Hamilton's Blakeley neighbourhood, on the fringes of Gage Park. This was the version of Pantychrist Delottinville wanted to focus on.

The group was, and remains, four friends united by apathy and raw aggression, eager to leave Hamilton's male-dominated punk and hardcore community with a pair of black eyes. The *Silhouette* published an extended piece on the band following the release of their debut full-length record, *Never Love Anything*. I was immediately hooked. Delottinville – along with original bandmates Izabelle Steele, Amy Hell and Patty Christ – had crafted thirteen tales of feminism, nihilism, violence and urban decay so honest and unfiltered they were undeniable.

For Delottinville, the songs that comprised *Never Love Anything* represented everything she loved and despised about Hamilton. "Hamilton is an industrial, working city, right? So a lot of people are really hard workers, and because they work so hard they either turn to drugs or alcohol to cope. So their kids are brought up, I know because I'm one of them, these kids are brought up in kind of rough homes," she explains. "I walk down the street and I see a lot of sadness in Hamilton. I see a lot of sick people, really worn-down, used-up people ... it just kind of feels like a dead city, but it's beautiful to me."

Pantychrist began in 2003, when its four founding members crossed paths in the women's washroom at the Underground and soon decided to combine their passion for music into a new project. The band's reckless frontwoman, only nineteen at the time, had been a long-time fan of local punk institution Riotstar and wanted to bring her own unique brand of chaos to the stage – only this time with women playing all the instruments and writing all the songs.

A regular at punk haunts such as the Corktown Tavern on Young Street and the newly opened Underground, Delottinville was inspired by the danger, abandon and unique camaraderie that Hamilton's increasingly dissident punk rock community offered. It was the thrill of the unknown that fuelled her desire to attend more and more shows – and that more often than not put her directly in harm's way.

"I really liked Riotstar and I liked the Sinisters because I was fearful at those shows," she begins, without a hint of hyperbole. "It was exciting, you know what I mean? I wanted to feel scared when I went to those shows. I think that rock and roll, and punk rock, it should scare people."

Pantychrist played their first official gig on September 28, 2003, at the Underground, and quickly developed a rabid fanbase around the commuter caves of Southern Ontario. From day one, the group's mandate was simple: don't take shit from anyone, including other bands, crooked promoters, venue owners or drunken voyeurs eager to gawk at Delottinville's Runaways-esque leggings, leather and lingerie.

More shows followed at the Underground, the Corktown Tavern and Mermaid's Lounge in Hess Village as the band slowly expanded their touring circle to include London, Toronto, Brantford, Kingston and other towns along Highway 401. Given that some members of Pantychrist had young children at home, each gig had to be within a relatively short drive of Hamilton. Aside from the odd overnight trip, extensive touring was out of the question. In early 2004, capitalizing on their immediate and growing popularity, the band released the popular *ShEPeed* EP and soon after produced a special demo CD for high-profile showcase events – the aptly titled *Demo-lition Dirty*.

By 2005, Pantychrist was ready to enter the studio to begin work on their highly anticipated debut record, the brilliantly titled and brutally caustic *Never Love Anything*. To capture the sound and fury of their unpredictable live show, the band joined forces with former Sailboats Are White guitarist Jamie Andrew and scheduled a one-day session at Andrew's Valleyview Studios in suburban Ancaster – a location that, geographically and ideologically, couldn't be further from the inner-city nightmares the band so often sang about. Delottinville doesn't remember much from the breakneck speed of the sessions, but Andrew still recalls his first encounter with Pantychrist.

"I recorded a bunch of girl bands around that time: Pantychrist, the Lorrainas, Buckshot Bebee, the Sheanderthals, Rackula," recalls Andrew. "I think Pantychrist recorded with me because I knew Patty and her husband, Larry, through the local scene. They were like the mom and dad of the band, since they organized and produced the recording sessions. Musically, the band clearly belonged to Danielle and Izabelle. I was so blown away by their talent, and Izzy's guitar playing in particular since I was also a guitarist. When I first met them, Danielle and Izzy, they were so young and rabid-looking that I wondered if they were going to trash my studio. They were actually really cool and easy to work with. It was an exciting time and we all had fun."

"It was obviously the first time I had been in a recording studio," says Delottinville. "It was actually pretty comfortable because it was in someone's house, and Jamie was really cool...I know it didn't take long at all. If anything, two days."

Despite the hasty recording session, *Never Love Anything* was a perfect snapshot of the band. In the years that followed its release on Hamilton-based AMP Records – spurred on by the word-of-mouth buzz in the regional punk scene – Pantychrist continued to hone their live presence and become a much tighter unit on stage. Since touring was out of the question, the band became highly selective in selecting their gigs in order to avoid over saturating their core audience in Hamilton. While Delottinville struggles to name many musical peers in the city, the band developed a close connection with a pair of British Columbia punk icons in Vancouver's D.O.A. and Victoria's Dayglo Abortions in the years that followed *Never Love Anything*'s release.

Not long after the release of *Never Love Anything*, AMP Records unveiled a DVD entitled *Skirting With Disaster*, which included a number of engaging interviews and scathing live performances from Pantychrist's early years. The film was well received, but the cracks were beginning to show. As early as December 2006, the band's original lineup was already drifting apart. Original drummer Patty Christ was the first to leave in 2007, temporarily replaced by ex–G-Men drummer Nick Tops while the band searched for a permanent female timekeeper. This transitional lineup released a limited-edition, live-off-the-floor CD that was sold exclusively at concerts, but it wasn't enough to hold everything together. With the search for a new drummer proving impossible, Pantychrist went on indefinite hiatus in June 2008. When the band rebooted several years later, Delottinville was the only founding member still on board. Still, the original lineup holds a special place in her heart.

"I want Pantychrist to be remembered for ... that's a pretty powerful question," says Delottinville, who takes a long pause to gather her thoughts. "I want us to be remembered for being not just your everyday, typical female band. I want us to be remembered as musicians. I don't want people to think of us as a gimmick band because we're female."

2007

IN THE PARKING LOT OF MISSISSAUGA'S cavernous Arrow Hall, we unzipped a baggie of magic mushrooms and carefully sorted the pieces. I was with a group of friends from McMaster, and it was only the second time I had planned to ingest the powerful psychedelic fungi ahead of a concert. The first was at a gig by Texas rockers ... And You Will Know Us by the Trail of Dead at the Opera House in Toronto, during the band's *Worlds Apart* tour in the spring of 2005. That evening ended with a full-on laugh attack in a dark alleyway near the club, followed by a lone figure asking if he could "have some of our shit." He said he would shoot us if we didn't comply. We took one look at each other and darted back into the crowd on Queen Street East, glancing over our shoulders before seeking refuge in a nearby bar. It was a memorable night, to say the least.

Regardless, I was eager to give it another go. I collected a gram in the palm of my hand and stared at the white-brown stems before tipping my head back and throwing the whole lot into my mouth. The bitterness was overpowering. I fought the urge to spit everything out and vomit all over the pavement. The taste of hairspray and mould lingered on the insides of my cheeks and underneath my tongue. I held my breath and closed my eyes.

Then suddenly it was down. The drugs were in my system and there was no turning back. I glanced around at our circle of friends. Everyone was grinning. Not the kind of grin where you're expecting something good to happen, but something much more sinister. We were on a mission now. A quest to survive. A journey of dizzying delights and unspeakable horrors.

We were about to watch Daft Punk's first Canadian show in more than a decade, and it wasn't going to be easy. For electronic music fans in Hamilton, this was destined to be the concert event of the decade. The importance of Daft Punk cannot be overstated here.

For a certain generation of music lovers born between the late 1970s and mid-1980s, Daft Punk offered a gateway into an entirely new musical universe of loops and sound effects, vocal samples and drumbeats, that later dominated the underground club scene in Hamilton. This was music that was far beyond the four-chord rock that populated the airwaves during the North American alternative boom of the 1990s. Daft Punk offered a fresh and fun alternative to distorted guitars and introspective lyrics. It was bright. It was danceable. It made going to night-clubs fashionable again. In 2005 – nearly a decade after the release of their landmark *Homework* LP – the Parisian duo's fourth release, *Human After All*, helped usher in a whole new generation of French electro that included the likes of Justice,

Uffie, Cassius, Feadz, Kavinsky, Mirwais, Breakbot and Boston Bun, among many others. We were all captivated.

As we joined the massive line outside Arrow Hall, I noticed groups of other attendees with that exact same stupid grin. Dozens of them, bug-eyed and giggling, surveying the scene, taking it all in. Shuffling along as the line inched forward and sipping from large bottles of water. We were desperately trying to look normal. I watched the sun slip behind the venue as we made our way toward the front door. IDs were checked, hands were stamped and we were thrown into the fray.

Two members of our crew purchased plastic cups full of beer and we regrouped in a loose semicircle behind the soundboard in the middle of the hall. The mushrooms were slowly waking up, but it was still early. I stared at the ceiling in the massive airport hangar, and slowly rolled my head down and looked toward the main stage. We were all grinning. Soon, the grins turned to giggles.

Then, without warning, chaos ensued.

SebastiAn, a French electronic artist on tour with Daft Punk, started performing from the soundboard in the middle of the arena, not twenty feet from where we were standing. But it wasn't just any track; SebastiAn dropped a monstrously loud, furious remix of Rage Against the Machine's "Killing in the Name" as fans craned their necks toward the grinding noise. The house lights were still on and it all seemed surreal.

"Is this really happening right now? Am I hearing this?"

"I think so. Are you seeing this?"

"Is that Rage Against the Machine?"

"Why do I know that song?"

"Where is the music coming from?"

"Is that Daft Punk?"

"Ohhhhhhhhhh mannnnnnnnnnnn…"

The drugs were coming on strong and it was too late to bail – the switch had been flipped. All we could do was stare and giggle at the situation. Then the giggles turned to laughter. Then we were laughing at each other laughing. Then we were laughing at everything and nothing at the same time. We must have looked insane. But I could see others in the arena laughing and pointing as well. I knew we weren't the only ones setting off on this electronic vision quest. SebastiAn hovered over the soundboard and nodded, flipping switches and tapping buttons with a menacing scowl on his face. He looked exactly like Keith Richards circa 1965, which only enhanced our confusion. I watched "Keith" DJ for what seemed like an hour, but time quickly became irrelevant. We were measuring things in blinks and bleeps, and flashes of light and cups of beer.

By the time Daft Punk hit the stage, it was a full-on sensory overload. We were all zooming. During the *Alive 2007* tour, Daft Punk performed on top of a massive LED pyramid in front of a colossal honeycomb of flashing lights and throbbing sensors that stretched from floor to ceiling, covering an entire wall of the concert hall. It was madness. With each new track, the band unveiled a more grotesque and overpowering layer of strobes and visual effects, until the entire pyramid and backdrop were awash in bright, pulsating lights. Those positioned in the middle of the hall were perfectly situated to take in the entire monstrous spectacle.

And then, halfway through one of the greatest concerts I had ever witnessed, we heard that quiet but urgent request that so often accompanies a bad trip.

"Uhh…I need to get out of here."

"What?"

"I need to leave. Right now. Get me out of here."

62

One of the boys, let's call him Paul, started to panic. His face was pale and covered with sweat. His pupils were fully dilated. He was fucked, and he knew it. We all did.

We forced our way out of the main hall and came upon a quiet, fully lit room at the end of a long, dark corridor. The Comedown Room, as we later described it. Here, far from the pounding bass and nauseating neon glow, Paul slumped against a wall and slid down to a half-seated position, staring straight ahead, mouth agape and blinking slowly. Dozens of others soon joined us in the room, sipping from plastic water bottles and catching their breath. Paul stared blankly at the opposing wall until the colour returned to his cheeks and the sweat dried on his forehead. We returned to the main hall in time to see the last half-dozen songs. By that point the battle had been won. Content to stand at the rear of the hall while others waded back into the masses, we had a different kind of grin this time. One reserved for victors.

After the concert, the group of us walked over to a wide patch of greenery near the venue and stretched out on our backs. I unbuttoned my damp flannel shirt and felt the cool blades under my palms as I leaned back into a low hill. Mission accomplished. For ninety minutes, we sat motionless as the drugs wore off and watched massive commercial airplanes take off and land at nearby Pearson Airport. The sky was perfectly clear, the summer air still and warm and comforting.

• • •

While half of Hamilton's underground music community was tripping at the Daft Punk concert, two local record collectors were stumbling into a downtown burrito bar and inadvertently kick-starting the most outrageous dance party in the city's history.

EVENINGS & WEEKENDS

Che Burrito & Lounge stands at 38 Hess Street South, in the heart of the popular club-land playground just west of the downtown core known as Hess Village. The former home of a skateboarding shop called DMBC, the narrow red-brick house operates as a fantastic Mexican eatery and café during the day and a packed, sweaty, no-holds-barred nightclub once the sun goes down. From the beginning, owner Scott McDonald envisioned the kind of place where – much like nearby Club Absinthe – patrons could come as they are and cut loose. Featuring a small but vibrant main room, a large and well-staffed bar and an expansive two-level front patio, the place was built for good times. Having live DJs on the weekend was always part of the plan.

"Che actually means friend, or buddy, and the whole purpose of starting the bar was to open a place that was a friend to everybody. No dress code, no rules and no standards. Basically a party-rocking bar that is open to everyone. Aaron and Chris fit right into that mould," McDonald explains.

The story of Che's outrageous No Standards Night began on a sweltering Sunday afternoon in August 2007, when roommates Aaron Gurman and Christopher McNamee had more time, alcohol and music than they knew what to do with. With most of their friends having purchased tickets to the Daft Punk concert months in advance, the long-time fans were left stranded in Hamilton. One drink led to another as the two pals attempted to wash away the afternoon and forget about their misfortune.

"We sat in the backyard drinking sangria all day and we just got hammered," says McNamee. He's seated next to Gurman at Gallagher's Bar and Lounge on John Street South, reflecting on what has since become one of the most eventful nights of their lives. It's a cool spring evening in 2012, and the bar is quiet and nearly empty. "Gurm was really eager to go down to Che and

64

have some drinks, and I honestly didn't think he could handle it," he continues.

After a little coaxing, Gurman and McNamee sauntered down to Che and began ordering more pitchers of sangria while chatting about music. Not long afterward, a mutual friend who worked at the bar asked if the pair would be interested in stepping into the DJ booth for a few hours. With nothing better to do, McNamee made a quick trip home and burned several mixed CDs with ten tracks each – including the Dandy Warhols, Minus the Bear and Lupe Fiasco – and set out for Che once more. All things considered, the event was a huge success.

"We were drunk, so we decided we were just going to play songs that we would want to hear while drinking," says McNamee. Venue owner McDonald was interested in hiring the duo, but not without a few more auditions. "We were kind of on a trial basis, because of the fact that we just showed up there loaded and played these songs. We weren't really like a 'sure bet' of actually knowing what we were doing."

"When they first started, they had no idea what they were doing, but they knew a lot of people and could draw a crowd," McDonald adds. "I remember they made the front cover of *View*, and my Saturday DJs at the time were so rattled and jealous because they were getting such notoriety while being completely unseasoned. It was awesome."

• • •

Gurman and McNamee met at Sir Winston Churchill Secondary School in east Hamilton during the mid-1990s, not far from the towering smokestacks of the Dofasco steel plant. They immediately bonded over a shared love of music – not only listening to it, but also actively seeking out new sounds and reading about the latest groups and trends in local and international magazines.

The vibe at Churchill was similar to many high schools throughout the greater Hamilton area – weekend parties, lots of bands, independent shows and the beginnings of an Internet music boom that brought new music to those who craved more than what commercial radio had to offer. At the time, the residential neighbourhoods between Churchill, Delta Secondary and Bishop Ryan Catholic Secondary were home to a number of new Hamilton musicians and promoters, including future San Sebastian guitarists Sean and Brodie Dawson, live-to-air hype man Adam Burchill, Cities in Dust's Simon Toye and future Young Rival bandmates Aron D'Alesio and Noah Fralick – all of whom were breaking into the local underground in small but eager steps. Other groups such as Threat Signal, June & July, Vatican Chainsaw Massacre, Pantychrist and Tell the Divers would soon emerge from the same collection of neighbourhoods, stretching from Gage Park to Centennial Parkway.

"That area's kind of dingy, but not," says Social Divorce guitarist Dan Troup. "Not to say that Delta's in a dingy area, but like, crazier stuff happened there. We had a good history and art program [at Churchill], and that's what makes bands."

Vatican Chainsaw Massacre vocalist and former Die Hard Losers' member Kevin Sheeler developed a simple explanation for the east-end music boom. "Boredom breeds creativity. Bishop Ryan was just so mundane. Not to shit on the school or anything, but you want to get out and experience something different than you were exposed to."

"At the time, I was in a couple of shitty garage bands, playing shows at Transit Union and the Corktown," offers Gurman. "But my main thing with music back in the day, and Chris was the same way, is that whenever we went to house parties, I was always the guy who stood up at the CD player back before iPods were invented, throwing in mixed CDs. Even mixed cassettes at that point." McNamee agrees, even with the "music snob" handle offered by his cohort.

"Growing up, I was always around music and I always tried to have my finger on the pulse – although it was tougher in those days. Before the Internet was that common, the way that you heard about music was through friends and stuff like that. Or we'd go down to Sonic Unyon and go through their records. I was kind of anti-mainstream, not to say that I wasn't an elitist or anything like that. For me, I couldn't just like something because somebody said it was good. I had to listen to it for myself."

In an era when Korn, Limp Bizkit and Incubus had dominated MuchMusic and mainstream radio, the duo developed a mutual interest in melodic Britpop and indie rock and roll filtering out of the UK – favouring the sounds of Blur, Pulp, Super Furry Animals, Oasis, Suede and other British imports. Punk and hardcore music also became more accessible with the advent of Internet downloading. The pair gravitated toward new records from the likes of Small Brown Bike, Poison the Well, Glassjaw, Taken, Converge, Between the Buried and Me, Refused and Every Time I Die.

"We would hang out a lot and just talk about music, and we would share bands and CDs and stuff like that," says McNamee. "That was just before the re-emergence of rock, before the Strokes and Franz Ferdinand and all that kind of stuff took flight. That was the type of music we both really liked, so once it came back and was more mainstream we just bonded even more. That was around the time that a lot of our friends started writing music and playing shows."

As the 1990s wrapped up and rolled into a new decade, with new musical possibilities, the pair began attending east-end house parties with a side-bag of their favourite CDs and a Discman – armed and ready to take over a stereo whenever the opportunity presented itself. In the pre-garage rock revival years, it didn't take long once a party got going for either DJ to take full advantage of the sound system.

"Gurm was the guy who, no matter how drunk he was or how many people were there, would always be putting on music. If you put something else on, walked out of the room and came back, he'd already have something else on. You knew it was him, too, because you'd look around and he'd be the guy throwing down and getting rowdy."

After finishing high school and bouncing around the Hamilton music scene for several years, Gurman and McNamee began taking their casual hobby to a whole new level. They moved into a house on Dundurn Street South – affectionately known as the Lodge due to its wood-panelled interior, bearskin rug and fireplace – and began hosting themed parties on the expansive second and third floors. "It was a disaster, to be honest with you," Gurman admits.

"When we first started spinning…we played some seriously tiny, 'personal' clubs, where we were pretty much on the dance floor with everyone else," McNamee recalled in a 2009 interview. "As a result of that, we lost three decks and two mixers. Because we're such avid collectors of vinyl, we'd hate to lose them because of drunken hijinks. Even though those were some pretty rad parties."

It wasn't long before the duo made the switch to digital CD turntables, settling on a pair of white Vestax CDR-07s and a basic mixer, although the move wasn't universally well received. "Once, this fucking drunk dude came up to the booth and he was beaking off about us not using vinyl," recalls Gurman. "When we asked him if he was a DJ, he said, 'no, but [my] friend is.' So really, the idiot had no idea what he was talking about."

The flexibility of using CD turntables meant that a wide variety of music could be carted to any given show – including hundreds of burned albums, singles and remixes. From a musical standpoint, almost nothing was out of bounds during the earliest days of No Standards Night. The duo mixed emerging French electro with classic hip-hop, Britpop, punk, hardcore and house music. Sets would include everything from Kings of Leon, the Strokes and Blink-182 to Dr. Dre, Snoop Dogg and Biggie Smalls. MGMT's groovy mid-tempo cut "Electric Feel" from 2007's *Oracular Spectacular* was a big hit at the club, along with "This Charming Man" by the Smiths, "Day 'n' Night" by Kid Cudi, "Bohemian Like You" by the Dandy Warhols, "Jerk It" by Thunderheist and "Bounce" by MSTRKRFT. The latter featured the looping vocal hook, "All I do is party/ha, ha, ha, ha," and always pushed the dance floor into overdrive.

For Gurman, making selections at random was equal parts challenging and exciting – especially with a capacity crowd falling over the DJ table and screaming requests.

"Everything we do is on the fly. We never really plan too much for it, because we feel it takes away from the night," he told me in 2009. "If we're too serious about it, then it's not fun anymore. We know what goes well together, but it's all about reading the crowd and the dance floor. The whole point is to make it fun for everyone, even ourselves. Our idea for the No Standards Night at Che has always been that it should be just like wicked awesome house party, and not a lame club feeling."

• • •

No Standards Night wasn't the only underground dance party giving local rock and roll a shot in the arm. Ten blocks east, on a thin stretch of King Street known as the International Village, a growing number of students, musicians, DJs, artists and degenerates were getting down to vintage soul from Detroit, Memphis and Muscle Shoals at a two-storey venue called Club Absinthe. It was hot. It was sticky. It was dirty. It was undeniably Hamilton.

By the middle of the decade, Motown Wednesdays had emerged as one of the go-to weekly parties in the downtown core. It was where you went to see and be seen, debut a new pair of shoes, mingle with musicians and other DJs and take the edge off. Classic Motown and Stax anthems were dusted off and reborn in the dark, sweat-soaked basement of Club Absinthe, including classic hits such as the Temptations's "Ain't Too Proud to Beg," Stevie Wonder's "Superstition," Aretha Franklin's "Respect," Edwin Starr's "Twenty-Five Miles," the Contours's "Do You Love Me" and the Marvin Gaye/Tammi Terrell anthem "Ain't No Mountain High Enough." The night's main DJs, Owen Smith and Ashish Sharma, also went to great lengths to dig up or burn vintage rock and roll cuts from the 1960s and 1970s, including landmark tracks by the Beatles, Rolling Stones, the Kinks, the Zombies, the Meters, Wilson Pickett and Booker T. & the M.G.'s.

The groove was undeniable. It hit you like a tonne of bricks. You had to move at Club Absinthe – get lost in the moment and soak up the vibes. And it all started with a flash of inspiration from local musician and budding entrepreneur Marko Lubarda.

Born and raised in Montenegro, Lubarda relocated to Hamilton in 1995 and immediately dove into the city's punishing heavy metal scene. He formed popular local outfit Hypodust in the early 2000s, where he played bass and guitar alongside lead singer and local producer Julius Butty, drummer Dan Fila, guitarists Terry D'Andrea and Sean Williamson and, later, ex-Threat

Signal shredder Marco Bressette. The group cut two full-length records before quietly disbanding.

Despite his metal and hard rock leanings, Lubarda also recognized a developing niche market in Hamilton for out-of-the-ordinary musical events – DJ nights, bizarre themed parties, burlesque shows and anything that didn't already fit the standard format of a traditional rock or dance venue. All he needed was the right space to make it happen.

In 2003, Lubarda took control of a defunct two-floor night-club at 233 King Street East, formerly known as the Hudson. The old blues and hard rock bar had been shuttered for roughly eighteen months. Lubarda set about rebranding the murky hall for a new generation of live music fans – dubbing it Club Absinthe with a splash of neon-blue lettering atop a black marquee hovering over the street. From day one, the mandate at Club Absinthe was fairly simple: it was all about cheap drinks, positive energy and keeping an open mind to whatever was going to walk through the front door. The space provided another stage for emerging talent in the Hamilton area, and – along with Che and No Standards Night – helped reinforce the cultural cachet of the underground club DJ, a new hero into the city's music community. When the first Motown-themed event at Club Absinthe was held in 2003, it didn't take long for the city to latch on.

"Bobby Sockett [a close friend] and I were at a bar tossing ideas around," recalls Lubarda. "I had done a night with Jimmy Vapid, sort of like 1950s and 1960s and early punk music, and we always had a tendency to do something old, because we loved everything about it, the whole imagery, the clothing, the music, everything."

After developing a loose but promising concept, Lubarda hired Toronto-based club DJ Owen Smith to spin at his new weekly themed party. After two weeks on the job, Smith recruited

Ashish Sharma, a friend since high school, to help reinforce and polish the four-to-five hour set of music and add a new voice to the party. The pair would depart from downtown Toronto every Wednesday as the sun went down – their car stocked with the finest collection of soul, blues, rock and R&B music Hamilton's millennial generation had ever heard. For Smith, heavily polished Motown jams went hand in hand with vintage garage rock, southern soul, proto-punk and the more danceable side of British invasion produced during the same time period. Ironically, the challenge quickly became limiting the amount of Motown and keeping a fresh supply of tunes flowing through the speakers each week.

"I was bringing in all the records that applied, so maybe fifty to seventy records, and [Ashish] would bring a shitload of CDs," says Smith, over a pair of ice-cold Carlsberg pints at the Powerhouse in Stoney Creek – his adopted hometown for the past several years. One day shy of his thirty-sixth birthday, he's still sporting the exact same newsboy cap and fiery red beard that commanded so many parties from behind the DJ booth at Club Absinthe.

"When you first start you're like, 'fuck, I know tons of Motown, but do I know four hours of it? Do I know four hours that you want to hear of it? Do I want to play, like, Roberta Flack B-sides?'"

With no cover charge, cheap drinks and a live band or secondary DJ crew often booked for the main floor, Motown Wednesdays became the perfect fit for the city's growing student population. Twentysomethings from McMaster University and Mohawk College began venturing farther east from the pubs and clubs of Hess Village – reigniting the struggling International Village neighbourhood while helping to build a mid-week party scene in the downtown core.

During its first few years on King Street East, the club became infamous for three things: beer, sweat and out-of-control partying. Fights on the dance floor were uncommon, but certainly not unheard of, and the polished concrete floor in the basement was usually covered in spilled booze and broken glass well before last call.

"If those walls could talk. They definitely did sweat," says Billy Pozeg, a long-time associate of Lubarda's and one of the driving forces behind Club Absinthe. "As dank and dark as that basement was, it added a ton to the overall feel and vibe. Getting sweaty on Motown Wednesdays was almost a badge of honour, to say you did it all night and didn't stop. You had somehow survived."

On any given Wednesday night, lines stretched down the block toward Walnut Street, culminating in a loose mob of smokers, drunks and line-jumpers all vying for position at the front entrance. Some patrons would bypass the line entirely via the parking lot at the rear of the building. With a friend on the inside, one could sneak down the outdoor basement staircase, slip through a propped-open emergency exit and enter near the men's washroom – so long as a bouncer didn't catch you in the act. Regardless of how one got into the club, everyone was welcome.

"You'd walk in and there would be three punk kids, four metalheads and seven well-dressed club girls. It was just a mishmash of absolutely everything," explains Lubarda. "What girls loved about it was it almost felt like they were in a safe house party where they could dance without being bothered. And the guys that would normally be laughed at, they would let loose and do goofy moves and stuff like that. It was a good environment, and a safe environment for everybody."

"People were looking for a mid-week release," Pozeg adds. "It wasn't even young people, as we carried ages from nineteen to forty-five. Thing is, everybody fit in. Whether you were metal or punk or went clubbing on weekends. Motown was chosen specifically for that reason. It has a beat and funk that all genres appreciate, and was the one sound that everybody could agree on."

For Smith, the run of Motown Wednesdays toward the end of the decade comprised the event's golden era. What began as an untested musical and cultural experiment soon became the crown jewel of Hamilton's blossoming alternative club scene – a consistent and uncompromising staple with a throng of patrons crashing the front gates each week. Local DJs such as Andy Inglis would often stop by the club for impromptu guest sets, and each week's party brought in a new cast of characters culled from the hottest and most innovative bands in Hamilton, among them Arkells, San Sebastian, Cities in Dust and Huron. Despite the newfound popularity and attention that Motown Wednesdays afforded Smith and Sharma – in foreign territory, no less – Smith's fondest memory to this day is simply being able to share classic hits with young, inspired patrons.

"You kind of felt like, 'yeah, maybe I struck out with a chick that night,' or maybe you got lucky, whatever. But you came home with more of an education – like new knowledge, you know what I mean? It's cool that people like that," says Smith. "And there were no dumb questions. If someone came up during 'Satisfaction' and said, 'what is this?' I'd be like, 'oh, it's "Satisfaction." Have you heard of it?' I would never be like, 'you fucking loser.' I hate people like that...I don't like the nose-up-in-the-air bullshit."

· · ·

As the underground dance scene in Hamilton continued to expand and evolve, so too did Charlemagne. The band had garnered a passionate following in the west end and downtown core, and continued to book gigs across Southern Ontario. For shows in the Toronto area, Kerman and co. became infamous for loading their guitars and amps into the underside of a GO Transit bus and riding high along the Queen Elizabeth Way en route to Union Station, before carting their gear over to a local venue. Once new drummer Tim Oxford was comfortable and confident, the band wasted little time preparing to record.

"I think we spent six days rehearsing right after we met Tim," recalls former keyboardist Dan Griffin. "We were just so hot to record, and we needed an EP so we could start giving it out to people."

Independently released in 2007 – and reissued the following year by Dine Alone Records – the *Deadlines* recording showed a great deal of promise in the band's songwriting abilities, and was a big step from their previous effort, *The Broken Tapes*. The new CD included an early version of the band's first hit radio single, "Oh, The Boss is Coming!" and four other tracks that would make their way onto *Jackson Square*, the band's full-length debut, in one form or another: "Tragic Flaw," "The Ballad of Hugo Chavez," "No Champagne Socialist" and the album's closer, "Blueprint."

All five tracks from the sixteen-minute EP demonstrated a keen awareness for balancing tough, hard-driving rhythms with sensitive, introspective lyrics and sing-along melodies – two pillars that would come to define the band's sound in the years ahead. The *Deadlines* EP also offered a legitimate shot at finding a fanbase beyond the outer reaches of Highway 401 – a dream of Kerman's since the band's inception as Charlemagne in their dorm room at McMaster.

But getting just five songs on tape proved to be a major logistical challenge. When recording began in earnest, four of the five band members were still immersed in their undergraduate studies at McMaster. Guitarist Mike DeAngelis recalls struggling to find a balance between writing essays, studying for exams and navigating the ins and outs of a professional studio with an up-and-coming band.

"It was sort of an interesting time for me, especially because I had a bunch of papers due," says DeAngelis. "It was sort of this series of going to record, leaving, starting a paper, doing the paper all night, handing it in during the morning, sleeping all day and then just getting up again. We got late studio time because it was cheaper. So we would record from eight p.m. to twelve at night, and then drive back from Scarborough to Hamilton every night. The whole experience was so stressful and difficult, and it definitely had a lot to do with school."

The band continued gigging regularly throughout Southern Ontario as four of the five members tried to focus on completing their studies at McMaster. With exams wrapped up and the school year behind them, come May, the group landed a gig at the 2007 North by Northeast music festival the following month. It was an afternoon slot on the open-air stage in heavily trafficked Yonge and Dundas Square, not far from the sprawling Toronto Eaton Centre.

The gig proved to be one of the most fruitful of the group's career, past or present. During the set, Dakota Tavern owner Shawn Creamer happened to be walking along Yonge Street and paused to take in a few of the band's songs. Creamer bought several copies of the *Deadlines* EP after the show, and later passed a CD along to Joel Carriere of Dine Alone Records. The local imprint was already making waves in the Canadian music industry with acts like Bedouin Soundclash, Attack in Black, and City and Colour, and was eager to bring a new local group into the fold.

With a record deal on the horizon, the band hit a snag when an American group successfully claimed ownership over the name Charlemagne. The Canadian five-piece was forced to find a new handle as soon as possible. One name that stood out from the pack was the Surly Young Bucks – the name reserved for the old west-end jam band featuring Kerman, DeAngelis, Dan Griffin, Aaron Goldstein and a rotating cast of characters. While some members of Charlemagne considered the name a good fit, Goldstein wouldn't have it.

"Aaron was like, 'absolutely not,'" recalls DeAngelis with a laugh. "We were so lost in the naming process that we were kind of just grasping at straws at that point. We knew that the Surly Young Bucks name had worked to some degree, and the band really wasn't doing as much at that point and people were pursuing different projects. I think Max said, 'I'll just see what Aaron thinks,' and [Aaron] couldn't even believe it...he just thought it was its own entity."

The group eventually settled on the name Arkells, a nod to a student house at 85 Arkell Street in Westdale Village that Kerman and DeAngelis both lived in. A post on *Indie Music Filter* dated February 26, 2008, reads: "Update your notes, the band formerly known as Charlemagne are now called Arkells. Check out 'Oh, the Boss Is Coming!' on *MTV Live*. Their EP is available now on Dine Alone Records." The main hook from the song "John Lennon" – with its singalong vocal refrain, "I'm so lost/ and I live just around the corner" – is a reference to the distance between the band's student house at 85 Arkell and a string of pubs that runs through the city's west end, including a popular student hangout known as the Snooty Fox.

They would soon be singing that hook in student pubs and packed concert halls all over the country.

. . .

As the year progressed and Arkells fine-tuned their repertoire, two other Hamilton bands saw their own projects sputter. The first, Neighbourhood Noise, played their final show at a New Year's Eve party at Club Absinthe and decided to call it quits soon afterward. The second, a three-piece rock and roll outfit known as the Racket, was looking to expand their sound and explore new opportunities in the local music scene.

Two sets of brothers from both groups – Brodie and Sean Dawson from Neighbourhood Noise, and Greg and Mike Veerman from the Racket, along with drummer and mutual acquaintance Ted Paterson – went on to form Pumps within the following year, which slowly morphed into San Sebastian. Bassist Greg Veerman remembers this transition period, as well as the members' early days in the Hamilton music scene, with sparkling clarity.

"We played a show with Neighbourhood Noise at the Westside Concert Theatre, and it was a funny show for us because we had this girl come from EMI Publishing," says Veerman, leaning over a table at the Mulberry Coffeehouse in January 2012. Handsome and charming, he has the clean-cut look of a teen heartthrob plucked from the pages of *Tiger Beat* magazine.

"No one was there, and it was the first time we saw those guys play. It was the first time we met them. We thought their songs were really cool. We loved the guitar playing and they looked really cool on stage."

Formed in 2004, the Racket were considered veterans of the Hamilton music scene by the time they connected with the Dawson brothers. With a brand new album to their name, the trio arranged a self-booked tour to British Columbia and back, which proved to be somewhat of an ill-fated venture.

78

A friend of the Veerman brothers was hoping to visit a love interest out west that very summer. He offered to book a tour for the Racket, sell merchandise and do all of the legwork, if he could simply hitch a ride out to the coast and back. The band agreed and set out for the Pacific in a borrowed minivan with a small gear trailer. "He booked it kind of self-serving, because he knew there was a girl in Vancouver he wanted to see," Veerman says with a laugh.

The Racket had a steady and successful run of gigs until they hit the coast, at which point their tour manager had scheduled nearly two weeks in the city without much for his companions to do. But after a long haul across the Prairies – a journey that involved cheap and greasy fast food, sleeping at promoters' homes and one or two nights curled up inside the van – the band was happy to at least have a roof over their heads.

Being stranded in Vancouver wasn't the only spot of trouble on that first tour. After their first out-of-town gig, the club owner was looking to pay the group for their evening's work. By the time staff eventually located him, the band's rookie tour manager was already passed out drunk in the van. "We quickly realized he was there strictly to party, and that was fine with us," says Veerman. "That tour was more of a vacation. It was just fun to play shows, and it was a cool thing to do when I was twenty or whatever. It was a good experience."

Brodie Dawson and his older brother Sean grew up in the quiet, blue-collar community of Rosedale in the east end of the city, along with many of the budding tastemakers who would eventually make up the present-day Hamilton music scene. Much like Simon Toye, Aaron Gurman, Young Rival's Aron D'Alesio and Noah Fralick, and other musicians from that end of town, Dawson talks fondly of a musical upbringing driven by two factors: a passion for loud music and a lack of anything else to do. Everyone was young, bored and looking for an outlet. Along with their crosstown peers at Westdale Secondary and other area high schools, Transit Union Hall on Wilson Street became the natural hub for live music in the downtown core – especially for those not yet old enough to enter nineteen-plus venues such as the Underground and the Casbah.

"The bar manager had his own little deep fryer for French fries for people, and there was a beer selection for the nineteen-plus crowd," recalls Dawson. "But he was too old and couldn't go up the steps. So everyone upstairs, like fifteen year olds, were drinking forties of Olde English and, like, smoking weed and shit. You had fourteen-year-old kids smoking cigars because they could. It was awesome. What a tease for our future … somehow that lawless environment was okay. No one ever complained."

Monster Truck's Jon Harvey, a Transit Union regular while playing with his former punk band Hoosier Poet, had a similar experience. "I mean it was young, seventeen-year-old kids running these shows for four hundred or five hundred kids from all over the city. So it kind of made a scene. Or for lack of a better word, a 'scene,' I guess. It made something, you know? You always had something to do. If there were no shows on a Friday, someone would make a show."

Dawson earned his stripes playing Sunday afternoon basement shows in the east end with the band Halfway There, charging three dollars for admission. Their neighbours were not nearly as enthused. "Every time we played a show the cops would show up," he admits.

Almost immediately after, the two sets of brothers joined forces and Pumps exploded onto the city's music scene. The band members had individually earned a reputation as ferocious local party rockers before playing a single show together.

Now they had Greg and Mike Veerman on bass and lead vocals respectively, Brodie and Sean Dawson on guitar and friend Ted Paterson behind the kit. In addition to being a talented player, Paterson was also a calming presence from the get-go. And they needed it.

"That's why we have Ted in the band," Veerman told the *Hamilton Spectator* in 2011. "He's the mediator. Whenever we fight in the band, it's always Mike and I fighting each other, or Brodie and Sean fighting each other. There's not really any cross-brother fighting; it's always inter-brother. That's when Ted comes into the picture. He's our rock. He's our guiding light."

With ties to the reckless Rockstars for Hire crew, and the underground dance scenes at Club Absinthe and Che, Pumps quickly became regulars at down-and-out watering holes and sweaty nightclubs in the city's downtown core. If a case of Pabst Blue Ribbon was chilling next to a bottle of Jägermeister, chances are Pumps were nearby – with or without their instruments. It wasn't long before a large crop of local music fans, including a growing number of beautiful young women, joined the party.

"We called it the Year of Pumps," says Brodie Dawson, referring to the band's increasingly wild urban excursions throughout the ensuing year. "Every bar we went to on the weekend, it was always me, Greg, Sean and Mike. The four of us. The brothers. At this point, Ted was pretty much just a guy who played with us. We didn't know him very well. Our friend Shane Cunningham did a ton of pro bono video work for us. He would buy weird cameras and find the film on eBay, just so he could film us. He has tons and tons and tons of cool footage of that shit."

Naturally, they soon moved into a cramped and scummy band house and nearly killed each other.

• • •

EVENINGS & WEEKENDS

In September, I moved into a three-bedroom student bungalow near Churchill Park, along with Chris Arnett – my close pal from the *Silhouette* – and a mutual friend, Cameron Thomas. Chris and I each took a room on the main floor of the house, while Cam claimed a large, dark hovel on the lower level as his personal space.

The house had been trashed with confidence and gusto. The carpet on the main floor was so old and musty that we had to wear slippers to keep our white socks from turning black. The orange kitchen tiles were swarming with tiny black ants that flocked to leftover pizza boxes left by the rear entrance. The original deadbolt on the front door had been smashed – in some kind of overnight grow-op bust, it was rumoured – and its replacement was loosely fixed to the rotting wooden frame. The basement bathroom was caked in black grime and mould, and required several days of manual scrubbing on our hands and knees to become usable. There was a second kitchen in the basement that was entirely off limits – filled with rotting cabinetry, an old white stove covered in grey dust and cobwebs, cracked cardboard boxes and green mason jars piled in the middle of the floor. However, the basement fridge was still plugged in and working fine. It was immediately stocked with bottles of Labatt 50, large plastic jugs of orange juice and boxes of frozen pizzas.

On the plus side, the basement had a proper bar built into one of the walls in the wood-panelled recreation room. That was all we needed to see before signing the lease.

We moved a set of drums and all our guitars and amplifiers into the lower level, along with an old plaid couch, a television, two stereo speakers, a turntable and a receiver, a set of golf clubs and piles of old footballs, hockey sticks and skateboards. The upstairs was reserved for reading books and writing articles, while the basement quickly became our party den. Friends and coworkers from the *Silhouette* would come over at all hours of the night, puff thin joints and play old British blues songs. Sometimes we'd watch classic movies like *Easy Rider, Blue Velvet, Mean Streets* and *Chinatown*. We'd host house parties on weekends, complete with a basement dance floor cordoned off with white Christmas lights strung along the wooden baseboard and all the overhead lamps turned off. Friends from campus would tend bar on a rotating basis, pouring out huge shots of Jack Daniel's and peach schnapps, and cracking the tabs on cold cans of beer. At times, it was like running our own nightclub, flophouse and greasy spoon. The side door of the house, which led to the basement, was rarely locked.

During the first week of school – the night before attending Virgin Fest on Toronto Island to catch Arctic Monkeys, M.I.A. and Interpol – myself, Chris and a group of staffers from the *Silhouette* walked from our house in Westdale Village over to a gigantic house party on Bowman Street. We made the trek on foot, passing through the park and across McMaster's bustling nighttime campus. We crossed six lanes of traffic on Main Street West and carted a large case of beer over the railroad tracks before arriving at a white vinyl-sided bungalow near the foot of the Escarpment. The backyard was already rammed with students, the grass soaked in beer. Chris plunked down our case of Labatt 50 on the stone patio, twisted the caps from two bottles and handed me one.

Twenty minutes later, I met Terra Lightfoot.

• • •

Long before joining the Dinner Belles and launching a successful solo career as an acclaimed singer-songwriter, Terra Lightfoot was just Terra – another McMaster student with an acoustic guitar playing clubs and coffeehouses in the west end of the city, still getting a feel for performing in front of other people. Like myself, Lightfoot was also a townie – a local who chose to stick around Hamilton when most of her peers couldn't wait to flee for much larger scenes. Our upbringings in the city were entirely different, but vaguely familiar in a comforting way.

"I grew up in Waterdown," Lightfoot begins, corresponding via email throughout the summer of 2012. "I lived on Beach Road, right on the water, sometime before I turned five with my mom in a little apartment above a garage. I went to school in Waterdown and did the normal run of schools there – Mary Hopkins, Flamborough Centre and Waterdown High School. I played bass in the jazz band so I could get in on the trips to Cuba and Ottawa. My music teacher was Craig Hunter, who used to play drums in the Philosopher Kings and was a really, really, great teacher. We're still friends."

"My mom took me to the Suzuki School of Music when I was five. I took those lessons until I was ten, and then she bought me a guitar at a garage sale," she explained to the *Silhouette* in 2015. "It's actually the worst guitar ever. I didn't start singing until I was sixteen, probably. I used to always sing in my bedroom and my mom would always think that I had a friend over. She would ask 'who is your friend with the nice voice?' and I would pretend not to know what she was talking about. I was trying to be really quiet because I was really embarrassed."

Lightfoot is a fierce and uncompromising frontwoman with a strong command of her instrument and her voice, but she's equally comfortable stepping out of the spotlight and allowing others to shine. Primarily known for her alt-country leanings, Lightfoot has also cultivated a reputation as a talented lead guitarist who's more than capable of hanging with Southern Ontario's rock and punk communities. One of those projects involved a short-lived collaboration with Don Vail, a popular underground band comprised of former members of Chore and Treble Charger that released a self-titled record in 2008. When the opportunity arose to temporarily swap her acoustic guitar for a Gibson SG, it was too good to pass up.

"I've loved playing loud, overdriven electric guitar since I strummed my first note through an amplifier. I think everyone does," says Lightfoot. "The Don Vail thing happened because I've always loved Chore and was immediately available when they needed a guitar player for those few shows. I was neighbours with Mike Bell [Chore] and from there I got to know Dave Dunham, who asked me to sing on his electronic stuff. By the time those shows rolled around, they all had enough confidence in me to let me do those shows, which was a big thing for me. Still is."

"My parents have pictures of me falling asleep with my guitar on me," she told the *Hamilton Spectator* in 2015. "I would come home from school, I'd get together with some friends and I'd be still playing when they left. It was always electric."

Toward the end of the 2000s, Lightfoot continued to hone her craft, recording new songs in a number of complimentary and contrasting genres. But as her writing and personality matured, so too did the music. The year she turned twenty-five turned out to be her most prolific to date.

In spring 2011, she retreated to a remote campground on the shores of Koshlong Lake to record an EP with Huron guitarist Cam Malcolm. Billed as Secret Heights, the duo released a gentle, self-produced seven-track offering of the same name later that summer, before Lightfoot shifted her focus to a pair of projects that would formally launch her career.

Almost immediately following the release of the Secret Heights material, Lightfoot unveiled her long-awaited, self-titled solo record. Originally recorded on Toronto Island with the help of Pete Hall – along with Secret Heights collaborator Cam Malcolm and Dale Morningstar of The Dinner is Ruined – a remastered version of the album was released by Sonic Unyon in September 2011. The disc was amalgam of "really old songs I needed to get on tape," and new material the twenty-five-year-old had been experimenting with during the months leading up to recording.

That same fall, Lightfoot embarked on her first cross-Canada tour as a member of Hamilton folk-roots collective the Dinner Belles. The band was a blossoming side project featuring Monster Truck organist Brandon Bliss and former Marble Index frontman Brad Germain alongside veteran musicians Greg Brisco, Scott Bell, Jonathan Ely Cass and Melanie Pothier.

"The Dinner Belles are a really cool band," says Harlan Pepper frontman Dan Edmonds. "When we first heard them we really loved it, but we didn't really know any of them. We knew Terra, but not that well. Slowly, over time, we've played some shows with them and we've met them all in different situations around the city. They're a fantastic band and fantastic people, too. They're some of the best players in Hamilton."

The group released their debut record *West Simcoe County* one month prior to Lightfoot's solo disc, and booked a tour to the Pacific coast and back to promote the new material and fine-tune their dynamic live show. Having never visited the western provinces, let alone criss-crossing the Prairies in a cramped, stinking caravan of touring vehicles, it was an experience Lightfoot had mixed feelings about.

"It was amazing, it was horrible. The best, the worst. The most fun and the least sleep," she begins. "It was a lot of driving, and a lot of meeting new people and having to be on my game every night. I had never been west, however, so it was a really great experience. Driving through the mountains while my pal Scotty

slept in the passenger seat of my Cavalier – her name is Caroline
– was one of the highlights. I'd never been in a mountain range
like that before, and I won't ever forget seeing them for the first
time, even though it was foggy and raining."

"I always forget that she's still so young. She seems to have
been around forever," says 93.3 CFMU program director James
Tennant, reflecting on his long-time admiration for Lightfoot,
both as a solo artist and a member of the Dinner Belles.

"Terra's a funny one, because the second you hear that voice
...I remember Gunner and I were hosting the *C+C Music Show*
in maybe 2008, and we were in the studio with my buddy Afternoons in Stereo, and she came in and played and we all just kind
of gasped. It was beautiful. It was amazing. And we literally, I'm
not even kidding, almost cried. How crazy is that?"

• • •

As Motown Wednesdays continued to grow in popularity and
the Hamilton rock scene expanded alongside it, Marko Lubarda
was eager to stake a claim on the coveted Saturday slot – still
one of the most popular and lucrative dates on the weekly club
calendar.

By the middle of the decade, half a dozen bars in Hamilton
offered regular Saturday night dance parties. At McMaster
University, Quarters was home to a popular Top 40 night that
boasted a lineup stretching into the middle of the Student Centre.
The rapidly expanding nightclub scene in Hess Village offered
similar fare at a number of massive venues, including Sizzle &
Koi, Elixir and Funky Munky. A few blocks east, Seventy-Seven
and the adjoining Dirty Dog Saloon were also popular weekend
destinations for thirsty club-goers, with the latter favouring
cowboy hats and flannel as much as Calvin Klein and Polo.

EVENINGS & WEEKENDS

Still, Lubarda saw an opening. To counter the saturation of Top 40 pop music at most downtown venues, Club Absinthe officially launched I Say Disco/You Say Punk in 2006 – a brand new Saturday party that offered a bold mixture of techno, house, hip-hop, indie rock and hardcore punk. Around the same time, local on-air personality and Indi 101 program director Jamie Smith had been flirting with the idea of a live-to-air nightclub broadcast in Hamilton. He was just looking for the right team to back his vision.

A former tour manager with Junkhouse and the Killjoys, Smith's love affair with radio emerged during countless overland runs to the Pacific shore and back. Stuck behind the wheel of a tour van for long hauls across the Canadian Prairies, he developed a true appreciation for the local radio personalities that crackled over the airwaves in the middle of the night, telling stories of small-town misery, community politics, minor league hockey and good old-fashioned Canadian rock and roll.

With a background in tour managing and music promotion, combined with a raw passion for community radio, it wasn't long before Smith was hitting the clubs in search of the perfect venue to host his experimental live-to-air broadcast. He finally made a connection with Lubarda and a trio of McMaster University students turned amateur DJs – ex–Cities in Dust bandmates Simon Toye and Zach Frank, and their mutual friend Justin Wood. Soon after, a live-to-air, unfiltered showcase for Hamilton's alternative nightclub scene was born.

"One of the nights they were doing [at Club Absinthe] was called I Say Disco/You Say Punk…they were struggling, but they saw the product and what they could do with it," recalls Smith, hunched over a control board at McMaster's CFMU radio station during the coldest week of the year in 2013. "It was the right

88

move and the right time, and it was the right scene. There were lineups out the door to come and see Disco/Punk."

As a former music editor of the *Silhouette*, Toye had already developed a knack for finding and promoting underground trends well before the mainstream caught on. He later used that same adventurous, anything-goes mentality to help spearhead the innovative Disco/Punk series, spurred on by the same interest in unscripted, live broadcasting that captured Smith's imagination. Although his own fascination with broadcasting stemmed from late nights spent listening to alternative radio programs from the other side of Lake Ontario.

"The only reason I ever wanted to start playing records is because the Edge did live-to-air nights," recalls Toye. "Sunday night, they used to have a retro night at Whiskey Saigon in Toronto. It was kind of weird, but that new wave and synth-pop was always something I was very, very drawn to. I remember on Sunday nights I would listen from ten o'clock until whenever, and I would write down songs and set lists as they were playing. I'd try to remember, 'oh, this is this song,' and 'this is this song,' and then I'd go out and try to buy some of these records."

By the summer of 2007, Disco/Punk had absolutely exploded. With Toye now working steadily with Frank and Wood to grow the event, and Smith expressing real interest in promoting the DJs far and wide, the group began perfecting a set of uptempo, electro-infused rock and roll to spin at their weekly residency. They mixed new singles with old favourites from the likes of the Strokes, MSTRKRFT, Interpol, Refused, Bloc Party, Daft Punk, Jay Z and the Yeah Yeah Yeahs – each track infused with a perfect blend of raw power and dance-ability that attracted young crowds in increasingly large numbers. The grinding Justice remix of Simian's "We Are Your Friends" was an early favourite, along with the Ratatat remix of the Notorious B.I.G. cut "Party and Bullshit" from the former's 2007 album *Ratatat Remixes Vol. II*, and the Strokes's breakout garage-rock single "Last Nite" off 2001's *Is This It*.

With the new Saturday showcase growing in popularity, east-ender Adam Burchill soon came into the fold as MC Uncle Buck, adding another stick of dynamite to the already cramped and volatile DJ booth. "We would have just absolute shenanigans downstairs, and it was a lot of fun," recalls Smith. "I'd have Adam do throws over the air with me. He'd get the crowd going, and I'd back-sell the music. I was trying to keep it like a radio show, but if you listen to it, it wasn't a radio show. It was just a free-for-all party that was going over the air. And people loved it."

Lubarda agrees: "Usually what happens is: things start in places like New York and London, Toronto steals it from them and then we take it from Toronto," he says. "But with this Disco/Punk thing, it was very unique. A lot of people that came from LA, or photographers and DJs from New York, they were like, 'man, this is really cool' . . . it seemed like there was no other world once you were in that basement. It was sweaty, and it was packed. It was a scene, for sure, man."

"It was balls-to-the-wall parties every week, but it felt like you were in your friend's basement with the furniture and dimly lit corners," says Club Absinthe manager Billy Pozeg. "But then out of nowhere someone like Albert Hammond Jr. of the Strokes would come onto the decks. It was a night of surprises you want-ed to be a part of, regardless of what was going on, because the party was always insane and next level."

Pumps guitarist Brodie Dawson was hired as a bartender to help staff the increasingly wild and weird dance parties at Club Absinthe during Motown Wednesdays and Disco/Punk. Already familiar with the regular cast of students and musicians who frequented the bar, it was an easy sell.

"If you remember the old Absinthe [prior to relocating to its current location], we had that little DJ booth with the step up," recalls Dawson. "There are so many photos from Disco/Punk nights where the whole booth is just full of people standing on the equipment and, like, spilling beer and shit. There was no one grabbing them and throwing them off...no one gave a damn about anything. It was like a punk rock show. It was almost a controlled recklessness, where you expect stuff to happen but nothing really bad is going to happen."

2008

IN SPRING 2008, the members of Arkells were preparing to not only graduate from McMaster, but to digitally re-release their *Deadlines* EP on Toronto's Dine Alone Records. With undergraduate degrees framed and mounted and *Jackson Square* on the horizon, the band geared-up to hit the road harder than ever before.

"When we finished school, we did a tour with Saint Alvia Cartel," says lead guitarist Mike DeAngelis. "We basically toured all the way across Canada with them to the west. Then we did City and Colour after-parties on the way back. The shows pretty much both ways were ghost towns. They were super empty. Some of the guys from Dallas's band would come – the drummer and the bass player. We were also touring with Jim Ward from At the Drive-In. His band Sleepercar was opening for City and Colour on that tour, and they would come out. They were all really nice, and they thought it was cool that we were just trying to do it or whatever."

"The first tour is always exciting, because you're just in a van with your pals and you can kind of sweep aside any of the crappy parts of it," adds Kerman. "But the whole tour was full of pretty empty shows. Later that summer, we did three dates with the Black Crowes in western Canada as well. We went back out to play these big theatres, and that was really amazing. I think everyone was genuinely excited."

. . .

That April, we held a small party in the office for the newspaper's graduating staff. Everyone sipped from plastic Solo cups filled with Jack Daniel's and cheap, sweet champagne while putting our final issue of the year to bed. I slid my chair under my desk at the *Silhouette* for the last time, and Chris Arnett and I walked across Churchill Park to our student bungalow as the sun came up. Beyond passing my final exams and receiving my undergraduate degree in June, the rest of my year was wide open.

I bumped into Ciara again during a late night at the Phoenix at McMaster. Myself, Chris Arnett and two of our good friends from the *Silhouette*, Jeff Green and Adam Owen, were shooting pool and slowly working our way through two large jugs of beer and a platter of deep-fried bar snacks, reflecting on the year gone by. We were listening to the latest albums from the Kooks and MGMT on the bar's old stereo. Ciara was wearing a long-sleeve silver top with tiny sequins, a slim-fitting black skirt, sheer tights and glossy black ballet flats. She looked beautiful. Her own crew was heading out the door, en route to Club Absinthe for Motown Wednesdays, when she caught my eye for a split second.

"Andrew?" she called across the bar, skipping over to our table.

"How are you? I haven't seen you in forever!"

As we embraced, I knocked a full pint off the edge of the pool table, sending foam and beer all over the carpet. Adam picked up the glass and nudged me toward Ciara in one motion, without saying a word.

Ciara and I had shared a handful of English and film classes the previous term, but failed to progress beyond friendly waves and smiles and quick hellos. Ciara was always one of the brightest students in class, fearless in a large lecture hall or small senior seminar. She always maintained a long-term boyfriend and I was all over the map, busy with the *Silhouette* and other pursuits. It never seemed to click while we were at university. But there was always a spark – an unspoken connection between us. I knew we both felt it.

"I'm heading back home next week, but we should keep in touch. I want to know what you get up to," she said, smiling. Adam was grinning across the table, hands clasped atop an upright pool cue. Ciara's friends were calling down the corridor leading out of the bar.

"Sorry, but I have to leave now. Let's talk soon!"

She jogged around the corner and down the long corridor to join her friends, their laughter echoing as someone called for a taxi. It would be another full year before we crossed paths again. I glanced back at the game and watched as Jeff sunk the eight ball. "Rack 'em!" he yelled, taking a long haul from his pint. Chris and I lost the next two games.

• • •

It was around this time that I reconnected with an old group of friends from Westdale – Tom Shepherd, Mike Lawson, Stevie Ledlie and a handful others. We were all back in town following stints at university and college with varying degrees of success. I bumped into Mike and Tom first, during an evening in Hess Village. I was sipping a pint on the patio and watching crowds of people drift into the strip when my old high school crew arrived suddenly.

Mike was tall and tough, with a scruffy beard. He was dressed in a tight-fitting green jacket with a wide hood, skinny jeans and ratty black Chuck Taylors with white laces. He looked vaguely threatening. Casually menacing. Especially with a cigarette dangling from his lips. But Mike also had a warm smile and a wicked sense of humour, and was generally down for anything. He had just returned from a stint in Alaska and northern British Columbia, working heavy labour jobs in the backcountry. He was flush with cash and eager to burn off a little steam.

Tom was long and wiry, built like a long-distance runner. He could make a white T-shirt and blue jeans appropriate for any occasion with a few subtle touches, like an expensive watch or new pair of brown leather shoes from England. He always had a fresh bottle of beer dangling from his fingertips, and tonight was no exception. At home, he favoured drinking whisky and red wine from a set of antique glass tumblers he'd purchased from an antique market. Tom was a casual smoker, but it never showed.

"Drew, what's happening?" Mike asked, dragging a pair of metal chairs across the patio to my table. "Long time no see."

"Yeah man, what's good?" Tom chimed in. He pulled out a cigarette and tossed the pack toward Mike. I asked for one as well, and Tom lit all three with a single match before leaning back in his chair and exhaling into the sky. We ordered another round of drinks and caught up as groups of young girls yelled into their cellphones and clicked their heels on the cobblestone street. A few moments later, Stevie arrived.

"Fuck, Andrew? What's up, man?" I stood and Stevie wrapped his arms around me in a tight bear hug, slapping my back and squeezing my ribs. "You look good, man. Really tasty." He grinned and winked, then started giggling.

Short and stout, with shoulders almost as wide as he was long, Stevie was a ball of fun. He loved to crack jokes and squeal from deep within his belly whenever he got silly, which was often. He was also a diplomat who could diffuse any situation with a sly grin and a quick flick of his eyebrows. Stevie was always a little aloof, though – difficult to connect with in any deep, meaningful way, unless you were someone he could trust and confide in. And there were very few of us.

During our days at Westdale Secondary, Stevie and I had spent countless afternoons hanging around his parents' suburban home on the Mountain – playing guitar and video games, skateboarding curbs and mini-ramps, lacing up our skates when the local parks were frozen over. We'd drifted apart slightly when university and college came knocking, but remained in touch over the years, always making time to play music and share a few beers during summer breaks. We exchanged numbers on the Ceilidh House patio and agreed to catch up again soon. There were very few nights the remainder of the year when the group of us weren't up to something. Our gang became inseparable.

• • •

Meanwhile, Hamilton – along with much of North America – was about to slide into a prolonged economic recession. That fall, as Detroit automakers prepared to ask Congress for a multibillion-dollar bailout, the demand for steel dipped significantly as production of domestic cars began to wane. Hundreds of auto-sector layoffs soon swept across Southern Ontario, crippling the province's once-strong manufacturing sector. U.S. Steel, an American juggernaut now in control of the city's historic Stelco steel-making plant, would idle the factory the following spring. Multiple generations of local shift workers and pensioners were left holding their breath, waiting for scattered updates.

The city's annual unemployment rate was also rising. From November to December alone, the Social Planning & Research Council of Hamilton recorded an increase of nearly four hundred Ontario Works government assistance cases – the largest one-month climb since the late 1990s. The *Hamilton Spectator*, a local institution since 1846 and the city's only daily newspaper, was beginning to sputter. As advertising revenues dipped in the wake of an unprecedented digital news boom, parent company Torstar announced plans in February 2009 to layoff five-dozen employees in Hamilton, Guelph and Waterloo. Later that year, the company told designers in Hamilton and Waterloo they would be outsourcing twenty local jobs to Asia. The paper's prestigious summer intern program was also temporarily scrapped.

Local university students and recent alumni were beginning to feel the pinch. As the end of the decade drew closer, the total amount of student loans owed to the Government of Canada crept toward $15 billion. Many Hamilton-based graduates of the double-cohort generation were already drowning in debt by the time they received their degrees. Even the Hamilton Tiger-Cats finished dead last in the CFL that year. The whole city was hurting.

• • •

As summer turned to fall, I accepted a part-time job at my neighbourhood grocery store, Metro. It was hard work, but enjoyable, too. I had several good friends in my department, including my old pal Mike Tufts, and got along well with my boss. The store was close enough to my childhood home that I could walk to work. The monotony was agonizing at times, but we always left with a sense of satisfaction, our muscles aching, undershirts damp with perspiration, hands shaking from too much watered-down coffee. A typical evening shift went something like this:

Load up a metal supply truck in the receiving bay. Wheel it onto the floor. Stock the shelves with soup cans and bags of milk and frozen peas. Wheel the remaining goods to the storage room. Tie-off the store's overflowing garbage bags and throw them into the compactor. Collect the grocery carts in the parking lot and push them back into the store in a long row. Help an irate customer find the last bag of something. Clean up a spill in aisle four. Return a misplaced item to aisle six. Sweep the floor in aisle two. Face-up the cardboard boxes and metal tins on the shelves. Pile the skids. Stack the milk crates. Cut each other up in the break room. Turn off the lights, lock the doors, share a smoke and go home.

I'd often return home after a hectic evening shift at the grocery store, pour a cup of coffee, toast a sesame seed bagel and start writing. Most of it was garbage – short stories that went nowhere, album reviews for records I'd purchased years earlier. Still, I found comfort in the routine – in the quiet hum of energy that comes between midnight and sunrise. I began turning down extra shifts at the grocery store to transcribe interviews and write new stories. I filed the articles to a local alt-weekly newspaper, *View*, which soon took me on as a staff writer. I brought home copies of the paper to show off my byline, and let them stack up on the table beside the couch in the family room. Those I didn't save were tossed into the fireplace. But I also kept a growing pile of clippings under my bed. I wasn't finished as a writer just yet, though there were dark forces pulling me away from the craft.

. . .

Stevie, Mike and I entered the basement level of Club Absinthe. Voices from upstairs trailed behind us as we jogged into the darkness of the dance hall. We ducked and weaved through the warm mass of swaying bodies and surged toward the bar on the far side of the basement, beyond the DJ booth and a group of students laughing and taking photos. Mike elbowed his way to the front of the line and ordered three bottles of Labatt 50.

I leaned back on the slick countertop and surveyed the madness unfolding in front of us. Male dancers in neon plaid shirts and skinny jeans jostled against young women with long, straight hair held back from their eyes with thin cotton head-bands. Everything was damp. Tiny plastic cups and broken glass littered the concrete dance floor. Long-time couples and one-night stands made out in a dim lounge area full of plush couches at one end of the bar. Across the hall, at the far side of the room, twenty people were stuffed into the DJ booth. Two young men appeared to be selecting tracks, but several others were likely in the mix as well. Someone brought over a tray of shots and the entire booth reached out for one, limbs and hair caught in a swirling entanglement. Ratatat's "Party and Bullshit" came on next, blasting at full volume. The dance floor was suddenly over-run and everyone was screaming.

Mike wasn't finished with the bar yet. I wheeled back around and caught him leaning over the rail, mouthing one word and holding up three fingers. The music was pounding, but I knew exactly what he called for. My whole body froze.

"Absinthe."

The drinks arrived and I exhaled. Mike and Stevie laughed and knocked theirs back as I stared at the murky, swirling abyss in my glass. I knew it was all over after this. I took the drink and spun to look at the surging crowd. My head stopped but my vision didn't. The entire room was spinning.

We slid onto the dance floor as the entire scene became a sketch for an oil painting, delivered in broad, gloopy strokes. Legs flailing. Hands pointed toward the ceiling. Hot sweat rolling down my forehead and back. Bodies crashing into one another and ricocheting in another direction. Mike arrived with another three bottles of beer. One immediately fell to the floor and exploded, drawing cheers and boos from the crowd. We pushed through the bodies, away from the mess, and edged closer to the DJ booth.

Arctic Monkeys's "I Bet You Look Good On The Dancefloor" came on next, and Mike rubbed his hands over his face, sprinting in place. Stevie punched Mike in the shoulder. Lights flashed. Faces melted. The room spun in circles. We lost it.

I woke up the following morning in a daze. My forehead throbbed and my mouth tasted like stale beer. I was on a couch in a west-end student house, fully clothed, including my shoes. Harsh sunlight was peeking through the blinds on the back door. I looked at my wristwatch. It was 8:40 a.m.

"Drewwwww," a voice muttered from somewhere below the couch. It was Mike, sprawled across the hardwood floor, a pillow tucked under his head, flipping through his phone.

"Let's make some fucking coffee."

• • •

Hamilton at the turn of the millennium had evolved into a truly sinister battleground. For all of the suggestive and literal violence that swirled around Teenage Head, the Viletones, the Diodes and other Southern Ontario bands who garnered national and international attention during the late 1970s, these songs were more punishing and unforgiving. I was too young to experience much of it first hand, but those who were there speak of a scene that always walked a fine line between exhilarating and absolutely fucking terrifying.

"I went to a punk show with D.O.A., and I met some people there who were going to kick the shit out of me because of the laces and suspenders I had on," recalls Brett Hawley. The Gunnar Hansen frontman takes a deep breath and folds his heavily tattooed forearms behind the checkout counter at Hammer City Records – a hole-in-the-wall basement shop off a James Street North alleyway, and one of the city's modern punk institutions.

"I had white laces, black army boots and white suspenders that were down, and a Mohawk. The reason they didn't jump me is because I was wearing a Dead Kennedys shirt. So they said, 'what's your deal? You know what that shit means.' I was like, 'no. I'm from Milton, and I'm the only punk I know.'"

Hawley laughs and offers a big smile. The tension immediately breaks.

The soft-spoken punk rock lifer moved to Hamilton with his mother during the mid-1990s, and immediately fell in love with Hamilton's no-nonsense punk and hardcore scene. He attended shows at X Club on King William Street, the Corktown Tavern on Young Street – affectionately known in its pre-renovated state as the Dirt-town by local punks – and the legendary Transit Union on Wilson Street, with a group of like-minded disenfranchised youth.

Between the mid-1990s and the turn of the millennium, local bands such as the Swarm, Left for Dead, Chokehold, Riotstar and Haymaker ruled Hamilton's frenzied punk scene with little regard for audience or performer safety.

"Haymaker was the band you'd go and see, and it was, like, scary," says Alexisonfire's George Pettit. "It was kind of like how you imagined punk shows to be in the 1970s or something like that. There was always that element of danger around them, and there were all these vicious rumours about, you know, 'they beat up this guy,' or 'they slashed this van's tires.' They had that element to them that was very, very true-to-life hardcore."

But for Hawley – and just about every punk rock aficionado within a fifty-kilometre radius of downtown Hamilton – no band represents the chaos, ruin and utter despair of modern Hamilton punk better than a prolific group of misfits with roots in the east Mountain suburbs surrounding St. Jean de Brébeuf Catholic Secondary School. Between 2001 and 2008, one band defined the scene and put Hamilton on everyone's radar.

That band was Cursed, in every sense of the word.

Even the name is whispered in hushed tones among industry heavyweights – *Cursed*. Say it too many times in front of a mirror in a darkened bathroom and something bad is going to happen. Although its members resided in several cities between Southern Ontario and Québec during their seven-year run, Hamilton always served as a home base for the group, for better or worse.

• • •

My first real introduction to Cursed came in January 2005, when I heard a copy of the band's sophomore record *II* playing at the *Silhouette*. I had always maintained a cursory interest in dark music, but the furthest I'd ventured into the abyss was politicized art-punk from the likes of …And You Will Know Us by the Trail of Dead, At the Drive-In and Refused. I loved music that was loud and fast, and occasionally nihilistic and self-loathing, but usually from a safe distance.

Cursed was something different altogether. There was so much more mystery and intrigue surrounding the band. I remember being mesmerized by the album's grim cover – a black and grey scene with Baphomet the goat lurking at the edge of the frame, staring at the listener from behind a set of blank, dead eye sockets. There was no lettering, no colour and no informational markings of any kind. It was simple and striking. Pure nightmare fuel.

"They bridged gaps between, like, doom metal and punk, to me," says Snake Charmer guitarist Daniel Troup, over a round of afternoon beers at Homegrown Hamilton in 2013. "It was just, like, two worlds coming together. It was just such a nice meshing of vocals, drums, guitar. It was loud and it was very Hamilton."

For Dave Nardi, bassist in Dundas punks the Dirty Nil, the band represented something entirely new and completely removed from their rural suburban roots. Musically, it was a shock to the system. "We were so young, I never had the chance to see them. It's all just hearsay to me," Nardi offers. "It's like a strange dream that it happened in our city; thinking about the fact that a band like Cursed is from Hamilton is mind blowing. It's crazy. They're one of my favourite bands, and easily my favourite local band of all time."

TV Freaks lead singer David O'Connor still refers to the band as one of the most powerful and significant acts to shape his outlook in music, art and life – "keeping punk in the hands of the punks," he explains. From a lyrical perspective, lead singer Chris Colohan remains an intriguing and inspirational figure for O'Connor – an imposing frontman who, to the outside observer, is seemingly full of contradictions.

"I think people who had maybe never met him or just seen him play live, or just heard Cursed or Left For Dead, they feel like, 'oh dude, that guy must be so angry and so dark.' But he's not. He's the fucking complete opposite," says O'Connor, who played bass alongside Colohan in Burning Love and spent plenty of time on the road with the former Cursed frontman. "His upbringing in Hamilton has a lot to do with the way he writes and what he's into and stuff like that. But he's just, like, a really smart guy, really well spoken and written . . . in Burning Love, especially, he's good at making satire out of any social situation."

. . .

Although Cursed released just three full-length records during a chaotic and unpredictable seven-year career, *I*, *II* and *III: Architects of Troubled Sleep* will undoubtedly resonate for decades. In many ways, Cursed are a genre-bending anomaly – a universally respected tour de force in a scene traditionally plagued by elitism, infighting and a desire to separate the "real" from the "fake." No Canadian punk band to emerge in the last decade commands the same level of universal respect bestowed upon Cursed.

"Radwan [Moumneh, bass and guitar] and I were living in Montréal, Mike [Maxymuik, drums] and Christian [McMaster, guitar] were in Hamilton," explains lead vocalist Colohan, corresponding via email while on tour in the Prairies with his current band, Burning Love, in early 2013.

"But having grown up there and using it as one of a few home bases, I think it's safe to say Cursed was a product of Hamilton more than Toronto or anything else, in terms of that cynicism, violence and desperation. The Hamilton we grew up in was a very different world than the new one of condos and Art Crawls. You got jumped a lot and there was no vegan food, but the skateboarding spots were great and the rent was cheap because nothing really mattered there."

Not long after forming, the band's lineup began shifting. A friend of the group, Tom Piraino, filled in on bass for a time while Moumneh decamped to Lebanon to tend to a family issue. When he returned in 2003, they decided to bump the roster up to five, with Moumneh transitioning to guitar alongside McMaster. Piraino was replaced by Dan Dunham in late-2004, who remained with the group until the bitter end.

In 2005, Cursed released their sophomore full-length album, *II*, to rave critical reviews and a rapidly expanding fanbase. "It actually did really well. It was just before CDs bottomed out and I think ten thousand of them went pretty fast," recalls Colohan. "I had to twist their arm to press the vinyl in 2005 though, and it was gone in two weeks and fell out of print, that's my only regret with that."

In the whirlwind year following the release of *II*, the band played more than two hundred shows and spent eight weeks in Europe while continually pushing their physical and mental limits. More often than not, the concerts weren't great. Colohan recalls plenty of sparsely attended shows in distant American suburbs, tearing through a set of fierce intellectual doom while disinterested teenagers waited for their friends' mall-punk band to take the stage. But in spite of it all, or perhaps because of it, the band pushed forward.

"We hit the road a lot harder than it was asking us to," says Colohan. "But we had some stupid and self-punishing ethos that got wrapped up in it, like we had to do it in a way that made us hate life or it didn't count. So by the end of most days the only thing you could do with that was play and kick it out."

In 2008, Cursed released their highly anticipated third record, *III: Architects of Troubled Sleep*, on Goodfellow Records.

The album opened with a spoken-word collage of various philo-sophical and socio-political sound bites layered over a droning bass guitar and ominous feedback. The final line of the intro is as follows: "Go shopping, go back to the mall, go back to your normal lives...WE'LL TAKE CARE OF IT." The band then immediately tears into the lead track, "Night Terrors," with such fury that it's at once exhilarating and terrifying. Colohan, screaming at the top of his lungs, never sounded more unhinged than in the open-ing five seconds of that song.

But by the time the record came out, years of hard touring had taken their toll. While traversing Europe that spring in sup-port of their new record, the band's van was broken into outside of a punk squat in Germany and all of their money and passports were stolen. A much younger, more financially stable and less road-weary band may have found a way to push forward. Colo-han described it as a "bullet to the head." On the band's official website, he offered a detailed, passionate statement to fans not long after news of the break-in reached Hamilton:

"Yeah, you heard. Apparently, it gets even worse. That's all I know or even want to know for now. We got robbed at the very end of tour in a totally unreal, extremely sketchy series of events that still makes no sense at all, only leads to paranoia, anger and a total loss of faith. Passports, money, all the costs of the tour. Either way, whoever did it, it was a bullet in the head, the end of the line. A sudden and totally fucked up way for it to end, which I know will be fitting when I look back on it. All we could do was play the show, badly, and go our ways with whatever money we could muster. I hitched a ride back to Prague with Tomas. Since I can't do a fucking thing about it, I'm going to hang out with my girl, and friends, stare at some Czech mountains and try not to think about it. Needless to say, all outstanding plans are off. All this shit aside, thanks to everyone that helped out and travelled from all over for the shows on this tour, all the kids and bands we played and stayed with. Minus a few fucked up shows, it was probably the best tour we ever had. Thanks everyone for your good wishes. I'll elaborate when I'm home next week, for now – yes it's true, and yes it's over."

"When everything happened, it was like waking up to your partner being dead in bed beside you," Colohan tells me, five years after writing the band's now infamous epitaph. "I'd played with Christian since we were both sixteen, so it was a crash-landing to Cursed and the eight years we put into it. But beyond that, it was really a sudden end and forced letting go of a part of my life that stretched back to adolescence – more than half my life at that point. It was hard to wrap my head around and honestly still feels very fresh and probably will for a long time."

With Cursed in ruins, the band's final lineup shifted their focus to new and ongoing projects upon their return to Canada. Drummer Mike Maxymuik began playing full time with Toronto-based Quest for Fire. Dan Dunham pushed forward with Crux of Aux, an experimental thrash super-group featuring members of Chore, Sailboats Are White and Shallow North Dakota. Cursed frontman Chris Colohan focused his efforts on a new project, Burning Love.

"I think it's organic and it's good for a band, when you take it for granted and it's gone," says Kevin Sheeler, lead vocalist for Social Divorce and Vatican Chainsaw Massacre. "I kind of like that, as opposed to something just sticking around and everyone gets their chance to see it."

• • •

While Cursed was falling apart in Europe, a worthy successor was already taking shape back home in Hamilton. Former Die

Hard Losers frontman and Stoney Creek teenage outcast Kevin Sheeler was preparing to unleash his Dead Kennedys–infused Vatican Chainsaw Massacre on the unsuspecting masses.

The band – which included future TV Freaks frontman David O'Connor on bass, former Hoosier Poet and PFA drummer Nick Daleo, Patrick Marshall on guitar and Sheeler up front – wasted little time signing a deal with Goodfellow Records for the release of their debut LP, *Hazy Skies Over Martha's Vineyard*. The music was loud and turbulent, but it was Sheeler's bizarre, confrontational vocal style and maniacal stage presence that made the band an instant favourite in the latest iteration of Hamilton's punk scene.

Prior to the recording of *Hazy Skies* in 2008, O'Connor was holed up on a friend's couch in Hamilton for three weeks while the band rehearsed at Sonic Unyon and fine-tuned the material for their debut full-length. Despite having some experience on guitar with Niagara-based Get Loose and Toronto punks Our Father, it was the first time O'Connor had actually picked up a bass. Even though his roots were in Niagara, as a native of blue-collar border town Fort Erie, he was already developing a keen interest in Hamilton's cheap rent, sketchy undertones and active countercultural movement.

"Our Father had played with Hoosier Poet before, and I was super stoked on them," explains O'Connor. "I had heard Cursed, Shallow North Dakota and Chore, and I liked all those bands a lot. I was like, 'oh, Hamilton's cool.' It's like this dirty, weird, dirge-y kind of place. The music that comes out of here, at least for indie, hardcore and punk, sounds exactly like the city is."

As we chat, he sinks deeper into the couch inside his tiny bachelor apartment on James Street North, a walk-up unit above a family-owned jewellery store and one of the city's numerous Good Shepherd centres. Vintage garage rock plays at low volume. It's warm inside the sparsely furnished room, but O'Connor never removes his black toque. The dark walls are plastered in original drawings, gig posters and tattoo flash, a by-product of his current apprenticeship at Anchor's Tattoo Studio in Burlington.

More than anything, Vatican Chainsaw Massacre offered Kevin Sheeler a chance to take his onstage mania to a whole new level, O'Connor tells me. Remarkably tall and rail-thin, with thick Buddy Holly–style glasses permanently fixed to his nose, Sheeler seemed to transform into an entirely different person on record, and especially on stage.

"Kevin is a really, really funny guy," offers O'Connor. "If you met him once, you'd never know how he actually is because he's such a mild-mannered and really intelligent, soft-spoken guy, and a really fucking smart guy. But he kind of doesn't come out of his shell right away, you know what I mean? Even when I first joined the band, I kind of felt that he kept his distance a little bit. Not from me so much, but just not really coming out of his shell, vocal-wise."

Once O'Connor was up to speed on bass duties, the band's full-length album came together quickly. Everyone was eager to take a big step forward, especially Sheeler. "We were a band for a couple of years, and all we had was a shitty EP to show for it," he explains. We're sipping light beers at a small table at Home-grown Hamilton, a quaint hippie café located at 27 King William Street, alongside Social Divorce guitarist and close friend Daniel Troup.

"I was super self-conscious about recording vocals, though. I hated when they played the vocal track back and it would just be the vocals. But [album producer] Donny Cooper is just such a relaxing person ... I remember one of the days we recorded, I had no idea, and Donny's girlfriend showed up with an ice cream cake and was like, 'happy birthday, Donny!' I was like, 'it's your birthday, and you're here with us for eight hours?'"

Battling his own insecurities was one issue, but Sheeler also had to contend with an awkward situation at home. For as long as he had been performing in bands – even as far back as his teenage days with Die Hard Losers – Sheeler's considerably older parents remained blissfully unaware of their son's musical and political leanings. Even uttering the words "Vatican Chainsaw Massacre" would have been inexcusable, let alone trying to explain that he fronted a maniacal underground punk band with such a blasphemous handle.

"My folks are really old. My dad is seventy-one," Sheeler begins. "They don't even know who the Stooges are, never mind whatever the fuck I'm doing now. They've never even seen me perform. Not once. I remember when the Vatican record came out, my mom was a schoolteacher and we're an Irish Catholic family. One of the younger teachers at her school said, 'oh hey, your son is in Vatican Chainsaw Massacre?' My mom was like, 'what?' She was super embarrassed.

"They have no idea. I'd hide everything," he continues. "I'd make sure our band shirts were always at Sonic Unyon and I'd never bring them home. You know, shirts with upside-down crucifixes and stuff like that. They know I play music and they're supportive, but my parents aren't computer savvy so they never really saw me."

The finished Vatican record was every bit as acerbic, cutting and intense as Sheeler and company had wanted. "I don't know if you've heard that record, but it is fucked. It's so hard to play," offers O'Connor. "For a good bass player, that would be a pretty difficult record to play on. But I was like, 'Kevin, just let me do it.'" Tracks such as "The Not So Hidden Agenda" and "Insanity By Consensus" explode from the speakers with the same tightly wound energy that made Jello Biafra and Dead Kennedys a household name in underground punk circles during the early 1980s. Sheeler's vocals may as well have been recorded while receiving a root canal, with the drill bit striking a bundle of nerves just as the producer hit "record." Biafra is an obvious influence, but Sheeler also cites Sam Johnson from Orlando punks New Mexican Disaster Squad as a key source of inspiration. "Kevin's vocals really cut though," offers Troup. "Vatican was very low and heavy. Having a voice like that added another frequency to it."

While Vatican never achieved the level of fame or critical acclaim that some of their contemporaries enjoyed, *Hazy Skies* is about as close as a Hamilton band ever got to capturing raw chaos on tape. Musically, throw Propagandhi, Dead Kennedys, Cursed and Bad Brains in a blender full of piss and razor blades, and you'll come pretty close to achieving the record's dissonant blast. "*Hazy Skies* unites the cavernous bellowing of Cursed with the rabid vehemence of Disrupt," opined *Exclaim!* reporter Keith Carman in November of 2008. "It's terrific that Sheeler has enough gumption to ensure his words weigh heavy, but ultimately he could be shrieking about how much he loves puppies and this album would still be outstanding."

Ultimately, Vatican Chainsaw Massacre made their mark with just one record. When the band finally split, Sheeler regrouped with new hardcore project Social Divorce, while O'Connor emerged as the spastic frontman and chief lyricist of garage rock–infused TV Freaks. The latter released their fantastic debut self-titled record – recorded in a rural Niagara barn and mixed at Welland's Tapes and Plates, home base for Attack in Black – on Hamilton-based Schizophrenic Records in December 2011. For Chris Colohan, former lead singer of Cursed, the chance to see his old bandmate move to the front of the stage was a real treat.

114

"[Dave O'Connor] is a total piece of work and I love him for it. I love watching him sing in TV Freaks because he gets to just go full DOC," says Colohan. "It's like Bart Simpson ten years later, in 3D, drunk, just being a totally antagonizing little bastard. He gets it."

• • •

"There's soul in there. You can't do electronic music without soul," begins Graham Rockingham. He's passionately describing long-time U2 producer and famed Hamiltonian Daniel Lanois as the driving force behind the city's pioneering electronic music scene in the early 1980s.

"I don't need to tell you, but this is the home of ambient music. You talk about Lanois, and they'll tell you about the house they had up on Scenic Drive. [Brian] Eno was here with Danny for eighteen months, you know, just *getting sounds* ... they were going down to the tracks and getting sounds and recording dead air, things like that."

Rockingham is correct. Lanois was a pioneer. But the new electronic scene in Hamilton – one built around all-night raves in downtown and east-end warehouses, slow-drip coffee, designer drugs and late-night excursions to James Street North – was our world. It was darker. Grittier. Full of lost souls eager to escape the day-to-day grind of concrete corridors and dead-end jobs. Casual friends and young lovers who wanted to dance and find something new, something unique, to call their own.

"Hamilton has such a storied and interesting electronic music past," says Junior Boys singer and co-producer Jeremy Greenspan, "and for me, all of that past is what created [Junior Boys] sound. It was that, coupled with the fact that I lived in England and had a lot of influences there and stuff. But my initial interests in electronic music all come from a scene that happened in Hamilton that was very, very exciting."

"The atmosphere [in Hamilton] is diverse, interesting," Orphx's Christina Sealey explained to *Vice* in 2014. "It was certainly influential from our early start and there's a really good art scene there now. There are a lot of interesting people to work with. The smaller community helps you feel like you're really part of that, as opposed to a larger community like in Toronto."

"You know, it's funny," offers Jamie Smith. "You leave Hamilton and you mention Hamilton to someone and they'll say, 'oh, Caribou is from there. Oh, Junior Boys are from there.' And you're like, 'you know about them?' You have to say to yourself, 'Jesus Christ, man, get out of your goddamn bubble and believe that they're from here.' They are the ambassadors, and a lot of people follow them."

Smith wasn't exaggerating. By the fall of 2008, the Hamilton music community had been swept up in a new wave of electronic pandemonium. Established acts such as Junior Boys and Caribou led the charge, while the underground scene – including the likes of Motëm, Miramichi, En Francais, Electroluminescent, Orphx, HUREN and other talented producers – churned out an equally impressive array of bold new material.

Hamilton reached the summit of the modern electronic music scene on a warm September evening, when thirty-year-old Dan Snaith received the coveted Polaris Music Prize in front of a packed house at Toronto's Phoenix Concert Theatre. No one in attendance was more shocked than the recipient – an unassuming, bespectacled Dundas, Ontario native better known by his internationally-renowned stage handle, Caribou. Snaith declined to be interviewed for this book, but his impact on the Hamilton music scene has been monumental.

116

When I watched Snaith's acceptance speech for the first time, I was immediately taken by his honesty and humility in the face of tremendous critical acclaim. Here was a man who spoke my language – a punk rocker navigating electronic music circles; a mysterious superstar who quietly went about his business; a master craftsman wearing white sneakers, blue jeans and glasses, who favoured anonymity over mass acceptance. I was enamoured.

As host Grant Lawrence handed Snaith an oversized $20,000 cheque, you could almost hear his anxiety radiating from the stage.

"I didn't plan for this eventuality at all," Snaith began. "So I guess the most important thing I want to say is that I feel so lucky and so proud, not…um…to be included…uh…not, I mean …to be included amongst such an incredible, uh, group of musicians and group of albums. And, uh, not only that but, I mean, looking to the long list as well, there are so many incredible albums in there, so…uh…I really, I really feel humbled and proud to be included with everybody. So let's hear a round of applause for everybody who's here."

And with that, it was over. Snaith raised the cheque above his head and shuffled off stage to resounding applause. His speech was perfect. I played and replayed it over and over again, grinning wider each time. I marvelled as one of the most innovative musicians in Canada seemed to recoil from the spotlight.

The following morning, he reaffirmed this approach on the CBC.

"I make music in a very insular way. I make it at home, in my bedroom in my apartment. And it's so much just about making something that I'm happy with," Snaith told former Q host Jian Ghomeshi. "When I finished this album, I was happy to have made something that I was proud of. But that's so far from that gala last night, and being amongst lots of media and all that kind of stuff. But it's incredibly affirming, obviously."

"As far as I can tell, Dan seems to be quite a modest guy, and seemed pretty surprised and thrilled to win. I kind of remember him being a favourite, but perhaps that was just my bias coming into play," says local artist Becky Katz, who designed the print that accompanied Caribou's 2008 Polaris shortlist nomination. "*Andorra* clearly stood out among the other nine albums."

With his Polaris Prize-winning record *Andorra*, Snaith fused elements of psychedelia and electronica into an experimental masterpiece. The album was a revelation, a landmark feat of homegrown electronica. Bright and warm in spots, chilling and tense in others. During the 2008 Polaris Prize ceremony, *Andorra* was pitted against equally strong releases from the likes of Kathleen Edwards, Basia Bulat, Holy Fuck, Shad and the Weakerthans. But Snaith's Polaris Prize victory was no happy accident.

For nearly a decade leading up to that moment at the Phoenix Concert Theatre, Snaith had been writing and recording complex, orchestral pop music under the handle Manitoba. He had already released a series of EPs and LPs to increasing critical acclaim. His breakthrough 2003 full-length *Up In Flames* received an 8.6 rating on Pitchfork Media, and ranked among the website's Top 200 albums of the decade.

But with his career just beginning to gather momentum, New York punk icon Richard "Handsome Dick" Manitoba – frontman of the first-wave American punk band the Dictators and owner of the popular bar Manitoba's in Manhattan's East Village – threatened legal action over the use of his namesake. Snaith chose to adopt a new handle for all subsequent recordings rather than face legal action. Caribou was officially unveiled for 2005's *The Milk of Human Kindness* LP.

The years that followed were an increasing blur of monster world tours and critical acclaim, as Snaith emerged as one of the country's premier electronic artists. *Andorra* was followed by the release of *Swim* in 2010, a global sensation that catapulted Caribou even further into the stratosphere thanks in large part to the opening track and colossal lead single, "Odessa." That song was, and remains, one of the most popular and beloved tracks in Hamilton's nouveau dance club scene. Any time its distinct looping wail and smooth, rolling bass line is worked into the mix at Club Absinthe or Che, the crowd goes wild.

He followed *Swim* with the debut of a new alter ego, Daphni, in 2012 – releasing the Polaris Prize long-listed record *Jiaolong* on American label Merge Records that same year. Radiohead singer Thom Yorke famously became one of his biggest international boosters. Snaith would remix "Little by Little" off the band's *The King of Limbs* record, and also tour across Europe, America and Mexico with the hugely influential British quintet. *Our Love*, the sixth full-length Caribou album, was released in 2014 via Merge and German-based label City Slang.

• • •

"So are you going to put me into a section with Junior Boys and bands like that?"

Motëm is quick to reassure me this will not be a problem, but his point is well taken. Motëm is unclassifiable. Of all the electronic performers active during the mid-late 2000s, none came close to the sheer eccentricity of Hamilton's most prolific oddball virtuoso revolutionary. His music is informed by classic hip-hop, funk, jazz, house, hardcore punk and experimental noise, but somehow exists in its own astral dimension. His lyrical delivery is slow and methodical – like the comforting but confounding manner people speak to one another in dreams. It makes perfect sense, until you try to make sense of it.

I first encountered Motëm – otherwise known as Gebbz Steelo and, to family and friends, as Gregory Eberhard – at a summer job we both held following my first year at McMaster. Motëm was a sophomore at Bishop's University in Lennoxville, Québec, and back at his parents' home in an exclusive corner of Ancaster for the summer. We spent our days measuring wooden decks and in-ground pools in the sun-kissed Hamilton suburbs, and occasionally trade mixed CDs and MySpace links back at the office.

We both played guitar, and Motëm would occasionally invite me over to his home to jam in the basement and listen to rough demos he was working on. I was mystified not only by his creativity, but his willingness to record mountains of music spanning all genres and styles. If he liked a riff or drum loop, it was destined to wind up on his next homemade album. And there were already plenty of them.

Fast forward nearly a decade and we're seated across from one another on the back deck of Johnny's Coffee on Locke Street South. It's late August 2013, and the wooden patio furniture is dappled in warm sunlight cutting through the canopy. The location was Motëm's suggestion. "I love how quiet it is back here," he tells me. His face is hidden behind a pair of white sunglasses, a purple baseball cap and a thick blonde beard, but nothing obstructs his grin. "It's a great place to chill out and reflect."

The wild and weird Gebbz Steelo YouTube page currently boasts more than two hundred videos. The massive archive includes everything from homemade music videos and live concert footage to European tour diaries and record promos. He never stops producing and sharing new material.

"When I first heard him, I didn't get it," says Jamie Smith. "Like I just stood there for the first time and went, 'oh come on. What is this?' Then you go back and you see him again, and you go, 'oh! This is good.' It's the same thing you saw last time, you were just in a bad mood. Jamie Tennant and I talked about it years ago. We were listening to some of his music, and we were like, 'we get it. This is good.' That's the thing about music – sometimes you have to give it a chance. Don't buy into the hype, just listen to it and form your own opinion."

"Motëm is a good social experiment. He allows people to be free. If you can't enjoy Motëm you are too constricted by the music scene society tells us to live within," offers local music writer Nicole Nicolson.

"It's all good and nice to enjoy indie rock, but one day you've got to expand. There is no appreciating Motëm's art without seeing the bigger picture, which is why he's very smart to put out so many videos. Each piece plays a role. That silk scarf matches that silky beat, and you know he knows it. There's a reason why Greg and his music is almost universally liked in this city – he builds bridges and opens doors. He welcomes. I don't pretend to understand his music, but I know how to enjoy it and I think that may be the secret. To give up trying and just be," she adds.

"The first band I was ever in was this funk group with me and some high school friends. We called it the Balls Johnson Quartet, like super little pervo teenagers," Motëm begins. "That was when I played the bass and stuff."

But the music he really gravitated toward – besides Los Angeles-based Stones Throw Records and underground hip-hop from both coasts of America – was from Dischord and K Records, founded by DC hardcore icon Ian MacKaye and noted Olympia, Washington songwriter Calvin Johnson, respectively. The appeal of both operations, Motëm tells me, was absolute power and total artistic freedom. "I always liked having complete control over the music. Even to this day, the whole Gebbz

Steelo thing is kind of like a closed experience. The same way as, like, Macintosh computers. It's a controlled experience from the creator to the end user, you know? They don't allow outside software or hardware, and shit like that. With the videos and the music and stuff, it's direct from Motëm to the end listener.

"When you involve all these extra people, it's like anything else," he continues. "You get so many more opinions put at you. That works for some people, and that's super good, too. But for me, I just always wanted to have it be the expression of the individual. I always felt that's what I should do. I have a lot more quality control if I just do it."

After returning from his first year at Bishop's, Motëm reconnected with an old friend, Matt Baker, and played him a CD full of rough beats he had been working on. Baker was intrigued but didn't pounce on the material right away. Skip ahead to 2006, when Baker was living in a west-end apartment near Longwood Road North in Westdale Village. A group of friends, including Motëm, were invited over one evening to freestyle and listen to new music. That's where the idea for an eclectic hip-hop collective New Slang first clicked.

"I had all these beats, like gangs of beats at that point, because I had been making them for three years and I didn't know any rappers," says Motëm. "I was maybe doing a bit of rap-singing or whatever, but that was before Drake did the Auto-Tune rap singing. I was influenced by Andre 3000.

"Me and Baker really ran with it, and we came up with this whole album of New Slang stuff. We were like, 'okay, we're going to put that out on Gebbz Steelo.' We did a little handmade case for it and stuff. We did a few of those, and nobody really paid attention," he continues.

That all changed in 2008, when Baker came up with a loose idea for a New Slang concept album called *AndrogyNation*. The

122

premise involved a not-too-distant future where males and females have evolved into androgynous beings due to long-term exposure to chemicals and pharmaceuticals in municipal water supplies. Local rapper Lee Reed and *View* music columnist Ric Taylor began trumpeting the bold new project in local music circles, with Reed going so far as to offer New Slang joint billing at his release party for the *Introductory Offer* EP.

Support from Hamilton-based heavy-hitters was welcome, but not entirely necessary. Ironically, the scene that put Motëm on the map didn't involve Lee Reed, local hip-hop or even his hometown, but the remote reaches of Scandinavia.

One afternoon in 2007, bored at his summer job, Motëm happened upon a Wikipedia entry covering new global trends in electronic music. One of those genres was listed as "skweee" – a term coined by Swedish electro pioneer Daniel Savio to describe an emerging style of music that favoured a slower, stripped-down approach to crafting beats. The general aim is to "squeeze" as many bizarre sounds and samples out of vintage equipment as possible, and chop them up into twitchy, slightly off-beat electro loops. It wasn't long before Motëm reached out to some of the genre's leading underground artists in Sweden and Finland.

"I checked it out and I was like, 'these tunes are great,'" he tells me, eyes wide. "I guess they didn't get that many friend requests, because a lot of them friended me back pretty quick. Then I got this message from Frans [Carlqvist] and he was like, 'hey, I'm curious about your music, this funk music you're doing. Can you tell me more?'"

Motëm sent a number of stem files overseas, including "Contact Your Neighbours" off of his then-brand new *Nature's Beast* LP. Carlqvist asked if he could remix the track, and Motëm began his transition from being an indie basement funk producer to a Canadian-European skweee sensation.

"Motëm is, in his own weird way, doing very well," says James Tennant. "He's had a lot of success in Europe and a lot of success in Scandinavia. And by success, I mean he'll sell out a room. He's not going platinum or anything like that. But for a guy like him who's got a full-time job and does it part time and is still very prolific, he's just happy to get the love from anybody. He's a genuine oddball and a genuine nice guy at the same time."

In the years that followed, offers to remix more tracks turned into offers to perform and tour overseas, which Motëm gladly accepted. He was asked to contribute a track to the landmark compilation album *International Skweee (Vol. 1)*, released on vinyl via Harmönia. He became affiliated with Swedish rap prodigy and Sad Boys impresario Yung Lean, and established a reputation on both sides of the Atlantic as one of the most dynamic, progressive and utterly mystifying rapper-producers in modern underground music. Locally, Motëm continued to push boundaries and reinvent aesthetic conventions with the release of a dizzying number of homemade music videos in rapid succession.

Whether ghost-riding a blue Mazda Miata in a vacant suburban parking lot or skulking through acres of uninhabited woodlands that surround Ancaster, Motëm's on-screen persona became as important – if not more important – than the actual music. He was, and remains, a fearless style icon, pairing numerous layers of bright T-shirts and hoodies with an endless array of baseball caps, bucket hats, do-rags, dark sunglasses, ski goggles, scarves and fresh kicks. Whether playing on stage or leaning against the back wall of a club, he always commands the room.

Reflecting on the lasting legacy of Motëm proved more impossible than trying to fit him into a specific genre. He's too soft for the punks, too avant-garde for the hip-hop heads, too skweee for classic house lovers and too progressive for the mainstream rock crowd. In many ways, Motëm is a perfect amalgam of everything I loved about Hamilton during the 2000s – a fearless renegade, ready and willing to carve his own path and shape his own identity.

• • •

By 2008 the Ride Theory was rapidly evolving. It was around this time that the band shed their matching suits and ties for street clothes and formally dropped their old handle in favour of a new name, Young Rival.

They began taking the stage and appearing in press photos wearing Chuck Taylors, skinny jeans and vintage T-shirts. "New name, new look," Fralick reasoned. But there was much more involved than a simple wardrobe change. Older songs were slowly being phased out of the band's repertoire and there was a growing desire to mark a dividing line between the two projects. Young Rival represented a fresh start. It was the band Fralick and D'Alesio had envisioned from the beginning – cool, confident and undeniably talented, but without looking like they stepped out of 1966.

Anchored by the short, uptempo single "Your Island," the band's 2008 self-titled EP represented a bridge between two competing eras. Songs such as "Another Nobody" were clearly reminiscent of the group's early days as the Ride Theory – fast, thick, distorted, bursting with energy. Balancing the scales were tracks such as "4:15" and "Poisonous Moves," which presented a much more streamlined, restrained version of the band's classic garage rock sound.

If the Ride Theory was all flash and bravado, Young Rival was being presented as a more mature, sophisticated version of the exact same group of players. The licks and hooks were still there, but no longer buried under power chords, wailing solos and crashing cymbals. The new songs had room to breathe. They were dynamic and interesting. The Ride Theory was always cool, but Young Rival's self-titled EP represented a huge leap forward. In Hamilton, at least, long-time fans were more than happy to come along for the ride. Stevie and I were on board from day one.

• • •

In late November, I brushed a light dusting of snow off my mother's car and drove out to the city's west-end student ghetto. This was a rare night where no heavy drinking was involved. I was off to see a show at Club Absinthe with Stevie. Aaron Gurman and Chris McNamee, the Rockstars for Hire, had organized a Bank Holiday concert on the upstairs level of the club, featuring an incredible lineup of local bands. Stevie and I were eager to see Pumps and Young Rival.

On the car stereo that evening was Arkells' debut full-length record *Jackson Square*, released a few weeks earlier on October 28. The album was full of well-rehearsed, road-hardened bangers and delicate, well-composed ballads. Toronto-based Jon Drew was credited as the album's co-producer, but that said, Arkells knew exactly what they wanted to achieve before recording began in August at Mississauga's Metalworks Studios. And no member of the ensemble was more involved than keyboardist Dan Griffin.

"For *Jackson Square*, it was very much, 'okay, we've got the songs ready.' We had already done *Deadlines* and we were using a bunch of songs from that," recalls Griffin. "We refined them a bit and we had a bunch of ideas. Jon really helped us execute what we wanted to do. My job was to keep it moving in the right direction and keep us on track."

"I love Jon, and he's a really good engineer. He's credited as the producer, but to say he produced the record is totally inaccurate," says Max Kerman. "We're happy for Jon if it helped him in his professional career. That's great. But like, we did all the pre-production. I guess it depends on what your definition of a producer is. In my mind, a producer is pretty hands-on with the arrangement of a song, giving really critical feedback, not settling until it's just right. That's something more that Dan did.

"We were comfortable, because Jon Drew had done other, bigger records that we liked. So we figured it would sound fine," Kerman continues. "Our influences at the time were, like, Constantines, Wintersleep, the Weakerthans, and they all have really straightforward-sounding records. They're just rock bands playing rock music. So for *Jackson Square*, I think it sounds great, but it's a pretty conventional rock record."

Conventional or not, the album was a runaway hit. Lead-off single "Oh, the Boss is Coming!" was an instant sensation on MuchMusic and 102.1 the Edge in Toronto. The kitschy music video placed the band in a strip mall warehouse in yellow hardhats and navy blue coveralls, tasked with producing a work safety video for fellow employees at the boss's behest. Even though the band had toured extensively across western Canada by that point, for many new fans, the video offered their first real glimpse of Arkells in a "live" setting, albeit on a Toronto soundstage. The group soon expanded well beyond the Golden Horseshoe, and faster than anyone anticipated.

Follow-up singles included mid-tempo rocker "The Ballad of Hugo Chavez" and "Pullin' Punches," a fast and breezy staple of the band's live show anchored by the natural swing of drummer Tim Oxford. But the song that really captured old and new fans was "John Lennon" – a keyboard-driven stadium rocker that contained some of Kerman's most well written and introspective

lyrics to date. The song tells the story of a young student struggling to find his footing while navigating the pitfalls of adolescence, and features the infectious pre-chorus "I'm so lost/and I
live just around the corner" – a nod to the band's student days
at 85 Arkell Street in Westdale Village. "John Lennon" quickly
became a huge hit at live gigs across the country. Kerman would
often step away from the microphone for the second line, grinning
as the crowd carried the band into the fist-pumping chorus. When
Arkells performed the song at Toronto's Air Canada Centre
some eighteen months later – opening for Josh Homme, Dave
Grohl and John Paul Jones's supergroup Them Crooked Vultures
– you could hear the lyrics echoing around the gigantic twenty
thousand-seat stadium as fans streamed into the main room. It
was sensational.

. . .

I pulled into Stevie's long concrete driveway on Broadway Avenue and the car bounced over piles of ice and snow. The former
McMaster student house was relatively small but in good con-
dition. Two storeys, white vinyl siding, black shutters on the
windows, a big front porch and a spacious backyard with plenty
of tree coverage. Stevie occupied a large suite on the second floor
of the house, complete with a music room where we often sat
and played guitar. His roommate and older sister, Kristy, lived
in a tiny room on the main floor, right beside the kitchen. Mike
Lawson also lived in the house for a time.

Between the summers of 2008 and 2009 – the height of the
Hamilton nightlife boom – that house served as our west-end
launch pad for all things outrageous, nefarious and underhanded.
Our crew would pile onto a black leather couch and a handful of
bar stools in the tiny living room and plot the night ahead. Dank

weed and flat booze spilled onto the coffee table and all over the kitchen counter. The room was always full of laughter. We were constantly cutting each other up, playing darts and video games, and listening to new records on Stevie's hi-fi. On Wednesdays, Fridays and Saturdays, we'd take one final shot of Jack Daniel's or a cheap brand of tequila before piling into taxis and heading downtown to Club Absinthe or Che. It functioned like a club-house for man-children.

I knocked the snow off my white high-top Chuck Taylors, opened the front door and walked in. Doors were rarely locked at the Broadway house.

"Drew! Come on up," Stevie called from the second floor.

I slipped off my shoes and climbed up the winding wooden staircase. Stevie was sitting on a couch in his music room, shirt-less, with a teal Fender Stratocaster flat on his lap and two bottles of beer on his computer desk. Beads of condensation were forming on the labels. He twisted the cap off one and handed it to me with a nod and a grin. We sat and listened to music and sipped our drinks. Stevie played me some new recordings he'd been work-ing on, and we chatted and critiqued the songs. He was always tinkering with something new – folk tunes, uptempo garage rock numbers, experimental noise. Some of it was terrible, some showed great promise.

At the time, Stevie was the only member of our gang who col-lected vinyl records. He had stacks of blues, jazz and classic rock scattered all over the room, mixed in with contemporary albums from the Dead Weather, Justice, Ratatat, Arctic Monkeys and Phoenix.

"Ladies love vinyl," he explained to me once, eyebrows flick-ering, "the whole process of picking out a record, dropping the needle and blowing the dust off something that hasn't been heard in years. It's sexy."

I picked up an acoustic guitar as Stevie continued to noodle on his Stratocaster. We jammed for fifteen minutes before he slipped into the adjoining bedroom and pulled on a T-shirt.

"I think I want to be a long-haul truck driver," he suddenly called down the hallway.

"What?"

Stevie walked back in to the room and slumped on the couch.

"A truck driver, making big runs across the country. I want to load up a trailer in Toronto or Montréal and drive west non-stop, across the Prairies and through the Rocky Mountains to the ocean."

"Oh yeah?"

"Yeah. I'd buy a big cab with black leather seats and a sleeping compartment up top. I'd keep a handgun tucked in a secret panel beside the mattress."

"A gun?"

"Yeah."

"Sounds cool," I lied.

"Yeah, I don't know. I think it would be nice. I could see the country. And it would give me a lot of time to be alone. That's what I really want. Time for myself."

"Wouldn't you get lonely? Or bored?"

"Nah, man. I just want to go away for a while. Find some time to get lost."

He slapped both hands on his knees and then smacked me on the thigh. "Fuck it, let's get out of here."

• • •

I swung the car onto King Street East and made a hard right onto Ferguson. We parked in a municipal lot behind Club Absinthe, mere footsteps from a brick-lined apartment Ciara and I would one day share. We skulked across the parking lot on foot and slid into the venue under its blue neon sign.

Stevie and I held court at the quiet upstairs bar and nursed a round of Labatt 50 while stage techs tested the lights and set up microphones. It was still early, well before show time. I spotted Noah Fralick near the stage and he motioned for us to come over. As usual, his bright brown eyes and guileless smile lit up the room. With a new EP in his back pocket, the Young Rival drummer was even more enthused about music than usual – gesturing wildly with his hands while talking about the excitement surrounding the Bank Holiday showcase. His zeal was infectious. Stevie and I wished him well and watched as Fralick made a lap around the room, greeting an endless parade of friends and fans who'd begun streaming in. Gurman suddenly yelled from the stage, "I want to be on the cover of *View!*" before dropping a track from the Dandy Warhols. That dream would come true within six months, and I wrote the story.

• • •

The other main band on the bill at the Bank Holiday show was Pumps, the five-piece pop-punk-garage outfit born out of the demise and subsequent merger of the Racket and Neighbourhood Noise just one year prior.

The band was developed, and very nearly destroyed, in a modest family home down the street from an affluent elementary school, George R. Allan (now Cootes Paradise Elementary School). When I ask Greg Veerman about the band's tenure at that rented house on Kipling Road in Westdale Village in 2008, a wicked grin comes over his face.

"Through the summer when we became a band and started hanging out, we instantly fell in love with each other," says

Veerman. "We both had different groups of friends, but then we started hanging out together. Only certain people survived – it was kind of a weird meld of groups. Four people from their friend group and four people from our friend group, plus us, we kind of all started hanging out exclusively that summer. Then we started getting really into the band. Everyone's rent and lease was coming up at the same time, and we were like, 'we can get a house together.'"

As Pumps began to take shape throughout summer 2008, the Veermans and the Dawsons started hunting in the west end for a rental home that could also function as a rehearsal space. The brothers settled on a four-bedroom home on a quiet tree-lined street not far from Westdale Village, and proceeded to transport all of their worldly possessions and equipment into the tight living quarters that September. The storm clouds began gathering soon afterward.

"We were like a young couple getting engaged or something. All of our friends were like, 'this is all happening too fast, you guys are stupid, you're going to hate each other, don't do it.' And then we're like, 'nah, you're crazy,'" Veerman laughs.

"Then people started getting on each other's nerves. Sean bought a dog out of nowhere that, like, ate everything up. It was a husky-shepherd mix, so he was huge and just a terror, eating everything in sight, chewing up couches and everything. It was the messiest, dirtiest house of all time. My brother and Brodie both lived upstairs, and they're both pretty clean guys. Sean and I lived on the main floor, but we're both pretty messy and could kind of live in any circumstance."

"It was a nightmare," says Brodie Dawson. "At first it was perfect. There was not a lot of space, but there was just enough to have our shit in the basement – my recording stuff and all our guitars and whatnot. And then, something happened where it just became a fucking frat house. There wasn't a day that went by where four people who didn't live there were living there...at any given time, there would be eleven-plus people in this house."

Even with a basement jam space at their disposal, Pumps slowly disintegrated as the trees turned orange and brown. Rehearsals were few and far between, and by the time Stevie and I caught the band at Club Absinthe for the Bank Holiday show with Young Rival, morale was at an all-time low. The band was loose and sloppy, their interest in the project clearly waning. Everyone needed a jolt.

Enter Greig Nori and MuchMusic.

Eighteen months after nearly imploding while attempting to live and rehearse under one roof, Pumps – recently reborn as San Sebastian – were preparing to make their national television debut as part of MuchMusic's popular disBAND series. The concept of the show involved former Treble Charger lead singer and prominent rock producer Greig Nori plucking a rag-tag group of misfits from relative obscurity and turning them into a writing, recording, touring and hyper-stylized machine, with the help of industry heavyweights and major-label cash. To say that everyone in Canadian music was looking for the next Sum 41 would be an understatement. San Sebastian had the look, the raw talent and the right amount of youthful energy necessary for widespread commercial success. The band was bought in, a powerhouse management team assembled and, in the spring of 2010, the wave finally began to break.

"Hey buddies, just want to let all you know that we are overly excited for our DisBand Discovered episode tonight," Veerman wrote on a MuchMusic blog post dated May 5, 2010, the day of their premiere on the show. "I'm so excited about our episode tonight, I forgot to tell you that our first single 'Wake Up' is out on iTunes RIGHT NOW!!! My opinion may be a little biased, but I think it's great."

San Sebastian had officially broken through, but their ascent was hardly a smooth ride. At the band's all-important industry showcase surrounding their disBAND appearance, Veerman forgot to check the connection between his bass and the amp before the band went live. To make matters worse, the group's new manager had told every industry executive in attendance that they were about to witness the next big thing in Canadian rock and roll. The lights came up, and the band fell flat on their faces. Veerman felt two feet tall.

"We played, and it was a pretty bad show," he offers. "It started out without the bass, and we were pretty much dead in the water from that point on. I was looking around and nothing was working and I couldn't figure it out. Then I was like, 'well I'm not going to stand here and look dumb, I'm just going to fake it,' so I did. My brother was just giving me the death stare."

A stagehand ran from the wings as the first song finished and managed to fix the broken connection. But with no time to spare, the band dove into the next track with Veerman's amp cranked to maximum volume. "It totally ruined the flow of our set," he concedes. "Everyone was nervous and stiff, and we played like crap," Veerman explains. Jack Ross, head of the Agency Group and one of the most powerful men in Canadian music, didn't mince words when speaking to the Veerman brothers following the band's quick, disastrous set. "You've got a lot of work to do, guys," he offered.

Regardless, the disBAND television appearance rocketed San Sebastian into the Canadian music mainstream, and facilitated the release of their full-length LP *Relations*, issued October 4, 2011 via Universal Music Canada. Promotional excursions to Europe, Africa and Central America followed, and the band criss-crossed the country supporting some of the biggest names in Canadian rock and roll in large clubs and small hockey arenas. Still, the band's appearance on disBAND had tainted their brand a little – at least in the eyes of Canada's indie rock elite.

"We never really felt any of the backlash from it, necessarily," guitarist Brodie Dawson explains. "But we did get denied a couple tours. I won't put them on record, but we pitched a tour to two bands when we were coming right off the show. They were like, 'we don't want to tour with a TV band.'"

Touring woes aside, *Relations* is a perfect artifact of a band finally realizing their full potential. Featuring four singles – including the breakout hits "Wake Up" and "Baby," the latter of which was promoted with a humorous music video shot in Hess Village and around Hamilton's downtown core – the record still holds up as a fine piece of garage rock swagger from the final days of the genre's turn-of-the millennium revival. The songs are tight, well-written and sprinkled with just the right amount of studio magic to make them palatable for a more general audience while still appeasing long-time fans who followed the band all the way from Club Absinthe to MuchMusic and back again.

• • •

The unforgiving winter that bridged 2008 and 2009 was the apex of our rolling party. We moved around the city with ease, pouring ourselves in and out of taxis and floating between our usual haunts with bags of weed and bottles of whisky stashed in our heavy coats. It later became known as the Lost Winter.

By this time, the core members of our gang spent more time at Club Absinthe and Che Burrito than anywhere else. I'd leave an evening shift at the grocery store, hop on the bus at the corner of King Street West and Longwood Road, and cruise over to Stevie's house to plot the night ahead. I stopped shaving and let my hair grow into a nest of long brown twigs. I also lost the fifteen pounds I'd gained during university. I was a walking toothpick dressed in skinny jeans, black Chuck Taylors and bright plaid sweaters checked with neon green and blue squares. But goddamn if we weren't having fun.

The soundtrack to our destruction was the perfect blend of bone-crushing French electro, Canadian indie rock, classic New York hip-hop and a collection of stadium bands we had come of age worshiping – the Strokes, the White Stripes, Arctic Monkeys and Kings of Leon. When we weren't out at a club, we took the playlists made famous by Rockstars for Hire and the Disco/Punk crew and pumped them through gigantic stereo speakers until first light. One evening at Stevie's house, a group of us stripped down and streaked the length of the block in nothing more than our winter boots. Our damp clothes froze in a twisted pile on the front porch.

In late December, I saw Alexisonfire play at the Hamilton Convention Centre on the heels of a massive blizzard that crippled the southern tier of the province for days. That was the night George Pettit announced the band's forthcoming record, at the time simply titled *Young Cardinals*. As the show drew to a close, we surged through the pit and smashed into the barricade as the band ripped into "Polaroids of Polar Bears" from the *Alexisonfire* LP. A few days later, we went to the annual Young Rival Boxing Day extravaganza, and once again listened with great interest to new material from the band's latest EP. I continued to spin Arkells' *Jackson Square*, Cursed's *Architects of Troubled Sleep* and the latest offering from local folk-punk troubadour B.A. Johnston, *Stairway to Hamilton*. I also filed more stories with *View* and padded my portfolio. The scene improved, and my writing improved with it.

Around the same time, I began dating a beautiful girl with olive skin and starless black hair. Her name was Lily. She was born in Bulgaria but raised in the suburbs of Toronto. She was old-world beautiful, with deep, soulful eyes and a mysterious charm. Lily was four years my junior and studying in the Arts & Science Program at McMaster. We had met during a wild Halloween house party in Westdale Village, where people danced on couches and smoked cigarettes indoors. We kept in touch as fall tuned to winter. Stevie took to calling her "Spilly" after she accidentally dropped a full glass of wine on the floor at a party. Her student house was only a block from Stevie's rented home, in the heart of the McMaster student ghetto, and our mutual groups of friends soon began hitting the clubs together. During one of our runs downtown, I convinced the bouncer at Club Absinthe to usher Lily and two of her friends directly into the club, bypassing the massive line out front. It felt like we all owned a small share of the scene. Those who put in extra time and effort were often rewarded with small bonuses.

Our united crews rang in the new year at Tom's parents' home in Westdale Village. I offered to DJ, playing songs through Tom's laptop and an old set of speakers. Everyone took a shot of vodka and pomegranate seeds as the clock struck midnight. I wrapped my arms around Lily and leaned in for a kiss. Stevie beat me to it, lunging between us at the last possible second. He was the only person who could walk away from that scenario without a black eye and he knew it. Stevie winked at me, walked over to the stereo, turned up the volume and banged his head in time to the roaring techno. The little fucker.

2009

IN A DUSTY, OVERGROWN ALLEY not far from Jackson Square, one half of the Junior Boys is fumbling with a large set of keys. Jeremy Greenspan has just arrived for an evening session at his new personal recording studio. The industrial space is a big jump in size from his old digs on James Street North, and has the added advantage of allowing Greenspan to dip his toes in the river without being swept away in the current. Close to the action but not exposed.

"One of the things I like about Hamilton is that it feels very distant from the music world," he says. "I don't get caught up in a lot of things having to do with that. There's not, like, hit bands coming through all the time, or that pressure that comes with being in a real scenester situation. I like that. I like feeling quite isolated…Hamilton is so removed from international, national, even provincial discourse. But people are super engaged locally, and they take a keen interest in what's going on."

The Reason's lead guitarist James "Cubby" Nelan agrees: "Jeremy could just move to Europe and possibly become someone in the scene there. He could blow up and be doing stuff all the time. I like the idea of him being back here and just having the mindset of, 'I like being able to walk down the street and talk to people like a normal person.' That's a real Hamilton attitude to me – this idea that you're not placing yourself above someone else."

Greenspan wipes his forehead with his T-shirt. It's the beginning of summer 2012, and he's covered in a thin layer of sweat from the late-afternoon heat. The band's lead singer and co-writer is fresh from an extensive tour of South and Central America with his long-time Junior Boys co-conspirator Matt Didemus. He's eager to spend some time in his hometown to catch up on other musical projects and enjoy a much-needed break from the road.

As we enter the studio, Greenspan takes a seat in the main lounge chair and switches on a large fan in the middle of the windowless room. I take a seat opposite him and we chat casually about the mountain of gear surrounding us: a dozen keyboards, effects racks, samplers and a large mixing console line the walls of main room, with a vintage Gibson Les Paul, a Rickenbacker bass, and piles of guitar pedals and amplifiers the next room. Some of the gear is older than both the band and its frontman, while other pieces are still wrapped in the cardboard and Styrofoam packaging they were shipped in. It's a tech-head's playpen.

It's been nearly a year since Junior Boys released their acclaimed fourth LP, *It's All True* – a light, breezy ride that many critics viewed as a return to form for the band following the well-received but largely misunderstood conceptual album *Begone*

Dull Care. The thirty-three-year-old is pleased with the reviews of the band's latest offering, but remains somewhat mystified by the last decade-and-a-half of his life in the music business. He's now far removed from the group's earliest days of seeking out after-hours parties in long forgotten downtown dance caves. It was during this time, while experimenting with early Junior Boys collaborator Johnny Dark and others within the bourgeoning club scene, that Greenspan became fully immersed in the Hamilton underground.

"If you're on King William, and you're walking down and you get to John, on the corner of John there's a white building. And there was a door on King William, and it went upstairs, and the upstairs was the X Club," he recalls. "And the X Club had this night every first Wednesday of the month called Necropolis. You'd have these industrial bands from all over playing. You'd have Digital Poodle and Malhavoc and DHI, and then a couple of Hamilton bands like Orphx.... Just weird, noisy kind of stuff and I was into that."

A by-product of Hamilton's vibrant urban dance scene, Junior Boys officially formed in 1999. Didemus didn't enter the fold until a few years later, when founding member Dark prepared to embark on a solo career. All three contributed material to 2004's crisp and calculated *Last Exit*. Released on KIN in the United Kingdom and Domino Records in America, the album received a staggering 8.9 rating on *Pitchfork* – which praised its "high dance IQ" and "luxuriously monochromatic sensuality." That instantly vaulted the Hamiltonians to the top of Canada's electronic music mountain.

So This Is Goodbye, released in 2006 via Domino Records, made Junior Boys a truly global entity. Unveiled in August, the ten-track LP was heralded by critics and fans alike, and expanded the band's reach to a much larger and more diverse audience.

So This Is Goodbye was shortlisted for the 2007 Polaris Prize, ultimately losing to Patrick Watson's *Close to Paradise*. It was also named one of the best records of the year by *Pitchfork*, beating milestone offerings from the likes of Phoenix, T.I., Belle and Sebastian, Band of Horses, Lily Allen and Justin Timberlake, and landed at number eleven on the outlet's esteemed Top 50 Albums list. *Pitchfork* writer Jason Crock brilliantly described *So This Is Goodbye* as "music so smart, yet so obvious, that it must have been there all along, waiting for someone to snatch it from our collective subconscious and make it our soundtrack for late-night driving and pre-party preening."

But for all the accolades that surrounded the band after the release of *So This Is Goodbye*, it was Junior Boys' next project – the ambitious and conceptually-motivated *Begone Dull Care,* released in spring 2009 – that Greenspan thought of as his true masterpiece. Tempering the cold, menacing twitch of tracks such as album-opener "Parallel Lines" with the synth-pop sheen of tunes such as "Hazel" and "Bits & Pieces," the record is a polished, progressive piece of nouveau-electro that owes as much to Deutschland as it does Detroit.

The record Greenspan envisioned was to be both an homage to the underground electronica he first discovered as a teenager, as well as to the sounds and aesthetics involved in minimalist Canadian filmmaking. More than any of their previous work, *Begone Dull Care* represented new territory for Junior Boys – especially Greenspan. It was to be the epitome of a subtle, ongoing revolt against the mainstream. At the time, global electronic music was leaning hard. The beats were big and the festivals bigger. Household names such as Steve Aoki, Boyz Noise, Crookers, MSTRKRFT and Justice often favoured power over subtlety as producers worldwide opened up the throttle and let it rip. For the most part, Greenspan wasn't having it. "I felt like, 'whatever's happening in music right now, I don't want to be a part of it,'" he offers. "Then I was like, 'I need a hero. Somebody I can really look up to.'"

Enter Norman McLaren, a Canadian artist whose 1949 animated film *Begone Dull Care* and accompanying avant-garde jazz soundtrack not only inspired the album's title but part of its content and overall conceptual theme. McLaren was the breath of fresh air Greenspan had been searching for. "This guy embodies everything an artist should be, you know? All his art is about experimentation and the love of creating stuff. How it's packaged doesn't fucking matter, and how it does commercially isn't even a thought in his mind," says Greenspan, who spent nearly the entirely of 2008 crafting the lyrics and ethereal soundscapes for the new album. The frosty *Begone Dull Care* was recorded during stints at Didemus's apartment in Berlin, Germany and back home in Hamilton, with Greenspan working on most of the mixes in his former James Street North studio.

"We like the idea of songs that evolve over a longer period of time and force you to engage with them more," Didemus explained to German magazine *EXBERLINER* in 2009, not long after *Begone Dull Care*'s European release. "I think it's too much these days, especially with the Internet and iTunes and iPods – not that I have anything against these technologies – it's just that the culture of listening has become a little bit lazy. And people expect this big emotional payoff in a song in two seconds."

According to Greenspan, the band's label, Domino, wasn't enthused with the album's delicately nuanced soundscape, and pushed for an outside producer to rework some of the mixes. "I don't think [Domino] liked the record, and they didn't know what to do. So when it came out, they didn't push it that hard. It sucked. The whole third record experience sucked." Although well received in underground electro circles, the record ultimately failed to live up Greenspan's high expectations. Its success was further complicated by the obscure cultural references that informed the duo's writing around that time period, and by the singer's absolute rejection of the chic, carefully tailored style so often favoured by major club DJs.

"I've never really quite recovered from that. I put everything into that third album, and nobody got it," Greenspan continues. "The whole thing of the third record was weird. It was all like just me trying to lash out in this weird way. At one point, the label started talking to me about the way I looked, which was just so annoying to me...you can see it in pictures from that tour. I started purposefully wearing these fucking absurd outfits. I just started only wearing these plaid and Hawaiian shirts, and I was just like, 'fuck you.' I wanted to look as much not-the-part as possible."

After allowing time and space to temper their irritation, the band released the fun, nightclub-friendly *It's All True* in 2011 – their final effort for Domino – and once again began filling theatres and dance halls around the globe. "The Boys' beat-mongering has never been more efficient," Robert Everett-Green wrote in the *Globe and Mail* on June 11, 2011. "In that respect, listening to *It's All True* is like touring a series of apartments all decorated in the same minimalist fashion, with nothing left on a bed or coffee table to hint at unstructured habitation. In other words, the music is both physically involving and emotionally concealing."

In the years ahead, Greenspan would also lend his skills to a talented new artist in the Hamilton electro scene – Westdale Secondary School graduate and accomplished singer-songwriter Jessy Lanza. Released in the fall of 2013 on UK-based label Hyperdub, Lanza's breathy, R&B-informed debut album *Pull My Hair Back* was produced by the Junior Boys' frontman. The album was shortlisted for the 2014 Polaris Prize, further reinforcing

Hamilton's strong global reputation as an electronic music Mecca. "I think people think of Hamilton as being like a rockin', rock 'n' roll kind of city," Lanza explained to CBC Hamilton following the record's release. "They don't think of electronic music as being made there. But a lot of great electronic bands come out of the Hamilton area." While Greenspan and Lanza were busy collaborating, Didemus began issuing tracks under a new handle, DIVA, and launched his own record label, Obsession Recordings.

In 2016, Junior Boys returned with *Big Black Coat*, their fifth full-length album and first for new label City Slang. The disc was a smashing success, full of luscious grooves and dance floor-ready singles. Greenspan mixed the record and wrote five of the album's eleven tracks on his own, including much of the opening side, while Didemus is credited as a co-writer on five others. The duo also slipped a fun cover of Bobby Caldwell's 1978 easygoing single "What You Won't Do for Love" into the middle of the record, which acted as a buttery-smooth transition between sides. Even though they never really disappeared, Junior Boys were most certainly back. *Big Black Coat* was their best record in years, and Hamilton embraced it with open arms.

• • •

Partying at Embassy Club was always a wild ride. Located deep in the belly of a magnificent old stone building at 54 King Street East, the semi-secret downtown haunt was a magnet for after-hours revellers, house music lovers and beautiful, creative dancers of all colours, shapes and sexual persuasions. There's no marquee on the front of the club. You either know about it or you don't.

On a particularly cold and damp evening – the kind of late winter flash-freeze that seeps into your bones and snatches your breath – we decided to visit Embassy Club. Myself, Mike, Stevie and Tom were rubbing our hands together, scheming, plotting our next move at the corner of King and James. We were blood-thirsty, desperate for action. Stevie aimed a chubby index finger at the row of one hundred-year-old facades directly across the street. "Embassy," he said, nodding up and down in slow, calculated movements. He was already grinning.

Stevie always wanted to push the buttons of everyone around him. He was the true ringleader of our crew. The shit-disturber. More than willing to start a fight or finish someone else's, a fan of tipping over mailboxes and throwing rocks through windows of abandoned buildings. He was a juvenile delinquent who never quite grew out of it. And he wanted to get wild that night.

Mike glanced east down King Street and pivoted hard, looking west, squinting. He jammed his hands into his front pockets and motioned for us to follow him around the corner. We slipped into a piss-stained alley off James Street North, where Mike produced a small bottle of Jack Daniel's bourbon.

"Everybody hit this," he demanded, unscrewing the plastic cap and tossing it into a metal trashcan. "We're not leaving until it's finished."

One by one we tipped the bottle to our mouths and took long, hard plugs. I stepped back after my first gigantic gulp and felt vomit rise, which I quickly swallowed down. We sipped and stumbled around the alley for five minutes, until Mike's request had been fulfilled. Stevie passed around a pack of wine-dipped Colts cigars and everyone began puffing. Then it was time to dance.

The main entrance to Embassy Club was located behind the row of storefronts, nestled into a tiny alcove at the edge a dim city parking lot. We queued-up behind other late-night trippers, paid our cover charges, checked our coats and entered. I craned my neck and gazed at the fifty-foot ceiling as deep Chicago house music ricocheted off the walls. Dozens of male patrons in tight pants and T-shirts danced on black platforms and risers scattered around the dance floor. Bright neon lights and pulsating strobes illuminated the din of the hall in short, rapid flashes. Every time the lights flickered on, the dancers were frozen in a new position as if caught in a photograph: the shutter clicked every two or three seconds and a new image came into focus. I started nodding along to the flat, pounding bass as we floated toward the bar.

Mike ordered a round of beers and we waded into the centre of the dance floor, forming our own closed circle. Everyone cut loose. Wide rivers of sweat began pouring down my neck and back. My skin was damp and my black jeans were sticking to my thighs. In a flash of pure ecstasy, Tom peeled off his red T-shirt and climbed onto the nearest stage riser. The rest of us followed, joining a group of shirtless older men with thick bellies and tufts of dark curly hair poking out of their backs, chests and shoulders. Tom tucked his shirt into his waistband and swirled around our two collectives, hoisting our hands into the air and leading us in a group fist-pump in time to the music.

I watched as the tallest, widest, sweatiest older man on the riser snuck up behind Tom and draped meaty forearms over his shoulders and across his chest. The pair began swaying in unison. The older man leaned in close and whispered something into Tom's ear. They both began giggling and the dancing continued. It wasn't until the following morning that Tom revealed the details of their brief exchange.

"Don't worry," the older man had reassured him, "I'm only using you as bait."

We danced until well after last call before collecting our raincoats and slinking back into the night. Tom ordered four slices of thin, gooey pepperoni pizza from an all-night deli across the street and we feasted off paper plates as hot grease dribbled down our chins and dripped onto the sidewalk. Mike hailed a taxi in front of Jackson Square and we sped along King Street West under the twinkling corridor of ambient light. As we crossed the bridge over Highway 403 into Westdale Village, Stevie fell asleep in the back seat with his head resting on my shoulder.

. . .

Not long after our excursion to Embassy Club, I started working as a DJ at a tired sports bar across the street from McMaster University called Ramshead. Most of us simply referred to it as the Shed.

Adam Mitchell, an old friend from high school, was working there as a bartender while finding his footing in between graduate school and full-time employment. Another victim of the recession, he held degrees from Queen's University and the London School of Economics, but earned his wages pulling pints for students and softball teams.

One particularly slow night, Adam told me to select a few songs and play them over the club's ancient sound system. He didn't have to ask twice. Before long, I was being paid fifty dollars cash each week, entirely off the books, to play a few hours of music at the Shed on Thursday nights. I'd come straight home from an evening shift at the grocery store, round up a collection of CDs and take the bus over to bar – still reeking of stale milk and shredded cardboard. I called my event Everyone's a DJ.

Years of fighting, smoking, spilled drinks and dancing on tables had stripped away the sheen of the Shed. The dark main room was outfitted with a heavily stained carpet, chipped honey-brown wooden booths, faded sports posters and bright neon signs advertising all manner of beer and liquor. You could almost cut the air trapped inside. Most weeks, it was a good place to get lifted without slipping up in front of our regular crew of bartenders and bouncers. Nobody was getting kicked out of this place, no matter what happened inside. Plus, it was usually empty, save our motley crew of students, part-timers and a handful of old regulars. Within a matter of weeks, it became our west-end clubhouse.

Playing music at the bar was always a bit of an adventure. The DJ booth was equipped with an old computer tower and a grimy monitor, two CD decks and a dusty mixer. Everything was loaded onto a wobbly wooden podium beside the front entrance. Sometimes the whole system would shut down mid-song, or a crucial burned CD wouldn't load in one of the drives. Nobody seemed to notice once the booze started flowing.

Up to that point, I had only DJed a few house parties in Westdale Village. Playing a full set at an actual bar was new territory. Inspired by the raw and reckless DJ stylings of Gurman, McNamee, Frank and Toye, I would line up my weekly selections on a small table next to the podium and choose songs as the mood struck me. The sets always contained a mixture of hip-hop, punk rock and electro – bangers that were sure to get people moving. Nas, J Dilla, The Streets and Kanye West would bleed into Be Your Own Pet, Arctic Monkeys, Black Rebel Motorcycle Club and Queens of the Stone Age, which would lead into an extended dance set featuring Justice, Daft Punk, Chromeo, A-Trak, Cassius and Uffie. It was a poor man's Club Absinthe, but we always had fun.

At ten p.m., I'd claim my first free drink from the bar. Adam and I would chat over the sticky countertop until our friends started drifting in around eleven. Stevie would gather everyone around the DJ booth and order tray after tray of syrupy Jäger-bombs from Adam, who often joined us. We'd plunk the shot glasses into fizzing plastic cups of Red Bull and shoot everything back while New York hip-hop and French electro roared from the speakers. Lily was always close by, helping me sort through CDs and select new tracks.

Not long after launching the weekly series, I received an email from Ciara. We hadn't spoken in more than a year, since our brief encounter at the Phoenix a few weeks before gradua-tion. She told me she was living back home in St. Catharines and working a part-time job at a telemarking agency. I told her about my late-night writing sessions and my job at the grocery store. I also told her I was working as a DJ at the old sports bar across from McMaster on Thursday nights.

The following week, Ciara arrived at the Shed with two friends from university and quietly slipped into a booth near the back of the room. I didn't notice at first. The bar was packed and loud. I selected tracks and nursed a warm pint until one of her friends came over to say hello. Then she came over. She never left my side for the rest of the evening. We talked about music, work, mutual friends and missed opportunities. We laughed and brushed hands. She snapped blurry photos and sipped sug-ary mixed drinks. I loved the way her smile lit up the room when Stevie pulled her onto the dance floor. I couldn't look away and I didn't want to.

A few days later, lying side-by-side in my childhood bedroom, I suggested to Lily that perhaps we were better off as friends.

• • •

When I first met Lee Raback back in 2002, I expected to be lec-tured, berated or worse. Raback had a shaved head, a laser-focused gaze and a foul mouth. He was short but built like a linebacker. Openly confrontational and unflinching in his political and social beliefs, Raback was a renegade with a microphone and a loyal following, backed by an innovative and intimidating eight-piece jazz-rock-hip-hop click known as warsawpack. He was a legitimate force in the Hamilton arts community and, for a brief window of time, one of the most recognizable, charismatic figures in underground music circles from coast to coast.

"I remember Lee as a younger, almost shy dude coming through CFMU with Realistic," says Leon Robinson, better known as Eklipz in the tight Hamilton hip-hop trio Crown A Thornz. "He had a very sing-song, melodic style that almost had, like, a reggae influence to it. I was like, 'yo, who is this dude?' We'd freestyle and go back-to-back and it was just good vibes and good energy... even back then, he was always on some spiritual and scientific type of lyrical content."

During my final year of high school, I somehow managed to convince Raback and warsawpack to headline an afternoon concert at Westdale Secondary as part of a student-led discussion on music and politics. I expected the power to be cut during the first song, but Raback was far too savvy. He knew how to get his core messaging across, regardless of the scenario or circumstances. I watched from the wings as Raback pulled the microphone away from his mouth during every single "fuck" and "shit," never missing a beat in front of a packed auditorium full of nervous teachers and curious students. He spoke openly and eloquently between songs, encouraging dialogue and debate. He shook hands and chatted with teachers after the show, and seemed genuinely gracious for the opportunity to perform in front of such a young crowd.

When we finally had the chance to speak after the gig, Raback told me we should plan more events like this – that his band would perform anytime, at no cost to our meagre student events budget. I knew right then and there that he was the real deal.

In spring 2009, I stood on the balcony at the Pepper Jack Café and watched Raback set up his minimal gear on the club's tiny stage. It was April, and our crew was on hand to watch Raback – now performing under the handle Lee Reed – launch his debut solo album, *Introductory Offer*. The record was a tour de force, anchored by the biting lead single "Viral Rock" that instantly exposed Raback to a whole new generation of local hip-hop heads.

The intervening years had been both productive and destructive. Raback's band warsawpack called it quits in 2004, but not before releasing one final record on Winnipeg's G7 Welcoming Committee the previous summer, the fully antagonistic *Stocks and Bombs*. Following the dissolution of his main outlet for political and social commentary, Raback spent the next several years working odd jobs and dabbling in various collaborative projects with like-minded Hamilton musicians. This included a short-lived project known as Peoples Republic that served as an important stylistic bridge between warsawpack and Raback's breakout as a solo rapper.

"My friends who were really into hip-hop loved [Peoples Republic]. They preferred that to seeing the band," offers Raback. "Almost immediately, it opened me up to an audience that wasn't there before, you know? I mean, they were always there, but I could access them more easily. I had a lot of people tell me they preferred it."

Long-time warsawpack DJ and legendary mixtape producer Aaron Sakala – aka Realistic, described by Raback as "the Keith Richards of DJing" for Sakala's workmanlike attitude and musical intuition – served as the ad-hoc musical director behind Peoples

Republic. It wasn't exactly two turntables and a microphone, but it was all about stripping back layers of sound in favour of more restrained loops, beats and samples. The idea was to keep it pure, simple and to-the-point.

"With Peoples Republic, I had maybe two loop pedals, a delay pedal, a distortion pedal and another live looping pedal so I could layer things," says Sakala. "It was overtly hip-hop, but at the same time it had that live element to it...and then with Lee coming with his amazing lyrics for everything, we gathered a lot of those hip-hop heads who wouldn't come out to warsawpack shows."

But it wasn't until Raback officially re-branded as Lee Reed and made a concerted effort to go solo that his reputation as a biting, fearless MC began to take hold. The lasting appeal of warsawpack – it's large ensemble and avant-garde melding of jazz, rock, hip-hop and blues – always put the band in a league of their own. For Raback, the challenge had been finding his place *within* such a robust orchestra of competent players. Everyone wanted, and deserved, a chance to shine.

As a solo MC, however, he was free to test the limitations of his lyricism though longer, more complex rhyme schemes and less singing of hooks and choruses. His flow was delivered over much more utilitarian drum-and-bass beats. He suddenly had more room to breathe and opportunity to vent. The music may have changed, but abandoning his revolutionary political ideals was never going to happen. It was all about finding and maintaining the perfect balance.

"I actually was writing like that for a couple of years before I even started warsawpack," says Raback, reflecting on the dig-your-heels-in approach of the majority of his work. "It wasn't really a conscious decision, so much as that's just how I write.

I think what was consciously different [following warsawpack] was trying really hard to sound more in-step with hip-hop with my voice."

Introductory Offer was followed by the release of *Emergency Broadcast* in 2011 – a strong twelve-track album recorded by local producer Scott Peacock at his home studio in Westdale Village and mixed by Sean Pearson at Boxcar Sound Recording. After throwing out an earlier batch of recordings that Raback wasn't entirely happy with, he regrouped with Peacock in the spring of 2011 to take another stab at tracking the album.

"I'd leave work at four or four-thirty and immediately walk over to Scotty's place," Raback begins. "We'd do three hours or something and then I'd split. It was great. We had all the time in the world, and for me, that's worth more than the quality of the studio or the gear. How long do you have to fuss over it? Are you working with somebody who's happy to fuss over it with you? You need that kind of person."

"It took us a while, like, six months, to make that record," Peacock admits. "I had a closet upstairs that I treated as a vocal booth. So when Lee would cut records, he'd go upstairs, lock himself in that closet and I'd be downstairs. We had a talkback system so we could communicate with each other. We'd cut all his vocals, he'd do a few passes and then come down, go through them all and go back up again."

Featuring a collection of hard-hitting beats supplied by John P, Realistic, Nate Wize, Anonymous D and Canadian Winter's John Staples – with additional contributions from Leon Robinson and R&B songstress Sara London – *Emergency Broadcast* was Raback's coming out party. Poignant lyrics, sharp social commentary and smooth production shaped the album from top to bottom. To accompany the record's release, local artist Robert Michael produced a video for lead single "The Growth" that featured Raback walking around Hamilton's rugged Beasley neighbourhood in a Santa Claus costume collecting electronic goods in a canvas sack, before returning home, melting the items into a thick stew and mainlining the toxic goo into his forearm like heroin. "I think we're living too large," Raback repeatedly raps into the camera as the video cuts to black. "I think we're living too large…"

"I think he's incredible," says Robinson, reflecting on Raback's lyrics, demeanour and, at times, controversial ideologies. "His stage presence, and the way he engages the crowd, it's so authentic. That's why he gets the masses of people that come out to his shows and support him, because it's very genuine. He really believes in what he does, and he lives it. Some people talk a good game, but it's not really what they're about."

"He's very entertaining. He's a showman," Peacock adds. "He knows how to engage with his audience. He always has. I was the kid who was front row at warsawpack shows, just mesmerized by him and the rest of the band, but mainly him, you know? He was the head entertainer…he's a super cool, mild-mannered guy, and then he gets on stage and it just all comes out. The fierceness comes out, which is critical."

• • •

I still listen to Nas's *Illmatic* more than any other hip-hop record. I was ten years old when the album was released in 1994 – still far too young to fully grasp the vivid urban inferno depicted on the Queensbridge rapper's landmark debut, but old enough to know when something is good. And this one was *really fucking good*.

Nearly six thousand kilometres across the Atlantic Ocean, in a multicultural suburb of Surrey known as Woking, Kobi Annobil was becoming mesmerized by the very same verses and samples. Born in northwest London in 1979 to immigrant parents from Cape Coast, Ghana, Annobil says he first "caught the hip-hop bug" after catching wind of Nas during a summer 1993 family trip to New York City. Like me, he instantly knew when something was too good to ignore.

"When I got back to Woking, I really just started studying the mechanics behind the music," Annobil begins. "I ended up linking up with some guys the year ahead of me at school and we recorded a bunch of demos. They went to university and then we got offered a deal by a label a few of them had linked up with. We didn't sign, and the band sort of drifted apart. I ended up teaming up with another MC called Reality who I met in my first year at uni, and we'd do shows together completely freestyle, including one night when we randomly ended up rapping with Kool Herc, the godfather of hip-hop, in 1999."

In between writing rhymes and performing at local gigs, Annobil began spending more time with an old schoolmate, now known as DJ Merkin. Around the turn of the millennium, the pair would "knock off work on Fridays, share a bottle of rum and record freestyle sessions onto MiniDiscs," Annobil tells me. They'd occasionally venture down to Brighton, on the shores of the English Channel, to record and experiment with a local producer named Irwin Max.

Canadian hip-hop was still largely unknown in England, but Annobil had a few reference points to work with. He heard Saukrates' "Father Time" in 1996 on Tim Westwood's Radio 1 Rap Show, and randomly purchased the 1994 Maestro Fresh-Wes single "Naaah, Dis Kid Can't Be from Canada?!!" at a second-hand store in London. "But other than that, it never really popped-up on my radar," he explains.

Still, this affinity for exploring new sounds and studying worldwide approaches to hip-hop proved more important than

Annobil could have ever imagined. Especially when it came to the formation of Canadian Winter, his radically-inventive Hamilton hip-hop collective, not long after he relocated to this side of the pond to work on film and television scripts. "The first place I lived was Westdale. It reminded me of a bunch of sleepy English villages that I spent my youth running around," he says. "In the first few months out here, I really threw myself into getting out and about and exploring."

In many ways, the original lineup of Canadian Winter was an anomaly – a group that shouldn't be. The band comprised four new friends from diverse musical and cultural backgrounds, eager to carve their own path but not entirely sure where to begin.

"Ken Inouye introduced me to Johnny [Staples] the night of Lee Reed's *Introductory Offer* EP launch, and we got talking about the sneakers I was wearing that night – Nike ID Air Max 90s," says Annobil. "It turned out that he had been to school with some of my cousins, and we ended up exchanging details."

One of those cousins, Kojo Chintoh, already knew Staples from his early days DJing around the city. The trio met up a few weeks after the Lee Reed showcase, and Staples spun a few instrumentals over which the group started jamming. "I was not 100 percent sure I wanted to get back into making music at the time, but Johnny said if Kojo and I ended up doing something he wanted to be involved," says Annobil. Within a few weeks of this initial rehearsal, local producer Scott Peacock was brought in by Staples.

"The whole thing was really like this perfect storm," Peacock explains. "I don't even really remember what the hell happened or how I came into the fold, but I was just all of a sudden *there*. John and I were hanging out a bunch by that point. We were good buds and we're best buds to this day. So Johnny pulled me in, but we really didn't know what to do at first."

"The city as a whole was kind of an enigma to me," Annobil continues. "I didn't know anyone apart from my family. I was going home from my cousin's place one night and took a wrong turn on top of Jackson Square and ended up on James Street North. It was eleven o'clock at night and just looked like there was nothing there – almost like a vacant lot that stretched the length of a street. All the stores on the first block were closed and I'm probably exaggerating, but I don't even think the streetlights were on. It wasn't until I started hanging out with cats like Johnny and Kojo that I started to learn about the city's history."

According to Annobil, once he felt more settled in his new surroundings, he began searching for common musical ground upon which he could build a foundation for the new collaborators. Legendary Detroit beat maker J Dilla was an early inspiration, along with a host of American and UK-based performers who appealed to Canadian Winter's eclectic sensibilities.

"Musically, we found common ground in J Dilla's records. He kinda crossed everyone's musical boundaries. We all have pretty broad taste in music, but [J Dilla] was the middle of the Venn diagram," says Annobil. "Scotty was heavy into the *Ruff Draft* record at the time. Both Johnny and I were fans of *Beats, Rhymes & Life* by A Tribe Called Quest, which Dilla had a big hand in, as well as his work with Slum Village, Busta Rhymes and Common, among others. Kojo and I also jammed to his beats when it was just the two of us playing in his apartment, and 'Got Til It's Gone' by Janet Jackson, which was also produced by Dilla, is one of my favourite songs ever."

"Kobi and I really bonded over [British rapper] Roots Manuva," Peacock adds. "I wasn't super into English hip-hop, but Roots Manuva had this really interesting sound and I remember Kobi being really into it."

2009

After rehearsing in Staples's west-end home throughout the summer of 2009, Canadian Winter played their first official show at a September house party, according to Annobil – although Peacock cites a gig at This Ain't Hollywood supporting Micachu & the Shapes as the first "true" Canadian Winter concert. As the end of the year approached, the group had begun to take shape as a four-piece, featuring Annobil on vocals, Chintoh on percussion, Peacock on guitar and bass, and Staples manning two turntables and a mixer. It wasn't long before the band debuted popular live tracks such as "You Know What You Are" and "City Lights," and began cultivating a signature sound amid the cacophony of samples, scratches and live instrumentation that dominated early rehearsals.

"I had never been in another band, really" explains Peacock. "Kojo and I played on opposite sides of the stage, but him and I would just lock in. We had that classic feeling, but with a backing track and John laying samples over stuff. It was all very interesting. John was like the drummer in the band, in a way, and Kojo is just this free spirit of instrumentation. We just worked very well off of each other."

Two years after first connecting at the Lee Reed record release show, the band unleashed their debut full-length LP *Just Wait Till February* to a rabid following of local hip-hop fans. Featuring production from the likes of Motëm, Cheese Shop Paddy, SUPA 83 and Dex Brown – as well as the Winter's own John Staples and Scott Peacock – the seventeen-track disc was a sensation in the local underground music scene. This was partly due to Annobil's casual flow and unique English accent bobbing over top of the inventive and experimental backing tracks.

"He has his own unique perspective, coming from the UK and bringing that here," says Crown A Thornz MC Leon Robinson. "The way he sees Hamilton, and when he speaks about

Hamilton, it's a whole different view than somebody who's been here their whole life…he really feels the vibe of what Hamilton is, as an outsider coming in and looking at it."

"I think Canadian Winter has made a huge contribution to the music scene in Hamilton," says Afro-soul musician Kojo "Easy" Damptey, a native of Accra, Ghana who came to the city to study engineering at McMaster. "I remember when I went to the album release at This Ain't Hollywood, the place was packed like a sardine can, music was pumping, heads moving and everyone was having a great time. Like the musical genius Kobi is, he always shares the spotlight with his contributors. Hip-hop producers like SUPA 83, Cheese Shop Paddy, Motëm and Michael 'Dex' Brown showcased their music production chops, and Hamilton was introduced to hip-hop talent never seen before."

On the strength of *Just Wait Till February*, Canadian Winter took home the 2011 Hamilton Music Award for Hip-Hop Recording of the Year, and continued to garner an underground following in Southern Ontario and several new locales across Canada. But despite their early success, the founding lineup of Canadian Winter was not long for this world. Staples left the group prior to the release of 2013's *The Snowball Effect* and was replaced by DJ Close. Peacock also left the fold around the same time – eager to further his career as a record producer and engineer at Hamilton's Catherine North Studios – and local guitarist Jay Baggett entered the group in his stead.

"We really started to struggle with what to do next," says Peacock, looking back on his somewhat rocky departure from the group at the tail end of 2012. "We were sending stuff out, it was getting airplay and we were on a few top ten lists. We wanted to do it more seriously, but we were all in different points in our lives. We would have needed to tour, it was the only thing we could have done…I wasn't nineteen; I was thirty. I had a mortgage and a full-time job. I couldn't just throw all my crap in my parents' basement and be like, 'I'll see you in a bit,' and just hop in a van."

To help ease the transition period, Canadian Winter de-camped to Hive Studios on Cochrane Road near Stoney Creek to record a track with Kojo Damptey. Released in October 2012, "Daylight Robbery" is a smooth, guitar-heavy tune that show-cases Damptey's strong singing voice and Annobil's natural flair for documenting the struggles of everyday life.

"Aside from creating records that cut across various genres of music, I think the lasting impact Canadian Winter has had in Hamilton is fostering a community of musicians that just love music," says Damptey. "Many times we fall victim to the group-ings of music – rock and roll, R&B, hip-hop, indie rock, etc. But Canadian Winter has taught us to forget about those categories and make music that speaks to the soul and give audiences an experience they will never forget. At the end of the day, isn't that what music is all about?"

• • •

At the other end of the Hamilton club DJ spectrum – far from the mind-bending blowouts at Club Absinthe and Che – Flamborough native Rachael Henderson was quietly building a reputation for playing feel-good sets anchored by thick layers of dub, reggae, hip-hop and disco. Anything to get people moving and grooving on the dance floor.

Henderson, more commonly known as DJ Donna Lovejoy, developed her style with patience and care, thanks in large part to a sympathetic older sibling and an adventurous mother with a passion for new music. "I grew up making mixtapes to put in my mom's van, so we could drive around and listen to tunes," begins Henderson, wrapping her hands around a cup of herbal tea at a trendy, bustling café called Democracy on Locke Street South in November, 2013. He dark brown locks are cropped close like a French New Wave actress; her demure frame leans gingerly over the tabletop. She never stops smiling and laughing.

"That's just what we did, and that was my first foray into, just like, how songs can connect to one another – not necessarily because they're the same, but there's a tone about them that goes together. It's the combination of music that makes it a great overall mix, and that's how I DJ as well."

With a growing interest in electronic music and all-night raves in hidden warehouses in the city's downtown core and industrial northeast end, Henderson moved out of her rural family home at nineteen and landed in a tiny apartment on King Street West, not far from Jackson Square.

During the late 1990s, downtown Hamilton was still peppered with independent and chain record shops within walking distance from Henderson's newfound home base. Dr. Disc and Sonic Unyon were on Wilson Street; Sam the Record Man on James Street North; HMV within the Jackson Square shopping complex; and most importantly, In Yer Ear was at 172 King Street West, one floor below her new apartment. The latter proved to be a catalyst in the teen's newfound passion for collecting and spinning rare records, along with the perfect gift from her sibling.

"My brother Ira bought me a regular record player, just a regular belt-drive, and I had already started buying a couple of records here and there," recalls Henderson. "He bought me these great speakers and a receiver, it was a good set-up. He was like, 'you need to have these things.'"

Every Friday, Henderson would wander downstairs to In Yer Ear to pick up a handful of records for her growing collection. Her tastes included diverse and eclectic artists such as DJ Shadow and Blackalicious, along with plenty of reggae, hip-hop, dub and electronic music. These were the early days of her growing vinyl obsession, a key period that helped define her dance-heavy style as DJ Donna Lovejoy in the years ahead. It was also during this time that Henderson first made the switch from one turntable to two. "I met a guy who became my boyfriend for a little while, and he had turntables. I started to learn how to DJ from him," she explains.

Her first proper gig took place at the Casbah in 2001, opening up for a pair of bands in a largely empty room. Billed as DJ Go Down ("It was a really silly name," she says with a laugh), the nervous twenty-one-year-old pieced together a lighthearted, dance-heavy set full of Ugly Duckling, the Pharcyde, A Tribe Called Quest, Beastie Boys, Blackalicious and other "true school" hip-hop culled from her growing personal collection. By the end of her brief set, and with an enthusiastic reception from the crowd, she was hooked.

Soon afterward, Henderson began a regular residency at the new Pepper Jack Café on King William Street after catching the ear of talent buyer and local promoter Ken Inouye. The weekly "Big Box of Beats" event featured contributions from DJ Go Down, Rev Selecta, Nate Powers and Triple-X Girth. By the mid-late 2000s, Henderson was gigging regularly under the name DJ Donna Lovejoy – a combination of a "Lovejoy" steel product she noticed in a local hardware store and the random selection of "Donna" as a first name. It's not an ode to Reverend Lovejoy's gossip-hungry wife on *The Simpsons*, as is often assumed.

Once she was fully entrenched in the booming Hamilton club scene, Henderson began playing regular gigs at Inouye's Pepper Jack Café, and other venues along the rapidly evolving James Street North strip. These included the Brain – owned by Junior Boys' singer and producer Jeremy Greenspan – the Red Mill Theatre, Academica Hall and the Mulberry Coffeehouse.

"She plays 1980s retro songs as well as current dance music, and many songs with a female singer," offers Inouye. "Nothing too dark, and girls love her style. Guys too, but the ladies really come out for her the most."

Despite her growing popularity in the local dance scene toward the end of the decade, two key factors separated Henderson from her peers at the more reckless Club Absinthe and Che: first, an aversion to the kind of lose-your-mind partying that popularized both clubs; second, a newborn baby boy.

"The Rockstars for Hire guys, they were party animals," says Henderson, flashing a big smile. "I remember hearing about them and thinking, 'oh god, these young guys, all they want to do is party and drink and just get wasted.' And I never was into that when I would DJ. I might smoke a joint or something like that, but I would never get drunk, never lose control of my functions when I was DJing because I wanted to keep it in control."

Sleepless nights at local clubs were soon replaced with sleepless nights tending to a newborn child – putting a temporary halt to Henderson's DJing, but hardly cooling her passion for the craft. When her son Louis was born – the second true love of her life – his delivery was scored by none other than Hamilton's foremost electronic duo. "I've told Jeremy Greenspan this one, but when I was in labour in the hospital, we listened to Junior Boys' *Last Exit* album. That was one of the soundtracks for the birthing experience," she explains. "It isn't, like, an overwhelming record, but it has a really nice musicality to it and it also has a driving beat – something that I could close my eyes and just focus on."

More than a decade after initially crossing paths, long-time Pepper Jack Café owner Inouye still regards Henderson as one of the most important, influential and cross-generational performers to emerge during the city's club DJ explosion of the mid-late 2000s.

"She's the queen diva of Hamilton DJs," he explains. "Her taste is impeccable – there's rarely ever a stinker in her song selection for the night. She can play to an older crowd, late twenties to forties, even fifties, easily, and she also has a very graceful and genuinely fun manner when she DJs. It's pop music that does not suck."

Aaron Sakala, also known as DJ Realistic, agrees whole-heartedly. He also credits Henderson with having one of the best ears for mixing different styles of music in the city. She's simply a natural talent, he explains.

"A lot of people [in Hamilton] have been mixing different genres together, like house, pop-rock, older rock and hip-hop. I think people kind of do it, but she's found a way to blend it seamlessly," Sakala says. "And not just seamlessly. She makes it work. She's good 'cause she knows her music. She knows what will mix together and won't mix together. And she's really good at reading the crowd…a lot of people will throw something on and clear the floor, and they won't be able to get people back on. If that ever happens to her, she'll find something to mix in and get people going again."

• • •

Even as a student newspaper writer, I had long maintained a fascination with the allure of the road. The triumphs and the struggles. The temptation and the vices. The lingering threats. Back when I was pulling all-nighters at the *Silhouette* with Tim Robinson and Simon Toye, one line of dialogue from *The Last Waltz* held a great deal of significance for us. Toward the end of the film – reflecting on a sixteen-year career playing saloons, roadhouses and rugged concert halls around the globe – the Band's lead guitarist Robbie Robertson leans into the camera, grins and offers the following quip with the perfect balance of stoicism and self-pity:

"It's a goddamn impossible way of life … no question about it."

The road can make or break any band, and Canada is said to contain some of the most unforgiving terrain on the planet. Still, every single musician in the country wants a piece of it. Huron was no exception.

Cam Malcolm answers the door of his parents' Kirkendall home with what looks like a tobacco-coloured Fender Jazzmaster in hand. It's Super Bowl Sunday 2012, and the lanky twenty-five-year-old is dressed in faded blue jeans and a plaid button-down shirt.

"It's actually a Squire," says Malcolm, home for a weekend break from his graduate studies at York University. "I bought it from a friend for four hundred dollars. The pickups are Seymour Duncan and the finish is new, but everything else is stock. It doesn't play that well, I just really wanted to have a Fender again," he explains.

Striding into a well-appointed basement recreation room, he plugs the guitar into a silver-faced Fender amplifier. Warming up with a series of bright country scales, his playing is effortless. Trained as a jazz bassist, with a background in music theory and composition, Malcolm's fingers move over the fretboard with ease. The tone is clean and pure, and the warm sound resonates all over the room.

Eighteen months earlier, Malcolm was preparing to embark on a cross-country tour with Huron, originally known around their hometown as Jawbone. The band was formed with fellow guitarist and co-lead singer Aaron Goldstein, bassist Adam Melnick and drummer Pete Hall, formerly of Sonic Unyon psych-rockers A Northern Chorus. Their self-booked adventure would stretch to both sides of the continent and touch two oceans on the strength of *Huron*, their 2009 self-titled LP. The album was released on Toronto indie label Latent Recordings, home to Skydiggers, Cowboy Junkies and fellow Hamiltonian Tom Wilson and his LeE HARVeY OsMOND project.

In many ways, the tour was a last-gasp effort for the band. With an album in independent record stores and mounting pressure from their label to promote it, Malcolm and co-guitarist Aaron Goldstein knew the window was closing to get the most out of their investment. In other ways, it perhaps just delayed adulthood and responsibility for another year in favour of a strange and nomadic existence.

"Touring musicians always talk about, like, 'life on the road, man,'" says Malcolm, rolling his eyes. He's never viewed it as a chore, and never wants to.

"You sit on your ass all day, and then you play for forty-five minutes…it's pretty cushy compared to a lot of jobs. Touring is one hundred times easier than any full-time job, regardless of whether you're sleeping on people's floors. It can be hard. It can be draining and it's tiring. But how fun is it? You're on a road trip with your buddies, and you get to play for people who talk to you about how much they like your music. It's really gratifying."

It was a chance meeting at Goldstein's Rocky Saugeen band house on Carling Street that set Huron on the course toward recording a proper record. On the bill that night was C'mon, a Toronto-based power-rock trio fronted by none other than burly guitar god Ian Blurton – former lead singer of Change of Heart and one of the most in-demand producers in Canadian rock music.

"C'mon was playing at Rocky Saugeen, and we really wanted to do something with Ian," recalls Malcolm. "He came to the show and I think Aaron sort of meekly asked him if he would be interested in producing Huron." Blurton seemed interested and asked for a copy of a cassette containing some of the band's early demos. A friendship was quickly struck between the two camps.

Talks continued as Goldstein played on one of Blurton's 2008 projects, and later that year, Huron assembled in Toronto to begin work on a proposed EP with Blurton at the helm. The group laid down the bed tracks for several songs over a single weekend, and worked steadily over the next few months to put the finishing touches on the record. As soon as Huron heard the outstanding mixes from the Blurton sessions, they switched gears and committed to a full-length album – personally financing the recording sessions to the tune of three-to-four thousand dollars, Malcolm tells me.

Released in 2009, *Huron* perfectly captures the dynamic push-and-pull of the band's live shows – balancing thundering amps and towering classic rock riffs with softer, country-infused melodies and pop-rock sensibilities. Blurton, known for playing a role in crafting some of the heaviest records in Canadian rock history –including the brutal *II* from Hamilton's own Cursed – initially put some of the band members on edge.

"I mean, I was slightly intimidated," Malcolm admits, grinning. "When we were in the studio, we would do the hardest songs first, in terms of rock and roll. The loudest songs. I was hesitant to play some other country songs or pop numbers, but at the end of the day he's got an ear for both styles of music.

"He would, like, kick my amp or kick me when I was supposed to be doing a guitar solo," Malcolm continues. "He'd call me 'Joel Plaskett' or something like that on stage and make fun of me. I was kind of offended at first, but then afterward he

170

would always be like, 'I'm sorry I called you that.' He's become a good friend."

It wasn't long before the band set out on the Trans-Canada Highway with Blurton for their first real taste of touring the country as a fully formed unit. The group's initial run to the Maritimes and back offered a crash course in hard living, hard drinking and the virtues of finding a decent place to crash for the night.

"We played the Toucan in Kingston. It's not really a venue; it's like this long bowling alley of a club," says Malcolm. "So we played a set and partied afterward, and I remember we stayed at Ian's friend's place. We were going to bed and we all had our sleeping bags and toothbrushes and stuff, and Ian just slept on the floor in his winter jacket. He woke up in the morning and just pulled himself off the carpet and went out and had a smoke. I was just like, 'wow, I'm a total pussy compared to that guy.' That's rock and roll. That's why that guy is the real deal."

The band soon tried their luck in the western half of the country, booking the archetypal "shit-eating tour that every band that tours Canada goes on," Malcolm says. Huron first drove eighteen hours to play a deserted hall in Thunder Bay. The next two shows in Kenora and Gimli were cancelled while the band continued to push west. In Winnipeg, eager to pull in some cash following the scrapped gigs, Huron were a last-minute addition to a show featuring fellow Hamilton rockers San Sebastian, who were heading east toward home. For both bands, it was their first experience playing at legendary punk dive the Royal Albert Arms Hotel – an infamous, recently closed (2013) venue and flophouse in the city's downtown Exchange District. They barely left with their shirts.

"This is a good little Hamilton road story," Malcolm begins, leaning back in his seat.

"San Sebastian opened for Huron in Winnipeg, and we played at the Royal Albert, which is this notorious, crazy, shit venue. I remember it was pouring rain, and the ceiling was leaking. Like, there was actually water coming in through the drywall. I was literally waiting for the ceiling to collapse. So San Sebastian goes on, and I had never seen a crowd member throw a bottle at a band before. That was the first time. They start playing, and this guy finishes his beer and just tosses it behind his back toward the stage. Brodie [Dawson, guitar] had to duck, and I was just like, 'shit, the Royal Albert is living up to its reputation!' Luckily, that was one of those occasions where I was happy to be in a hard rock band. We could just pummel them with noise. If it had been my solo band, we would have been fucking eaten alive."

As Huron pushed farther into expanse of flat, dry earth that is the Canadian Prairies, the shows got better and better. They linked up with Arkells for a packed and rowdy show at a tiny club in Regina, before playing to a warm and receptive – albeit relatively small – crowd in nearby Swift Current. Alberta was a different story altogether. The band "really ate shit" in Edmonton, laughs Malcolm, playing to a minuscule crowd who couldn't care less about an independent riff-rock band from the other side of the country. The remaining dates on Huron's first and only west coast jaunt were entirely hit or miss.

"Touring is strange," offers Malcolm. "It will knock you down so, so hard, but it will lift you up, too. I've always had these experiences where I'll play a town like Vancouver, and it just sucks. It's this totally underwhelming show. And then you'll play Abbotsford on a Sunday night, and you think it's going to be terrible. Then it turns into this amazing show where you get to two encores and play the loudest rock and roll ever. That's the thing with touring Canada, especially when you're unknown. There's

172

this unpredictability, you know? You never know the way it's going to break at a show."

Arkells lead guitarist Mike DeAngelis cites the infamous Coquihalla Highway – a narrow and meandering stretch of highway between Kamloops and southwestern British Columbia, carved into the heart of the Rocky Mountains – as one of the most stress-inducing legs of any west coast run. This rings especially true for any Ontario band on their first tour to the Pacific and back.

"Whenever there's a sudden deceleration, even if it's to get gas or something, I wake up in this total terror that we're about to go off a cliff or something like that," he explains. "We've had some bad stretches there where if it's very snowy it gets really slippery, and there are some really steep sections. I've been driving when it was so slippery that the whole van and trailer and everything is just in a full-on uninhibited slide...it gets quite foggy, and the fog at night there is very frightening. You're going down a hill and there are sharp turns and you don't know what is going on. We've had some hairy experiences driving."

"I think a lot of bands tire of that west coast run," adds Malcolm. "You're waking up early and driving eight hours, a lot of the time to play for nobody. But I may be a glutton for punishment, because I just like doing it. It's kind of an adventure."

Lacking the funds and motivation to record a follow-up to *Huron*, and still aching from a hard year on the open road, the band fizzled out not long after opening for Arkells at the Hamilton Place Studio Theatre in December 2010. Within a year, the group's co-lead singers would be leading very different lives. Goldstein wound up playing pedal steel with City and Colour, travelling to Australia, Europe and the far corners of the globe with one of Canada's most successful musical exports. Malcolm regrouped with his long-running solo project, the Owls, and entered law school at Lakehead University in Thunder Bay, Ontario. Melnick lent his talents as a pianist and organist to a number of Canadian projects, and later recorded an experimental eleven-track album known as *Blackburn Hall* with Pete Hall and Dan Empringham, including contributions from Terra Lightfoot, Julie Fader, Alex McMaster and Holy Fuck's Graham Walsh.

• • •

Mike, Tom, Stevie, Jeff Green and I dropped our T-shirts on the couch in Stevie's new downtown high-rise apartment. We had tickets for a hockey game at Copps Coliseum (now FirstOntario Centre), and had decided to paint the name of one of the team's star players, P.K. Subban, across our chests. One or two letters per fan, in bright blue body paint. Everyone was laughing, snapping blurry cellphone photos and pulling warm cans of Pabst Blue Ribbon from a case on the kitchen floor. Rain pelted the sliding glass door leading out to the patio. The west end of the city twinkled in the distance.

Mike ordered pizza from a tiny shop around the corner, and we tore into it with blue-stained fingers. Justice's *Cross* was on the turntable, blasting through a pair of high-end studio monitors. Stevie began mouthing the opening lines to "Tthhee Ppaarrttyy" while standing on the couch, his voice mimicking the song's female vocalist, Uffie. I took a sip from a can of Pabst and jumped on the couch in time for the chorus. Stevie grabbed my shoulders and shook me back and forth during the last line, spilling foam on the cushions. We both burst out laughing.

Mike buttoned up his shirt and slid a bottle of whisky into the breast pocket of his heavy fall coat. I jumped off the couch and called downstairs for a taxi. We took a long elevator ride down to the lobby and watched as rain hit the cars parked out front.

After the game, I was already feeling light-headed from smuggled whisky and tall stadium beers when we decided to walk over to James Street North. Thick drops of water smashed against my black rain jacket as we trudged along Bay Street North and swung onto York Boulevard, passing the colossal Hamilton Public Library and the indoor farmers' market, both closed for the evening. My shoes were soaked from toe to heel, along with the bottom half of my jeans.

Stevie and I had been curious about a new event taking place that evening – a free festival billed as Supercrawl. One of my favourite new local bands, Burlington's Sandman Viper Command, was booked at This Ain't Hollywood at the north end of the strip, and I was excited to catch their melody-driven garage rock for the first time. I was equally intrigued by the band's commitment to producing a simple, pure sound by running vintage guitars through beat-up old amplifiers without adding layers of effects. We worked our way down James Street North in the rain and queued up at the side entrance to the club.

Since the middle of the decade, on the second Friday of every month, a loose collection of shop owners, artists, musicians, bartenders and entrepreneurs had banded together to host Art Crawls – an increasingly popular monthly event that capitalized on the growing energy of James Street North. People from all over the city would stream into the downtown core and stroll along the historic boulevard from dinnertime until the galleries closed.

"An Art Crawl consisted of a meal at Mex-I-Can, followed by a visit to the galleries that were around such as Loose Cannon, Blue Angel, the Print Studio, the Inc, and then a stop at Mixed Media's old location where most people would congregate to discuss the goings-on of the street," offers music writer Nicole Nicolson. "It was not so much a crawl as a jaunt – a step down the block. There was none of the fanfare, the spectacle, the food trucks, the pan flutes. Hell, I think the Mulberry (Coffeehouse, now a central hub) was still just a dream. The street had fewer options on where to spend your money, but everything felt honest. When those pan flute players show up, that surely signals the death of any event – kind of like when the university freshman picks up the acoustic guitar at a red cup party."

In those early days, our crew would assemble at Ola Bakery near the Hamilton Armoury for custard tarts and espresso at seven p.m., before setting off into the night to wander through independent art galleries that offered free wine and plates of salty hors d'oeuvres. Some nights we would hang around the old Portuguese sports bars in the area, sipping warm pints alongside regulars who had been sidling up to the bar since before we were born. Around midnight, we'd walk back down the strip, cut across the darkened Jackson Square rooftop plaza and head toward Hess Village, or veer further west and walk home over the bridge to Westdale.

It was a beautiful time in the city – a downtown economic boom driven by art, passion and genuine curiosity. It felt organic. Shop owners knew patrons by their first names, and you felt the love and freedom and unbridled creativity just by walking down the street. At the same time, James Street North had become the wild west of downtown Hamilton. Public drinking was rarely reprimanded, and all-night parties took place in long-forgotten concert halls and hidden warehouse spaces peppered throughout the core. You couldn't walk two blocks without bumping into a group of casual friends or old classmates, with someone mentioning an underground after-party that was being promoted solely by word of mouth.

By 2009, those at the heart of the scene began pushing for a much larger cultural festival anchored in the city centre. Enter Tim Potocic.

"Right from the conceptual moment of the event, it was always tied to, 'this is not just a music festival,'" says Potocic, co-founder of Sonic Unyon Records and the founding director of Supercrawl. "Of course, music was always the shiny ticket and the driver of what's going to draw the crowd. But, you know, there's an arts community there and it was really important to us to focus and shine that arts community."

We're seated across from one another in a crowded coffee shop called My Dog Joe in Westdale Village. Potocic is only a few weeks away from the opening night of the 2014 edition of festival – an event that Arkells will be headlining. By most estimates, roughly 130,000 guests are expected to pour into downtown Hamilton from all over the province and beyond for the four-day affair – a far cry from the three thousand curious on-lookers who braved the rain in 2009, during the first Supercrawl.

Potocic has a loving family and a beautiful home in the west end of the city, but maintains the raw ambition of a twenty-two-year-old bachelor, fresh out of university. He's far from naive and brazen, but has a distinct brand of confidence that is infectious. No idea is too bold. No plan too grandiose. Potocic is the living embodiment of Hamilton's traditional municipal slogan, the Ambitious City.

"We didn't think it would ever, honestly, be this big this fast," he continues. "The goal was always to drive crowds, but the free aspect of it was to try and change people's perceptions of what's going on in downtown Hamilton. [Sonic Unyon] had done business in downtown Hamilton for fifteen years prior to this happening, and we'd seen the changes…the festival will always be free, the major components of it. But we would like to get to the point in the evolution of the festival down the road where we can do a Copps Coliseum show, like, a Thursday-night launch at Copps with 'X' huge artist that's going to sell fifteen thousand tickets."

Despite the pouring rain and relatively low attendance, the 2009 incarnation of Supercrawl was deemed a success. The free street festival won the Tourism Hamilton Award for Best Small-Sized Festival of the Year. In the years ahead, the event would grow to include a board of directors, art curatorial committee, fashion committee, advisory committee, volunteer coordinator, media liaison and numerous others partners and organizational divisions. According to Supercrawl organizers, the 2014 affair resulted in an economic impact of more than $14 million. Non-local performers that year included the likes of Spoon, Kevin Drew, How to Dress Well, Operators, Shout Out Out Out Out, Hamilton Leithauser, Charles Bradley and A Tribe Called Red. The Hamilton contingent was equally impressive, offering Jessy Lanza, Jeremy Greenspan, Harlan Pepper, Canadian Winter, Terra Lightfoot, Lee Reed, WTCHS, the Dirty Nil, Dead Tired and Arkells to the crowds.

"I've lived here for ten years now, and back in 2004 there was no reason for tens of thousands of people to come into the downtown core like this," George Pettit explained to *Vice* in 2014, while discussing his new band Dead Tired's booking at Supercrawl. "The festival location is unique, because a lot of the bands are partaking as well as performing. It's a nice feeling, because we all have a vested interest in supporting the city and the local economy."

"Tim is shooting for the moon, and he's getting there. He's getting to Mars," says the *Hamilton Spectator*'s Graham Rockingham. "He first told me that his plan was to have Supercrawl run from the Escarpment to the Bay. I paused and I said, 'sure.'"

Rockingham doubles over laughing and continues. "That would have been after the first one. And now, he's almost there. It is the most important free musical event in Hamilton. There's no doubt about that."

• • •

The morning after Hamilton's first Supercrawl, I had a new text message on my phone from Stevie: I LOVE YOU. The message was written entirely in capital letters. The time stamp was 4:17 a.m. I called his cellphone but he didn't pick up, so I drifted back to sleep. Around noon, I woke and wandered into the kitchen for a bagel and fresh coffee. There were two missed calls from Stevie on my phone, but no new messages.

The house was quiet and empty. I sat in the sunroom and put my feet up on the couch, absently watching the news while smearing butter onto the bagel's crisp halves. Coffee was steaming in a brown ceramic cup I'd balanced on the couch's round armrest. I sipped and snacked until it was time to dress and walk to the grocery store for a long evening shift. It had just started raining.

• • •

Not long after Supercrawl, I helped launch a local newspaper-magazine hybrid with a tight collective of old and new friends, including Tom Shepherd and a few former staffers at the *Silhouette*. The twelve-page paper was called *Hamilton Review*.

Ad revenue came quickly, and we had a dedicated team of volunteer writers filing stories within a matter of weeks. Our print circulation was two thousand, and we distributed free copies to more than forty businesses around Hamilton – criss-crossing the city from east to west during snowy delivery runs in Tom's truck. We put Metric on the cover of one edition, and ran big-time features with the likes of Cancer Bats, Alexisonfire, Hollerado, Tokyo Police Club, Young Widows, the Danks and Attack in Black. It was turning into a real business and it caught all of us by surprise.

The magazine was very much on top of anything and everything happening in the city. We published interviews with local bands such as Young Rival and Sandman Viper Command, and Arkells band members Max Kerman and Nick Dika began filing sports and music columns. We covered the Bulldogs hockey team and the Tiger-Cats football team, and put our own spin on pro sports from a casual fan's perspective. We were the first publication to get the scoop on Junior Boys lead singer Jeremy Greenspan's new bar and music lounge, the Brain, which opened to rave reviews in a tiny cave-like space at 199 James Street North. We also remained on top of the downtown core's rapidly developing music and art scene. We started receiving free records, press releases and story tips from local readers. Tom and I even toured potential office spaces along the James Street North strip, and contemplated making the move from our part-time garage-and-attic operation into a real small business.

I was drunk with enthusiasm and naive optimism.

Then my world tipped upside down.

One morning in late November, I shot out of bed to the sound of frantic knocking at my parents' front door. My bedroom was located on the first floor of my family home. It was a little after ten but felt much earlier. Sunlight streamed through the blinds, carving tiny incisions into my sheets. I ignored the knocking and fell back onto the mattress, rolling away from the window. I was the only person there.

Silence for a few moments, then the doorbell began ringing. The knocking grew louder. My phone buzzed on the nightstand. I opened my eyes and stared at the wall against my bed, pulling the sheets higher. More silence, longer this time. I closed my eyes and drifted back into a light sleep.

The knocking was at my bedroom window now. Heavy and more urgent.

The caller was in the alley next to my parents' home. He knew someone was in the house. He knew where my bedroom was located. My phone continued to buzz, missed texts turning into missed calls. I peeled back the sheets and swung my legs over the edge of the mattress. I walked over to the window facing the alley and slipped my fingers between the slats. Tom was there, smacking the glass with an open palm.

Tom and I had put an edition of *Hamilton Review* to bed the night before, and it had taken a long time to come down from the high of a late-night production run after sending the pages to the printing house in Guelph. The following morning, my body was aching and my head throbbing. I fought the urge to close the blinds and retreat. I tapped on the inner pane and Tom peered up from the alleyway. He lowered his phone and pointed to the front of the house. His face was pale, his expression flat.

I pulled on a pair of dirty jeans and walked to the front door, barefoot, rubbing sleep from my eyes. I tiptoed into the foyer, feeling the sting of cold blue tile under my soles. The front door swung open and Tom entered without saying a word. Alain Wright, another close friend from high school, followed closely behind. We assembled in the living room, in between a long couch and two plush armchairs. Nobody sat down. I didn't know what to expect.

"We've got something to tell you ... I don't know how to say this," Alain stuttered. He couldn't look me in the eyes. Tom said nothing and stared at the ceiling, arms folded across his chest. My head swivelled back and forth as I tried to get a read on the situation. Tom shifted his weight, exhaled.

"Andrew," he began, his voice cracking. "Stevie died last night."

• • •

Reality always disappears in the face of great tragedy. Time slows down. Actions feel prolonged and cinematic. It becomes difficult to separate emotions, actions, thoughts and dreams. You're treading water. You simply exist.

You watch other people shuffle around you – rushing off to work, a job interview, an exam, a date. You smile and nod to the barista at the coffee shop, and wave to other drivers at stop signs. You make a little joke in the checkout line at the grocery store and leave an extra-large tip at the restaurant. You take the car for a midnight drive and roll down all the windows, staring at the muted lights of quiet office towers. You call in sick and sleep until noon. You fall asleep with a book in your lap. You laugh and you frown; you feel happy and you feel sad. But somehow, it all feels the same. Everything feels relatively normal. Static. Un-flinching. Safe. These tiny distractions are everywhere, and you welcome them.

At night, when you're alone with your thoughts and the dis-tractions are gone, reality returns and it destroys you.

You clench your knees and heave uncontrollably. You roll out of bed and claw at your chest. You reach for the desk lamp and wipe cold sweat from your forehead, running your hands through your hair. You cover your mouth, and hope that nobody on the upstairs floor of the house can hear you – that nobody will find you in this deplorable state at 3:30 in the morning. You dig your fingernails into the wooden surface of your desk and hold on tight until the room comes back into focus.

When your breathing slows and your heartbeat settles, you crawl back into bed and stare at the ceiling. You pull the sheets up to your chest, close your eyes and take a long, deep breath.

One of your best friends is gone, and he isn't coming back.

. . .

Stevie died November 30, 2009, after jumping from the top-floor balcony of his downtown high-rise apartment building. I became consumed with his final moments on that tiny concrete slab – where I had laughed and enjoyed drinks with friends so many times. Did he hesitate for a few moments, or was his mind made up? Did he take a giant leap from the railing, or roll slowly over the edge? Did he look up at the night sky while falling, or down toward the rapidly approaching concrete? Did he think about his family and friends, or was his mind entirely blank? Was he satisfied? Did he regret it? Did he care?

The funeral, held one week after his suicide, was a blur. All of our families were in attendance, and many old friends from Westdale. Lily was there as well, along with her group from Mc-Master. All the guys said a few words during the service – the core group of us. Our friend Ben Board was stranded on the tiny island of Fiji in the middle of the Pacific Ocean, en route to Canada following a year of teacher's college in Australia. Tom read a long, moving letter on his behalf. Near the end of the service, the entire room sang "Blackbird" – one of Stevie's favourite Beatles songs, which he often played on his acoustic guitar. Then it was all over. People offered quiet condolences and spoke with Stevie's family before putting on their winter coats and shuffling outside. I took one final look at the small metal urn containing his ashes and began sobbing uncontrollably. It was a full-blown heaving, coughing, sputtering breakdown in the middle of the empty funeral parlour with Ciara's arms wrapped around my shoulders and rubbing the back of my head. It was the worst moment of my life.

For weeks after it happened, I questioned everything. Every little conversation. The tiniest, most insignificant exchanges with Stevie. I reviewed old texts and sifted through photos. I paced around my bedroom and went on long, meandering walks down to Cootes Paradise and over the railroad tracks to the water. I don't know what I was searching for. Nothing, really. There was no question I could ask and no response that could be given.

Sleep never came easily. The drinking escalated, too. For a short time, a group of us were legitimately out of control. Rich brown bourbon flowed into bottomless glass tumblers every time we sat down for a conversation. Entire evenings were lost. My eyes were constantly red and swollen and dry. We devoured platters of greasy food and pitchers of flat, sticky beer during late-night missions to west-end pubs. Nobody wanted to stay home, but nobody wanted to talk about it, either. Ciara was always at my parents' house. She was a light in the darkness.

By New Year's Eve, the initial shock had subsided. I picked up more shifts at the grocery store and fell back into a somewhat normal routine. I began writing again and worked steadily on the next issue of the magazine. Music became more pleasurable. I wanted to read novels and exercise and not be drunk every day of the week.

I capped off the year by getting Stevie's initials etched into the left side of my chest at a little tattoo shop on King Street West. Thin, black, looping letters no larger than an exaggerated signature. Stevie and I had often talked about getting tattoos, and it felt good to do something for both of us. A final act of reckless abandon. One final moment with Stevie before he truly slipped out of reach.

. . .

Those who devote their lives to music often spend more time with bandmates than they do with family, friends, wives, boy-friends, partners and children. Those who travel by van know just how intimate these relationships can become. There's no separation. No distance. No private space to escape to when you simply need a breather. The longer you stay out on the road and the more difficult the journey, the more the cracks begin to show. Everyone has a breaking point.

For Ride Theory/Young Rival guitarist Kyle Kuchmey, that breaking point came in December of 2009.

The Ride Theory should have been a breakout band. They had the look, the drive and the honest-to-god raw talent nec-essary to make it happen. But with luck and timing always working against them, they never quite made it – at least not in the traditional sense.

By the time the Ride Theory had rebranded themselves as Young Rival and signed with Sonic Unyon Records, Arkells had already toured the country, released a hit record and been nominated for several major awards. As the latter's star began to rise, the former found themselves struggling with a litany of personal and professional challenges in the face of a rapidly evolving music industry. When bands such as the Strokes and the White Stripes fell out of favour toward the end of the decade, popular taste shifted away from high-voltage garage rock and toward a more earnest, roots-infused brand of songwriting. Cana-dian groups such as Attack in Black, Constantines, Two Hours Traffic, Hey Rosetta! and Ladyhawk led the charge, with Arkells'

Jackson Square cementing the band's reputation as a key player in this new movement. As if the sting of watching a fellow Hamilton rock band climb the charts wasn't bad enough, Young Rival would lose one of its own before the year was finished.

"The touring I think is what really got to him," offers drummer Noah Fralick. "We had done an admittedly shitty tour in August of 2009. A really long west coast tour. One thing you never do, unless you're a big band, is you never tour Canada in the summer. Who wants to be in a dingy club, unless you're seeing a big band? If you just wait a couple months and go out in the fall, all the students are back, they've got some money, they want to party."

With a devastatingly brutal western Canadian tour behind them – often playing to empty rooms for little or no money – morale in the band had hit an all-time low. Musically, Young Rival was also setting off in a new direction. Following the warm reception for 2008's *Young Rival* EP, the group decided to trek further into unknown territory for the next release, prompting feelings of excitement and uncertainty in equal measure.

"We decided to change our name and stop wearing the suits," adds Fralick. "And I guess with that came a bit of musical change. It wasn't a concerted effort to write different music, that's for sure. We were just growing up a bit, and you can only play those really straightforward blues-based thrashy guitar 'oh baby baby' songs so much. Then you kind of want to see where you can take that."

Young Rival played one final show in Hamilton – a support gig for former Smiths bassist Andy Rourke – before taking some much-needed personal time to regroup and plot their next move. The band's self-titled full-length record was already finished, and Hamilton imprint Sonic Unyon was gearing up for a spring release. After several weeks of inactivity, the band assembled for

186

what turned out to be their final rehearsal as a four-piece. That's when Kuchmey officially broke the news.

"Honestly, it was a bit of a surprise," says Fralick. "But I think even in my own head, Kyle was never going to be somebody who was necessarily touring into his thirties or forties.

"There's absolutely no way we could ever fault Kyle or hate that he left," he continues. "His leaving was totally understandable. Not that we're out of control guys, but Kyle wasn't a big partier or a big drinker. He loved playing music, he's an amazing guitar player and he loved the creative aspects of the band."

Kuchmey's final performance with the band took place at the Casbah on Boxing Day 2009, in front of a packed and humid room full of long-time fans sweating though their thick overcoats. I was there with our core group of friends. Everyone was camped out at the bar and drinking heavily before the band hit the stage. We were inseparable throughout the winter holidays. Nobody wanted to be alone. It had only been three weeks since Stevie's suicide, and it seemed impossible that we were at a Young Rival show without him. Or anywhere without him, for that matter.

I elbowed my way to the front of the hall and planted a fresh bottle of Labatt 50 on the edge of the stage. Kuchmey walked from the back of the club not long afterward, slinging a cherry-red Stratocaster over his shoulder and flicking the switch on his Fender half-stack for the last time.

"The whole month leading up to the final show was pretty nostalgic for me," says Kuchmey. "I was just kind of savouring every moment, every crappy show and every really good show. I knew it was the end of an era. I use the comparison a lot, that it's kind of like leaving high school. You had amazing times there, and you had terrible times there. But you come to a point where you know you gotta go. You gotta move on to the next thing."

2010

I DIDN'T TOUCH A DROP of alcohol for the entire month of January. I got a proper haircut and shaved my patchy beard. I stopped falling asleep in my clothes and didn't go out to the clubs as much. Ciara would pick me up from the grocery store on a Sunday evening and we'd drive over to Dundurn Plaza to rent a movie. We'd eat butter-soaked popcorn and sour candies in my parents' basement, and nod off on the couch in front of their old television.

I'd wake early the next morning and listen to the news, then I'd spend fifteen or twenty minutes responding to story pitches and advertising queries, sesame seeds and butter falling onto the keyboard. *Hamilton Review* was still producing new editions at our normal rate. I often stared at the screen and thought about Stevie; his goofy grin and infectious laugh drifted in and out of my mind. I instinctively checked my phone, expecting to find a new text message with an inside joke or a recap from a date.

There was never a new message, but I would often scroll through the old ones.

Night shifts at the store were always quiet in the winter. No barbecues, no outdoor parties. Customers bought whatever provisions they needed to survive for the week and little else. My work crew would stand shoulder to shoulder in deserted aisles as the clock ticked toward the end of a shift, facing-up cans of beans and boxes of oatmeal and wheeling out full crates of milk to stock the dairy counter. We'd line up grocery carts in long trails in the parking lot and push them through fresh snow back into the store, leaving tiny rows of black snaking lines behind us.

Most evenings, I'd simply punch out in silence at the end of the night and walk home in my uniform. But during one particularly slow evening, about six weeks after New Year's Eve, our grizzly old night manager called everyone to the receiving bay. When we arrived, he was standing in the middle of the cement floor with a large bottle of Baileys Irish Cream and four red Solo cups filled with crushed ice from the meat cooler.

"Everybody take one of these," he grumbled, passing around the cups. "You've earned it."

We sipped and chatted and laughed while the last remaining customers drifted out the front door. One of the crew members lit a thin joint and propped open the back door. The night manager refilled our cups until the bottle was nearly empty, which didn't take long. The Baileys was cool, creamy and sickly sweet. The weed was dry and harsh, but we passed it around eagerly.

"All right, let's load up the milk counter and call it," the night manager sputtered, jumping off a bale of compacted cardboard boxes. He lit a cigarette and drifted down the long, dark corridor to the dairy cooler, smoke trailing behind the metal supply cart. I closed the back door, locked up and tucked the remaining Baileys behind the compactor for another time.

In the months that followed, I started writing heavily again. It became more of an escape than ever. A dependable outlet. I assembled fresh clippings from *Hamilton Review* and pasted them into my portfolio with careful precision – adding an extra swipe of glue to loose corners before pressing them onto the black cardboard pages. We also hit the pubs less, and everyone seemed to level off for a little while. It was a welcomed change of pace, and things were about to get a lot more hectic.

. . .

Young Rival issued their eponymous debut album in April via Hamilton's Sonic Unyon Records. Like their 2008 EP, the album took another big step away from the band's mod roots and carried them deeper into uncharted territory, fusing elements of surf, psychedelia, jangle pop and droning stoner rock into one tight package. It was more mature and balanced than anything they'd done prior. It was the band's first release as a three-piece, although Kuchmey still contributed guitar tracks prior to his departure and was listed as a contributor in the liner notes.

"I was just kind of laying back," Kuchmey tells me, reflecting on the sessions. "I wouldn't say that I was faking it. I still loved the tunes. I was able to put parts in there that I think were significant for the songs. But I think if I was in the same mindset I was two albums ago, there would have been more there of my own sounds."

Former Arkells collaborator Jon Drew, who had worked with the band on *Jackson Square*, was recruited to help guide the recording sessions for *Young Rival*. "We went to Jon because his previous stuff sounded really big, and we always wanted our recordings to sound big and be powerful," D'Alesio explained to *ExploreMusic*. "I would say that Jon engineered the album. We essentially produced it...but he's just got a way of putting things together and representing bands in a large, powerful way."

Toronto media began to take note, and early reviews of the record were solid. Many critics hailed the band's flair for reinventing, but not destroying, what had become a somewhat stale genre during the previous decade.

"Now that the early '00s garage-rock revival is behind us, Young Rival's refined blend of Vines-era grunge and sunny, Kinksy pop-rock feels almost like it's on the vanguard," Chandler Levack wrote in *Eye Weekly* on the eve of the album's release. "Here's a band that should step out of the garage more often." Paul Terefenko echoed this sentiment in *NOW Magazine*: "Their self-titled debut nails '60s garage rock without the use of old, rusty nails. The trio succeeds by not succumbing to the artificial throwback throw-up danger faced by anyone toying with 'like your dad did it' sounds."

But even with the success of radio-friendly singles such as "The Ocean," which became a staple on *CBC Music*, the band failed to gather much momentum. They continued to play relatively small and familiar clubs in Ontario and Québec such as the Phog Lounge in Windsor, Café Dekcuf in Ottawa and Divan Orange in Montréal, and embarked on another long and winding tour to the west coast and back, including a huge run in the United States that was more road trip than major concert tour. Young Rival had released the best and most inspired music of their career, but couldn't quite reach the national stage. Regardless, they played with as much passion and purpose as ever. They still loved the craft and lived for the lifestyle, for better or worse. They became lifers.

• • •

Throughout the summer of 2010, I received a crash course in daily newspaper reporting. For many years, I had been trying to break into the *Hamilton Spectator* in one form or another. I desperately wanted to work at my hometown newspaper – situated atop a low hill at 44 Frid Street in the city's west end, not far from my childhood home.

In April, I finally slipped through a crack in the back door. I was offered a four-month paid internship over the summer months – in large part due to the surprising success of *Hamilton Review* – and the contract was set to begin the first week of May. I declined an acceptance letter to Western University's Master of Journalism program, took my name off the masthead of my own magazine and handed in my resignation at the grocery store. Then I bought a gently used, slate-grey, four-door Pontiac G5 with money I'd saved from the store. I was all in.

My cubicle at the *Hamilton Spectator* was situated in a pocket of veteran reporters not far from the main assignment desk. I was surrounded by three key figures: Wade Hemsworth, who earned his stripes covering the infamous Paul Bernardo trial as a young crime reporter and served as my first true mentor; Ken Peters, a long-time courtroom workhorse and recent Tiger-Cats beat reporter; and Denise Davy, my desk-mate and one of the kindest, sharpest and most intelligent writers I've ever had the pleasure of working with.

These reporters were warm, encouraging and merciful, along with many others in the newsroom. We chatted about music, art and travelling, swapped records and went on long, meandering walks around the paper's cavernous Frid Street offices – past an area known as the Zoo that offered a bird's-eye view of the colossal printing presses – while sipping from paper cups brimming with cold coffee. The veterans helped me gain confidence as a hard news reporter, and offered stern but fair criticisms of daily assignments. I sat in the press box at Tiger-Cats football games with Drew Edward and Steve Milton. I filed regular stories on emerging local bands for Graham Rockingham. I documented the expanding scene along James Street North and attended community events all over the city. I even waded into the fray as the G20 Toronto summit descended into chaos, snapping photos and dodging police while documenting the city-wide protests as Toronto burned.

Most senior editors wanted me to chase these kinds of stories, also known as "hard news" or "spot news." Disasters and tragedies. Car crashes. Accidental deaths. Robberies. Courtroom hearings. The nitty-gritty stuff most daily readers crave. Intern rocket fuel. It was exhilarating at times, but as the summer progressed I also struggled with a growing number of "pickup" assignments. Those went like this:

When a member of the community died suddenly, often tragically, a reporter would be tasked with tracking down quotes and photos from their next of kin in order to produce an accurate portrait of that person for the following day's paper. This task usually fell in the lap of a fresh-faced intern or rookie staffer. The secret to success, I was told, was to inform the family this was much better than simply reporting the death as a statistic – that we wanted to let the community know just how wonderful or influential that person had been. A noble sentiment in theory, not so easy in practice. Tears flowed, phones were slammed, vague threats were issued. Most family members were warm and receptive, even genuinely grateful for a call or visit. But I was also politely instructed to "fuck off" on more than one occasion. And I was happy to oblige.

One particularly difficult pickup still weighs heavy. I was charged with retracing the final moments of a teenage boy who had ridden his bicycle off a crude dirt jump in the northeast end of the city, crashed violently and died unexpectedly from internal injuries to his spleen and liver. He didn't even know he was injured after taking the fall. He later collapsed in front of a convenience store a few blocks from his home and couldn't be revived. It was a horrible situation that shook the close-knit neighbourhood to its foundation.

After connecting with a family member over the phone, I drove out to the boy's home and sat in the sparse living room with his father. He showed me class pictures of his son and we talked about what had happened only a few days prior – how inexplicable it all was. He was still in shock; he looked exhausted. We chatted a little more, about good memories and bad ones, and his voice grew faint. I thanked him for his time and hospitality, left the home and knocked on a few more doors. Then I wandered over to the spot where the dirt jump had been constructed, which wasn't far from the boy's home. There were no children playing outside that afternoon; the streets were eerily silent. That's when it all came flooding back – the sting of a young and tragic death. I drove back to the office with the windows rolled down and the radio turned off, filed my story and went home. I mailed the family a bouquet of flowers the following year, on the anniversary of the boy's death, but I never heard from them again.

As the weeks ticked by, I longed for an escape from the daily grind of the newsroom. I needed a respite from monitoring police scanners and cold-calling grieving family members. I quietly hatched a plan in my cubicle.

• • •

There was no escaping the rain at the SCENE Music Festival in St. Catharines. My navy blue T-shirt, black jeans and white high-top sneakers were soaked through. Strands of hair were plastered to my forehead. A stack of twenty-dollar bills in my front pocket were wrapped around my driver's license and clinging to the plastic.

At every intersection in the downtown core, crowds of young fans huddled together under umbrellas and makeshift garbage bag ponchos. They laughed and texted friends, wiping beads of rain off the glowing screens and shielding huge slices of thin pizza with paper plates or newspapers. Others had given up entirely – parading through the streets and jumping in and out of puddles, embracing the classic British festival weather with open arms, even though we were in Southern Ontario. Even in the cold afternoon downpour, spirits were high.

I was technically on assignment for the *Hamilton Spectator*, tasked with gathering updates from the festival that would be relayed on the newspaper's brand new Twitter account, launched earlier that year. Realistically, I was at the 2010 edition of SCENE to catch an amazing trio of rock and roll acts from Hamilton – Monster Truck, the Reason and Arkells. The former were a brand new hard rock sensation who'd torn the roof off L3 Nightclub during a hot and heavy mid-afternoon set in the upstairs half of the James Street venue. The latter had just shocked the country by winning a Juno Award for New Group of the Year in St. John's, Newfoundland, and delivered a strong, swagger-filled performance in front of a packed hall at Barracuda Pretty.

And right in the middle of both sets were the Reason – backs against the wall, facing a crossroads in their career, about to lose two members to a rival up-and-coming Hamilton band. Their own appearance at Barracuda Pretty, opening on an unseasonably cold June evening for close friends and musical peers Arkells, was a last stand of sorts. The beginning of the end – or at least, the beginning of a new chapter. The making of their latest record, *Fools*, had all but suffocated the band's ambition and pushed individual friendships to the brink. But if this was indeed going to be the last hurrah from the Reason, at least they were going out in top form.

. . .

The city of Asheville, North Carolina, is a little over 1,200 kilometres from Hamilton. Travelling by car, factoring in stops for gas, food, bathroom breaks and other roadside attractions, it would likely take the average driver between twelve and fourteen hours to traverse the winding highways that stretch from the bottom of the Great Lakes to the top of the Deep South. But despite the geographic and cultural divide, the two communities are a lot closer than one may think.

Situated on the western edge of the state – roughly halfway between Knoxville, Tennessee, and Atlanta, Georgia – Asheville is a renowned hub for live music and artistic expression. Like Hamilton, it has an urban population hovering around half a million, with a bustling city centre that boasts numerous bars, restaurants, independent shops, live music venues and seasonal festivals. Also, like Hamilton, Asheville exists in the shadow of much larger neighbouring metropolises, though that has never deterred the locals from staking their claim as one of America's best destinations to soak up new sounds. "It's kind of like the Austin of North Carolina," offers the Reason's lead guitarist James Nelan, likening Asheville to Texas's world-famous local music scene.

How the band arrived there was certainly an interesting ride.

The Reason, one of the most popular bands to emerge from Hamilton during the mid-2000s, was actually rooted in the punk rock underground of nearby Windsor, Ontario. Lead singer Adam White and bassist Ronson Armstrong met and became friends during their high school years in the blue-collar border town, and bonded over a shared desire to make music a full-time career. Living just far enough west to virtually ignore the Toronto music bubble, the pair instead gravitated toward the gritty rock and roll seeping out of neighbouring Detroit. As teens, White and Armstrong regularly slipped across the border via the Ambassador Bridge, to attend concerts or play underground punk shows all over the city.

With the drinking age in Michigan set at twenty-one, compared to nineteen in Ontario, the duo also developed a love for all-ages shows. It was a short-lived era of musical and personal freedom, but one that White looks back on fondly. "After 9/11, all the stuff at the border changed. When we were young, we used to be able to just go and play shows in the States. No passports, no work visas," he explains.

As the pair continued to make runs into Motown, their primitive pop-punk band, Sewing With Nancie, was slowly making a name for themselves in union halls and tiny clubs within a day's drive of Windsor. "We were a band for, like, half of high school, and a few years after," says White, sipping from a frothy pint at the Cat 'N' Fiddle on John Street South in late 2012. He's wearing a red plaid button-down shirt and tight blue jeans with boots, looking comfortable and relaxed inside the Corktown watering hole.

"When we finally started playing out of town, we met James [Nelan] through a band he was in called Little Red Wagon. We were a three-piece and we wanted to get a fourth member, and I just remember his energy on stage. He was the frontman for his band, and I wanted a guy like that."

Whenever Sewing With Nancie would travel up Highway 401 to play a show in Hamilton – usually at independent, all-ages shows at Transit Union or the Corktown Tavern – they often wound up sleeping on couches at Nelan's parents' house in suburban Dundas. It quickly became obvious that Nelan, a fellow punk rock devotee looking for a new adventure, was exactly what the band had been searching for.

"They probably stayed at my parents' house half a dozen times before we even had that conversation," recalls Nelan. "That's what you did back then. If you were the promoter and you put on a show for guys out of town, you either put them up or you found a good place for them to stay."

"I remember going to Transit Union Hall to see Cubby's old band, Two Bit Operation, I think. Dave Crosbie and Terris Taylor were eating takeout from the Chinese place across the street and yelling out the window to kids walking by," says Terra Lightfoot. "I was immediately in love with them. I think the floor was in serious danger of collapsing from all the teenagers jumping up and down in there."

As a brand new four-piece, the band toured all over North America as part of the Vans Warped Tour – an eye-opening experience that involved little food and many nights sleeping in the van. "We would spend as little money as possible, and still lose money," recalls Nelan. "That was the hardest touring I've ever done. We had per diems, but it was two dollars per day. If you had one dollar to tip at the end of the day, you could get into the band barbeque." With only one square meal in their bellies, each member of Sewing With Nancie would attempt to hustle ten burned CDs throughout the day to cover gas and other travel expenses, with varying degrees of success.

After touring to the west coast and back, the Windsor contingent decided it was time to get out of town and make a serious run at the music business. Armstrong and White moved up to Hamilton, staying at Nelan's parents' house for six weeks before getting jobs and moving into a downtown apartment together. The group played a handful of local shows as Sewing With

Nancie and then called it quits. But during that brief transition period, they wrote a whole new batch of new songs and officially started the Reason. Hamilton was their newfound home, but it was the emerging punk rock and hardcore scene in neighbouring Burlington that originally pushed the members of the Reason to expand their pop-punk sound into heavier, darker territory.

"I think we were a lot more involved with the bands in Burlington," White admits. "When we first started, we were hanging out with all the guys from Jersey, Grade and the Silverstein dudes."

The band released their debut EP *Problems Associated With Running* in 2003, followed one year later by a full-length album, *Ravenna*. Momentum continued to build and the Reason hit the road hard in support of both records. But it was the group's 2007 offering, *Things Couldn't Be Better*, that pushed them to the brink of mainstream success in Canada. Bolstered by the massively popular single "We're So Beyond This" – a duet featuring Sara Quin of Tegan and Sara fame – the band was suddenly all over MuchMusic and receiving more attention than ever before. A second single and video for "All I Ever Wanted" kept the band in high rotation on Canadian television and commercial rock radio. By this point, the group had also expanded to five members. New drummer Steve Kiely and lead guitarist Jeremy Widerman, along with core members White, Nelan and Armstrong, were poised to make the biggest leap of their careers in the years ahead.

Building on the success of *Things Couldn't Be Better*, the band regrouped in Asheville in the fall of 2008 to begin recording a much-anticipated follow-up. But White, bored with distortion pedals, his vocal cords scorched, was lobbying for a big-time change to the band's overall sound. "A lot of stuff happened when I was twenty and I had a lot of shit I needed to get out of my system," he offers. "But after the first two records, I was just like, 'I don't want to scream anymore.'"

Eager to explore new musical territory and record in surroundings that were both foreign and vaguely familiar, Asheville was chosen as the site to record the Reason's next full-length record, *Fools*. The five-piece band set out from Hamilton in the fall of 2008, hell-bent on making the best record of their careers and breaking into the Canadian mainstream in a big way. The former was a resounding success. The latter, depending on whom you ask, was not.

"We were there for a month," Nelan begins. "There was a band house we got to stay in that was about a mile away from the studio. It was phenomenal. The studio itself was a converted church. The main live room was awesome – super-high ceilings, it sounded fantastic and had some of the best gear that I've ever gotten to see in real life."

With famed American producer Steven Haigler manning the board at Echo Mountain Recording Studio, the Reason began tracking the eleven songs that would eventually comprise *Fools*. The sessions were productive, spirits were high and, as the album began to take shape, Nelan and White both had a feeling they were tapping into something groundbreaking and unique. *Fools* represented a major transition in the band's sound. Gone was the pop-punk sheen and thick distortion favoured on *Ravenna* and *Things Couldn't Be Better*. The new record was bigger in scope yet lighter, lean and stripped-back. The band played with precision and grace, using the perfect amount of restraint to allow songs such as album-opener "Come and Go" to unravel and breathe. The changes were so drastic, in fact, that the group briefly considered changing their name before the album was released.

"We played a show, I think with Moneen, and someone who hadn't seen us in five or six years was there," says White. "He pulled me aside and was like, 'your new shit's awesome. Your old shit's awesome. But this is completely fucking different, I had no idea you played guitar. You guys all look way different, and I haven't seen you in five years. You should change your name.'"

The band's management ultimately torpedoed the suggestion, and *Fools* was poised to be the Reason's third full-length record. The only problem was that the band couldn't get their magnum opus off the shelf and into the hands of fans. Months stretched into long, frustrating years as *Fools* languished in a state of perpetual limbo and the band's momentum died a slow, painful death. *Fools* was mixed in December 2008, but wouldn't see the light of day for another twenty months. "That almost destroyed the band. It came pretty damn close," Nelan admits. "If it wasn't for the fact that we were so proud of the strength of the record, I don't think it would have been possible for us to keep going."

Fools was finally released on August 24, 2010, through Universal Music Canada – nearly a full two years after production began in North Carolina. Despite the strong radio and video play of breakout single "The Longest Highway Home," the band failed to gain the national traction they so desperately desired. The long delay wasn't the only challenge facing the Reason. Widerman and Kiely were also on their way out the door, officially defecting to up-and-coming hard rock outfit Monster Truck not long after the album's release.

The period between *Fools* and *Hollow Tree*, a 2013 EP released on Toronto-based Anthem Records, was the most frustrating and confusing era in the band's long history. During our extended, meandering conversation, White likened the band's career to a painfully slow escalator ride on a very shallow incline.

"I don't know how shit works anymore. I just try to write songs, man. The business of the whole thing has kind of turned me sour and a little jaded. I'm thankful for the small success we've had and I look forward to the future, but, you know, there's so much wrong with the music industry ... I don't know, I don't want to be that guy who has a negative attitude about stuff. I'm just stoked to get back out on the road."

. . .

Jon Harvey is a badass motherfucker. He struts onto an outdoor stage at Toronto's Downsview Park in the summer of 2013 wearing a loose red-and-black plaid shirt, sleeves rolled up, collar flapping in the breeze. He approaches the microphone, a thick mane of curly brown hair at his shoulders. He plants a tall, brown cowboy boot on a bright red toolbox, rattling the steel clasps. His right forearm is covered in bright tattoos and is already glistening with sweat. Harvey surveys the crowd and slowly rolls the volume knob on his gigantic sunburst bass, allowing the feedback to hang thick in the air.

As the lead singer and most recognizable face of Monster Truck, Hamilton's premier hard rock export, Harvey commands the stage with authority. During the band's mid-afternoon set at Edgefest 2013, it becomes clear that Harvey was born to play the part of a big-time rock and roll frontman. Nothing is insincere or ironic about his approach. He seems to stand eight feet tall on stage, even from the back of the park. He looks like a medieval dragon slayer, and plays the part well.

When I meet with Harvey one week later in a quiet, band-friendly bar called WORK on James Street North, he's far from the Viking warrior most fans encounter on stage. Large glasses set in thin metal frames rest on the bridge of his nose, and his long hair is tied back in a loose ponytail. He comes over, shakes my hand and orders a gin and tonic. He waves to two friends on the other side of the room before turning his attention to the shallow glass.

"Mannnnn . . . I'm exhausted," he says, letting out a big sigh. It's not surprising.

During the last year alone, his four-piece band – featuring ex-Reason bandmates Jeremy Widerman on guitar and Steve Kiely on drums, along with former Saint Alvia keyboardist Brandon Bliss on organ – has won as CASBY Award, a Juno and released their debut full-length record *Furiosity* on Toronto's Dine Alone Records. They're in high demand by the time I finally catch up with Harvey, and the towering singer seems content to sit back and relax for a few hours in relative obscurity. It's a far cry from the band's beginnings as a lighthearted, beer-soaked side project for a group of friends and music lovers.

"Monster Truck Mondays was our thing, 'cause we were all bored with having so much time off from the other bands we were in," explains Kiely, during a short Dine Alone Records documentary about the band's rise to fame. "We all had a huge lull at the same time, and we said, 'let's start playing at the bar down the street and making some extra beer money and partying,' you know? We've never done a cover song or anything. As soon as we started jamming, we started pumping out stuff. In the end, we never ended up playing at that bar."

When I ask Harvey why he clicks so well with Monster Truck guitarist Jeremy Widerman, his eyes light up and he talks openly and passionately about a shared history in gritty Hamilton union halls that stretches back more than a decade. One could argue that the seed for Monster Truck was planted way back in 2002, when Harvey and Widerman were attending and booking local punk shows, and navigating an emerging underground scene in downtown Hamilton. The fact that both men are cut from the same cloth seems to be a major pride point. It's also what helps them stay grounded.

"Man, he was there. He was there when we were kids," offers Harvey. "Our old bands played all the same Transit Union shows, and he ran a bunch of Transit Union shows. He was in Hoosier Poet when we started, and then ended up leaving to start some other band. But I don't know, I always wanted to play with him. We had a really close relationship. So, when he was like, 'do you want to do a rock and roll band?' I said 'all right!' I pretty much met the other guys during that first practice. [Jeremy] is tight. He's good. He's got that fire, man. Not a lot of people have it. That kid's got the fire."

With Kiely and Bliss firmly in the mix, the band began rehearsing in a downtown jam space on a semi-regular basis – filling the gaps between breaks in the Reason's schedule and other musical projects. Cover songs were never part of the plan, though the group's early days are often painted in a classic bar-band-made-good narrative. That's only half the story, according to Harvey. The plan from day one was to write catchy tunes, get on the radio and make things happen as quickly as possible.

Harvey mentions Sum 41's rapid rise to popularity on the strength of their debut EP, 2000s hook-laden *Half Hour of Power*, and suggests that Monster Truck saw a similar path to success with the release of their own carefully crafted EPs – even if the release of a proper full-length was somewhat delayed. If the songs were good enough, people would listen, he reasoned.

Harvey's instincts paid off. Released in 2011, *The Brown EP* was packed with radio-friendly, monster-boogie jams such as "Righteous Smoke" and "Seven Seas Blues," both of which served as huge crossover hits on classic rock and alternative radio stations across Canada, and raised the band's profile almost overnight. Alexisonfire's George Pettit was also recruited to add his signature snarl to the EP's closing track, a punishing hard-rock fist-pumper known as "Sworded Beest." Pettit remembers the recording sessions well.

"I've known Brandon Bliss for a long time," he begins. "He called me up and was like, 'hey, we've got this song and it's kind of metal. We think you should come in and yell on it.' And I was like, 'of course!' Drop of a hat. It didn't matter what he was doing. He's a friend, so I came out and sang on it. I remember when Jon told me the song was called 'Sworded Beest,' and I had to write lyrics to fit it. Me and the producer kind of thought it was a double entendre, that the sword was some sort of phallus or something like that. I remember researching the names of swords and knives, and trying to stick as many of those in the lyrics as possible."

"The fact that we got two radio singles off a five-song EP, I'm pretty proud of that," adds Harvey. "It kind of worked out the way it should. All we were trying to write was pop songs. Monster Truck's not fucking rocket science. We're literally just playing pop-rock songs. We know that, but we like 'em. It's like saying to AC/DC, 'why don't you write a prog album?' Well, no, because they don't do that, and we don't do that."

During Monster Truck's first large-scale tours of North America, the band hit the road in a spacious fifteen-passenger van with a gear trailer, but still did all of the driving, loading and tour managing in between playing some of the biggest and most prestigious venues in the country every night.

"We never travelled with a crew until now. We were doing stadium shows as just the four of us. It was pretty stupid," says Harvey. "The last tour we did with Alice in Chains we got three crew guys, so we had a smaller bed in the back that nobody could fit on except our drummer, who sleeps on it every time we drive …so we had seven guys in this van, with three benches and two captain's chairs, and it was just so uncomfortable."

"We used to sleep on people's floors and now we get hotels," Harvey continues. He doesn't long for the former in any way, shape or form. "People just want you to party when you stay at their house. It's like an invitation to come and party, and I can't be doing that shit. To them it's a thing. Here I am out on a Friday night, this is my big night out, the kids have a babysitter and all that shit. So if you're going back to their house, they want to go. But they don't realize you have a show the next day. To them, it's like Friday fucking night! To you, it's Monday."

When it came time to record their first full-length record, the band was set-up with a talented producer – an "LA gun," Harvey jokes. But the resulting sessions at Sound City Studios in Van Nuys, California – a hallowed space that produced records from the likes of from Neil Young, Nirvana, Weezer, Fleetwood Mac, Tom Petty and Arctic Monkeys – simply didn't hit the mark.

For starters, the band was booked for a month-long stay in Los Angeles, which Harvey detested from the moment they touched down at LAX. "I don't like the way that place treats people, you know? There's a hunger for fame that makes a guy in a Denny's tell someone he's a producer. It's desperation, really."

To make matters worse, the band only had two reels of four hundred-dollar recording tape at their disposal to try and nail the entire twelve-song record. As days stretched into weeks and the songs still weren't coming together, the sessions quickly evaporated.

"[The producer] was a nice guy, and it was a great studio in the old Sound City," says Harvey. "But him and Jer rubbed each other the wrong way from the get-go, and it just fizzled out from there. Everyone's buzz systematically got killed. We were rushed, the tones weren't really there and we were doing everything to tape with zero edits. You're doing a take, right, and it's like, 'do you want to keep that?' If the answer is no, that take is erased. And you're like, 'well hold on, dude, what about that one we did five times ago that we erased?'"

Our drinks are freshened and he continues with even more vigour as the business side of our conversation winds down.

"If you can do it live off the floor, more power to you. You're a better band than mine. We could do it, too, but it's going to take three months. It depends on the time frame, and it depends on the vibe everyone's getting off the songs.

"I play just for me, man. I close my eyes when I play shows. I don't even care. If people like it, that's fine. I'm doing it for me.... It's a sure-fire sign you don't enjoy what you're doing if you can't play your own fucking song without a crowd. If you need a crowd to affirm yourself, do something else. Go get a factory or warehouse job, and hang that guitar up or sell it on Kijiji."

• • •

On a lazy Sunday afternoon in late July, as I was busy hauling a load of clean laundry from the dryer, my BlackBerry began to vibrate in my back pocket. I managed to palm the phone and field the call just before it went to voicemail. Max Kerman, who was about the take the stage with Arkells at a private concert in Muskoka, left me with these simple instructions:

"Hey, Andy, we'll meet you at the Town Ballroom in Buffalo. Your name is on the guest list," he said through the crackling reception. "There will be a tour laminate waiting for you. This is going to be a lot of fun."

Less than twenty-four hours later, I was behind the wheel of my Pontiac with a duffel bag full of clothes, a digital tape recorder, a point-and-shoot camera and an electric guitar. The latter was an absolute necessity, I told myself.

I pressed hard on the gas and roared over the Peace Bridge toward downtown Buffalo. The Niagara River glistened in the mid-afternoon sun, boats drifting along in its steady current. I rolled down the window and leaned back in my seat, gripping the bottom of the steering wheel with one hand. I glanced in the rear-view mirror and grinned as the border offices fell out of sight behind the bridge's apex.

Crossing into the United States on that sun-kissed Sunday afternoon was no easy task. I had arrived at the bridge alone, but explained to the border guards that I would be travelling with two Canadian bands for one week. I had no idea where I was staying, save a one-night reservation in Buffalo, and no idea what time the rest of the convoy was due to arrive. I had a *Hamilton Spectator* business card with my editor's name and home phone number written on the back, but my laminated newspaper ID was left behind in the rush to pack. I had little in the way of clothes or provisions and only a meagre wad of American money stuffed into my cracked leather wallet.

I smiled as the border guard returned my passport and business card through the window.

"Thanks, pull over to your right and please exit the vehicle."

"Sure. Is something wrong, Officer?"

"Please pull over and exit the vehicle."

"Yes, sir. Right away, sir. Thank you, sir."

I waved and nodded, and drove away slowly. I was nervous. I'd heard horror stories of bands being turned back at the border for simply looking odd. Vans torn apart. Clothing strewn across the pavement. Merchandise confiscated. Entire US tours cancelled. I was terrified of saying or doing the wrong thing and blowing the whole assignment. If I was already travelling with the band, I'm sure they'd know how to handle it. Arkells were already well versed in the fine art of hopping the border under suspicious pretences. During a 2009 trip to Austin, Texas, for the South by Southwest (SXSW) music festival, for example, things quickly went awry during a routine stop-and-search at the border into Michigan.

"Max and Nick had cleaned the van before we left, because it was super messy," Mike DeAngelis explains. "We were driving my minivan at the time, this old Dodge Caravan. Me and Max bought it together, because we needed a way to get around."

Instead of immediately throwing out the trash, Kerman and Dika decided to temporarily stash it in the band's new gear trailer, where it was promptly forgotten. Fast-forward to Arkells rolling through US customs for the very first time, and the van being pulled over and searched.

"As we were walking in, super nervous, they opened the back door of the trailer and all the garbage falls out. It just spills everywhere, all this crap that was in the van. It almost took the pressure off, because it was like, 'we are never getting in now.' Whatever happened when we went through those doors was such an aside to the fact that there was some guard out there cleaning up our garbage. But somehow we made it over."

Once safely through customs, I checked into my room at the Comfort Suites just after three p.m. Downtown shoppers were stepping around one another in slow motion, mouths agape, fanning themselves with magazines and newspapers. A construction worker at a nearby job site removed his helmet and wiped his forehead with a thin towel. Sunlight dazzled off his bright reflective vest. He was drenched, and I was thankful to be in a white T-shirt and shorts. Still, I could feel my boxers clinging to my thighs as I entered the air-conditioned lobby. Buffalo is a city of extremes, and temperature is one of them.

After dropping off my bags, taking a cold shower and changing into a fresh button-down and jeans, I made a reservation for one at the T.G.I. Friday's restaurant in the hotel lobby. I nursed a warm bottle of Corona and drummed my fingers on the table. The hotel was only a few blocks away from the Town Ballroom, but we hadn't established a firm plan for the evening. The band was due to hit the stage at the club in less than two hours, and was nowhere to be found. I finished the beer, slapped a crisp twenty-dollar bill on the table and walked back upstairs.

Pacing back and forth in the cool hotel room, I finally received word from Kerman. The band was also held up at the Peace Bridge, their brand new $24,000 touring van being ripped apart by border guards. Kerman wasn't sure if they were going to make it in time for the show. Panic set in. This was the first date on the band's inaugural American tour, and one of the only markets outside of Canada already familiar with Arkells. Missing this gig would be bad. Not quite disastrous, but a few notches above a pretty big fucking deal. To make matters worse, I was on the road to cover the band's tour. Eliminating one of the dates made for good drama, but didn't exactly add to the experience. I pictured spending my Sunday evening in a Buffalo T.G.I. Friday's while the band pleaded their case at the border. Kerman told me to head to the venue, that they'd be there soon. Hopefully. Fingers crossed.

By two a.m., I was hammering out copy at a large mahogany desk in my hotel room, Kerman passed out on the mattress in the adjoining bedroom. The band had made it. Barely. Their set was rushed but fine. The audience was pleased and tall stacks of merchandise were sold to sweaty, eager Buffalonians. After the show, we tipped a few casuals with headliners and tourmates Tokyo Police Club before wandering back to the hotel and parting ways for the night – Kerman in my room, the rest of the band in a last-minute reservation at the Comfort Suites.

Kerman woke suddenly to the sound of my frantic tapping.

"I didn't take you for a tattoo guy, Andy."

To this day, Max still calls me "Andy" while most of my friends prefer "Drew." It's an interesting distinction I've never had the heart to correct. The arts magazine I helmed at the *Silhouette* was called *andy*. But the *andy* name had been in place since before my time at McMaster – a clever play on words that stemmed from saying "Arts and Entertainment," or "A and E," a little too fast. When Kerman began hanging around the office back in 2006, I always let it slide. It was far too late to change things now.

I looked down. The top of Stevie's initials – two swirling loops of black ink – were peeking out of my button-down shirt, now wide open.

"It's the name of a friend of mine," I said. "He passed away last winter." I closed a few buttons and deflected. "What's the plan for tomorrow morning?" I asked.

"Sorry to hear that, Andy. What happened?"

"It was an accident." I hadn't talked openly about Stevie in months. Not since his twenty-sixth birthday, or what would have been his twenty-sixth birthday. Kerman took the hint.

"Very sorry, man."

"Thanks."

"Listen, there's no show tomorrow so we can take our time in the morning. Get some sleep. See you in the a.m. We'll all get breakfast together and figure out our next move."

"Perfect. See you tomorrow."

My mind was still humming, but my body was begging for rest. I closed my laptop, clicked off the gold desk lamp and climbed onto the pull out couch with my clothes still on. Sleep came quickly.

The following day, we were bound for a quiet roadside motel in rural Pennsylvania. Washington, DC, the next stop on the tour, was still a half-day's drive away. We had splintered off from the main convoy and spent the day carving our own path through the rolling backcountry of the Allegheny Plateau. I watched the sun rise and fall behind low ridges filled with tall green pines as our two vehicles drifted up and down the hills, like a pair of tiny grey fishing boats at the mercy of a gigantic mid-ocean storm. Kerman was riding in the passenger seat of my car, dark sunglasses covering his tired eyes. I leaned back in my chair, took one hand off the wheel and gave in to the power of the swell.

I managed to get Kerman on tape later that night in our grubby roadside motel room, while the rest of the band slept soundly in a clean and comfortable chain hotel across the street. After a surprisingly delicious, gravy-slathered home-cooked meal at a nearby greasy spoon – a welcomed change from ninety-nine-cent McDonald's cheeseburgers – we were forced to split up for the evening due to a lack of rooms at the hotel. I opted to stay with Kerman, seizing my chance to gather some new material, and talk about the temptations and vices that come with long-term travel.

"If you're drinking beer and you're only sleeping for, like, five or six hours, and then you're sitting in a van and talking, it's really bad," he explains. It's nearly eleven p.m. and the band's lead singer looks exhausted. He's reclining on one of the paper-thin twin mattresses in our cramped motel room, flicking through grainy sports and local news channels on the old television, one arm resting behind his head. Commercials for indoor gun ranges, fireworks depots and overflowing buckets of deep-fried food flicker across the screen.

"I try not to do any of that stuff when we know we're going to have a bunch of dates in a row. Today we have a day off, but I think we play Tuesday, Wednesday, Thursday, or something like that. Three in a row, and a lot of driving. So yeah, I like to take it easy."

"Does that ever make for any tension, if some of the guys really want to go out?" I asked.

"No. The lucky thing about our band is that we're all a bunch of nerds," he offers, letting out a big laugh. "If I had an enabler in the band, it would make that more difficult. I don't know, there are some bands that are, like, non-stop. Their energy level can go way past showtime and into the late hours. But with our band, I think we put so much energy into the lead-up to the show – in terms of getting the merch set up, getting all the gear loaded in and putting on a really energetic show. All that stuff is stressful enough, so when the show is actually over, everyone's kind of tired."

With that, Kerman flicked off the television, kicked his Converse sneakers onto the floor and bid me good night.

I woke the next morning to the unmistakable sound of a basketball hitting carpet. That perfectly annoying *thhhwunk* that somehow always seems louder than dribbling on hardwood or pavement. Scourge of parents with finished basements who scream "take it outside!" from the top of the stairs. I lifted my head from the pillow and squinted.

"Sorry, Andy. Want to go shoot some hoops?"

Kerman was wide awake, dressed in black mesh shorts and a faded McMaster Marauders T-shirt, hovering over my lopsided twin bed.

"I spoke to someone at the front desk," Kerman continued, producing a hand-drawn map on a piece of motel stationary. "There's an outdoor court at a high school not far from here."

I rolled out of bed and shuffled to the bathroom to glue moist contact lenses to dry eyeballs and brush my teeth. I had spent the previous winter playing on an intramural team full of student reporters, but the game was never my first love. I had always preferred hockey and football, and still do. I reached down and yanked on my feet, pulling them up toward my back until my quadriceps burned. I swung my free arm in quick circles and rocked my neck back and forth, side to side, in a misguided attempt to limber up. In our tiny hotel room, I could hear as Kerman resumed dribbling, listening for brief pauses in the rhythm when he crossed hands.

We climbed into my Pontiac and set off. It turned out the school was only a half-mile away. I pulled into a deserted blacktop parking lot and we jogged over to the nearby court. The sky was a stunning shade of bright blue, and the air was cool and comfortable before the midday summer heat set in. I remember thinking the basketball court was oddly out of place in this picturesque scene, nestled in a shallow valley and surrounded by trees, as if Kerman had somehow willed it into existence. I tightened the laces on my sneakers as Kerman took long, loose shots from the top of the key. We continued our chat about life on the road as the ball passed through the twine with a light *thwooop*.

Conducting another interview soon proved impossible. I placed the tape recorder on top of my wallet behind the iron goalpost and reached for my camera. Between driving all day, loading the gear, sitting down for a meal, playing the show, unloading the gear and scrambling to find a hotel, there wasn't a lot of downtime for any member of the band to simply unwind. I relished the opportunity to kick back for a few minutes as well, and soon put down the camera. By the time we returned to the motel, showered and packed, we were an hour behind schedule. Hard glares cut through the parking lot, but the convoy pushed forward without incident. I learned an important lesson of the road that afternoon: it's better for everyone if you can forgive and forget.

The ensuing drive through Pennsylvania and Maryland was relatively smooth, save rush-hour traffic in Bethesda and the surrounding commuter caves that feed into Washington, DC. The Pontiac crept forward in bumper-to-bumper traffic as Kerman kept an eye on the clock. We weren't late, but we definitely weren't early. I had loaned my GPS to the band in Buffalo, and knew if I lost Arkells's van in mid-city traffic with no directions to the venue we'd have a serious problem. I kept my eyes locked on the back door of the gear trailer, and made sure no other cars came between myself and the band as we pushed deeper into the heart of the capital.

I squinted through my sunglasses as we pulled into a dusty gravel lot behind the club, and helped carefully manoeuvre our convoy into a fenced-off enclosure reserved for performers. The Black Cat was situated a few blocks south of the U Street metro station, on the northern edge of the Logan Circle Historic District. I grabbed my shoulder bag and laptop from the trunk, and helped the band carry amplifiers and plastic tubs full of merchandise into the back of the venue. It was only the second show of a month-long tour, but the machine was already up and running.

Backstage at the Black Cat, I necked a bottle of Yuengling beer as the band checked emails and rifled through suitcases. Tim Oxford slipped out to have dinner with a friend in town, while the rest of us feasted on lasagne and towering sandwiches provided by the venue. Later, in the band's green room, Tokyo Police Club keyboardist Graham Wright opened up about playing pond hockey a few months earlier with Oxford, a fellow Newmarket native.

"We all went back to my parents' basement after, which was a super blast from the past," Wright begins. "I don't live with my folks anymore, and in fact they don't even live in the house I lived with them in. I don't even have a bedroom there. So [Tim and I] just barnstormed in and had some pizza. My mom was like,

218

'there's root beer in the fridge, but there's only a couple cans. The rest is warm. I don't know if your friends are okay.' They were okay," he laughed, "and it was great."

After chatting with Wright, I retrieved my tiny point-and-shoot camera from my duffel bag and followed Arkells into the main hall of the club, to document their soundcheck. The room was barren, save a few staff behind the bar and the odd stage tech drifting in and out of the wings. The band was still wearing cut-off denim shorts and T-shirts, fresh from the road and having not yet changed into their stage clothes. After watching a standard take of "The Ballad of Hugo Chavez" and snapping a few photos, I switched the camera's setting to video and steadied my hands to record the next tune. I was floored when the band unexpectedly debuted a new song. The melody was infectious, the chords bright and dynamic. The music had the same punch, but this was a softer, more spirited version of Arkells – a band that suddenly favoured space and subtlety over vigour and volume. It was the first time I ever heard the song "Book Club."

Rearranged and positioned as the opening track on 2011's *Michigan Left*, the song has since become my all-time favourite of the band's catalogue. Truthfully, I still prefer the original take performed in Washington – slightly faster, dropped a full step lower, and featuring the lyric, "and then you give me one/another you just finished/you're my library/always open for business," as the song's chorus. The signature "white shoes, blue collar" vocal refrain hadn't even been written yet. The original tune was also driven by a stop-start drum pattern that saw the band hammering the end of each measure in unison, adding a sense of urgency to the music. Unfortunately, this early demo has never seen the light of day.

"Max! What the hell was that?" I asked, eyes wide as the group walked off stage.

"A new one we're working on. Did you film that?"

"Yes! I have the whole thing on tape. I'm going to send it to the *Spectator* and post it online right now."

"Let's hold off on that for now, Andy. We're still working on it. I'm not sure if we'll even keep it."

"Are you sure? I think it sounds great."

"Let's just keep this one between us." Kerman loaded his Telecaster into the band's guitar caddy before disappearing backstage.

After the DC show, we decided to push toward the next gig rather than scouring the dark and unfamiliar streets for a hotel room. Tim Oxford elected to ride with me. We loaded the remaining Yuenglings into the trunk of my car before setting off into the backwoods of Maryland.

Rocketing through the countryside on a dark and deserted two-lane highway, I kept my eyes on two bright red specks floating over hills and through shallow valleys ahead of us. Once comfortable on the open road, I eased up on the gas and opened a long divide between us and the band, knowing we couldn't possibly lose them. I switched on the high beams and we sailed through the darkness with the windows cracked. It was well after midnight and we listened to the car's engine echoing through the hills. It was here that Oxford began opening up to me about life on the road and the success of Arkells.

"We've spent many nights sleeping in the van. Too many," Oxford noted. "If we can't find a place to sleep, usually on a night like this, we'll just roll into an empty parking lot and camp out."

I considered reaching for my tape recorder but let the moment pass. He spoke openly and candidly about the financial pressures of being on a colossal American tour, and the contrast between winning a Juno Award and playing NHL hockey arenas on one side of the border, and trying to win over thin pockets of casual fans on the other. He spoke warmly about his mother, Nancy, who lost her battle with cancer just as the band's career began to take off. I offered stories about Stevie, and spoke openly and at great length about his suicide for the first time in months. We talked and pushed through the night until our conversation fell silent through twenty miles of open road.

A little after two a.m., our convoy pulled into a Holiday Inn in rural Maryland and everyone spilled into the quiet parking lot. Oxford and I carried the remaining Yuenglings up to our hotel room and cracked open a pair of the warm beers while lounging in our sparse grey lodgings. I filed an update from the road for the *Spectator* as my new roommate watched television and slowly fell asleep in his clothes. I closed my laptop at 2:53 a.m. and collapsed onto the remaining twin bed, drifting off to the quiet hum of overhead lights in the parking lot below.

The Columbus, Ohio, gig, our next stop on the itinerary, was destined to be strong. Everyone was sealed up tight and ready to burst after a long day of driving under the boiling sun. We were taking shots of whisky and sipping tall cans of beer backstage, and spirits were high. The band wanted to kill. Kerman looked possessed. And, once again, we almost didn't make it.

Like the Buffalo show, Arkells had arrived at the last possible minute – this time due to a long stretch of highway maintenance leading into the eastern edge of the city. We'd spent several hours inching forward in a narrow line of traffic that extended well over the horizon. Kerman shifted in the passenger seat of the Pontiac as precious minutes ticked by. Hot clouds of gold dust swirled beside the car, forcing us to close all windows. The heat was stifling. Kerman texted his bandmates in the van every ten minutes. I ran a few interview questions but soon placed the tape recorder in the car's plastic drink holder. I knew his mind was elsewhere. He seemed calm, but was nervous.

When we finally pulled up to the brick-lined basement venue, Kerman leapt from the Pontiac and sprinted for the front door while the car was still rolling. The club was tucked into a bustling mid-city neighbourhood, halfway between Ohio State University and the shores of the Scioto River – the beating heart of the Buckeye State. I wheeled the car around back to meet the rest of the band in a parking lot across from Huntington Park, home of the Triple-A Columbus Clippers baseball team. After frantically loading their gear through the back entrance of the club, the band changed into their stage clothes in the parking lot and began to stretch and limber up for their opening set.

Moments before the curtain rose, they opted to begin with the slow, ominous build of "Deadlines" – the opening track on *Jackson Square* and a rarity on that first US run. The swirling crowd was packed into a long, thin dance floor and spilled onto the stage, close enough to twist the knobs on Mike DeAngelis's guitar. The set was hot. The band was wild and free. Kerman spun around from the microphone and conducted the group with the fiery conviction of a soul bandleader. Their quick opening set ended with a macho, fully flexed version of "Oh, the Boss Is Coming!" that had the crowd knocking heads and slamming shoulders in the pit. As the song drew to a close, Kerman aimed the head of his maroon Telecaster at the low ceiling and hammered open strings while staring deep into the breach. Tim Oxford smashed the hi-hat and crash cymbals as the final chord rang out, letting his drumsticks slip from his fingertips and tumble onto the kit. The battle of Columbus had been won.

The crowd was ravenous. The band was wired. It was a triumphant finish to the first week of the tour, and their best show to date. This was a side of Arkells I had yet to experience. Tough. Lean. "Black and blue-eyed soul," as Kerman once described it to me. No longer just a group of friends from university on another

222

cross-country adventure, they were a force to be reckoned with. By the end of the tour, I knew Hamilton would be welcoming home an entirely different band. I knew they had finally made it.

The following morning, I rapped on the band's door at the Red Roof Inn to say goodbye. Everyone was still fast asleep except for Dika, who offered a hearty handshake and a firm slap on the shoulder while standing in the threshold in white boxer shorts.

"See you soon, Andy. Safe drive home." He was still rubbing the sleep from his eyes as the door swung shut.

Tim Oxford, my roommate for the latter half of the tour, was awake when I returned to our room, sipping watery coffee from a Styrofoam cup. I gathered my things, bid him farewell and eased my car onto Interstate 71 at the north end of Columbus. *Jackson Square* was the first album I slid into the stereo. Fuelled by strawberry Pop-Tarts and a couple cigarettes supplied by DeAngelis the night before, I rode the Pontiac fast and loose all the way from Columbus through Pennsylvania and New York, to the eastern tip of Lake Erie.

I crossed back over the Niagara River into Canada, five days and some two thousand kilometres after the tour began. That same day, Arkells continued to push west, bound for Indianapolis, Omaha, Denver and the Pacific coast. I wouldn't see them again until December, when Ciara and I stood on the balcony for a sold-out homecoming concert at the Hamilton Place Studio Theatre. Naturally, they tore the roof off.

• • •

As Arkells's popularity grew, Supercrawl had also become a resounding success. One year after launching, Tim Potocic's team was overwhelmed when an estimated twenty thousand people flocked to the core for its second incarnation. The festival featured more high-profile performers that year, including folk-rockers Elliott Brood and Bruce Peninsula, and Edmonton rapper Cadence Weapon. That same year, the event won the Festival of the Year Award at the Hamilton Music Awards and earned the Best Mid-Sized Festival of the Year Award from Tourism Hamilton.

By fall 2010 the secret was out. Local promoters began hosting parties up and down James Street North, and the strip emerged as a magnet for independent culture, young entrepreneurs and free expression in Hamilton. Junior Boys singer and producer Jeremy Greenspan opened the Brain at 199 James Street North – a dimly lit bar and café with a small space in the back reserved for hosting DJs and groups of musicians. A few doors south, at 193 James Street North, the Mulberry Coffeehouse transformed the derelict Hotel Hamilton into a thriving community hub for a new wave of tenants and business owners flooding the area. This Ain't Hollywood, having opened a year earlier at 345 James Street North, had already earned a reputation as one of the city's best live music venues. Owned and operated by local punk icon and radio personality Lou Molinaro, This Ain't Hollywood would soon emerge as the strip's premier live concert venue.

Long-forgotten spaces such as Academica Hall and the century-old Red Mill Theatre – a beautiful Victorian-era concert hall located above a tiny Chinese restaurant near Jackson Square – were also being utilized for all-night raves and semi-legal after-parties following monthly Art Crawls. Long before *CBC Hamilton* and the Art Gallery of Hamilton moved into their new digs at 118 James Street North, the vacant building played host to a number of dance parties on the cavernous and dilapidated ground floor.

Montréal DJ Lunice headlined a wild Supercrawl after-party in this locale on September 25. Tom and I purchased a round of bathtub beers being sold at the back of the venue, and discussed the Wild West nature of the James Street strip with Mike and a small group of friends while the party bumped in the main room. The balance felt perfect in that moment. A fusion of old and new, with students and young entrepreneurs mingling with the Italian, Portuguese and blue-collar communities that had called James Street North home for several generations.

Around this time, I was also listening to a new record from Hamilton alt-rock band Cowlick, formed in 2006 by ex–By Divine Right member Dylan Hudecki and his younger brother Jackson. Their latest offering, *Wires*, was a jittery eight-song record slathered in distortion, and peppered with odd sound effects and instrumentation. Featuring contributions from Lee Reed, Huron's Aaron Goldstein and Cam Malcolm, Jeremy Fisher, Terra Lightfoot and several others, *Wires* received Alternative/Indie Recording of the Year honours at the 2010 Hamilton Music Awards. The elder Hudecki, like many young people in the Hamilton music scene, was becoming a champion of the city's burgeoning arts community. External validation meant little to Cowlick. They were happy just doing it.

"Originally, we thought about trying to make a record company take notice of us," Hudecki explained to the *Hamilton Spectator*. "But now record labels are less important to us. We've decided to just make great music and tour when we can. The object is to be self-sustaining. I don't mind being this secret band in Hamilton. The word is starting to spread. Things are happening here and you can really feel it."

I was soon hired as a full-time reporter at *Niagara This Week*, a weekly community newspaper based in Thorold, Ontario – a sister paper in the *Hamilton Spectator*'s corporate family. Ciara and I were also on the hunt for our first apartment together. Everything was buzzing. Everyone was excited. It was fantastic time to be young, adventurous and free in the downtown core.

. . .

In October, Ciara and I moved into an old walk-up apartment building on King Street East, in the heart of the International Village. Our two-bedroom unit was located on the third floor of a red brick building, above a popular Greek restaurant, a tiny cocktail lounge and a cheque-cashing outlet. Across the street were a Chinese restaurant and an after-hours Korean karaoke bar. Club Absinthe was only a few doors down – its secret basement entrance positioned a few metres from our driveway. Within a year, four of the six units in the building would be occupied by close friends.

Prior to moving in, Tom – who lived upstairs and served as the building's part-time manager – and I spent a week ripping out the old, grey carpet that covered the entire unit. We decided to replace it with new laminate hardwood flooring. Tom loaded a table saw onto the wooden deck behind our unit, and we carefully measured and cut long strips of flooring while sipping coffees and staring out across the north end of the core. On breaks between fitting strips of flooring, we'd climb down the wooden fire escape and walk over to James Street North for bagels and more coffee, knocking sawdust and dirt off our boots. When the flooring was nearly installed, I received a two-hundred-dollar cheque from the building's owner for my efforts. I was glad to have it. We signed our names and the date under the final floorboard in the living room before sealing it up.

On impulse, I painted two of the pristine white walls in the living room a heinous shade of soupy green. Ciara was not impressed.

Fortunately, I had a screen print from the 2008 North By Northeast music festival that perfectly matched the strange green-white-black-brown colour scheme. I had it framed and hung in the centre of the living room. Miraculously, it tied everything together.

Our first night in the apartment, Ciara made spaghetti and tomato sauce with toasted garlic bread. I hauled a pair of beige lawn chairs up the fire escape and into the back room. We had no couch, no coffee table and little else in the way of furniture. I slid the chairs underneath a glass dinette table left behind by a previous tenant, and piled some of our books and records on a leftover plywood shelf. I turned on an old jazz record from Cheapies and quietly set the table.

After dinner, I opened a bottle of sweet red wine and leaned against the towering windows in the living room. I peered down at the waves of traffic rolling west into the downtown core. Horns blared. Pedestrians ran back and forth across the street, shouting profanities at one another. Garbage bags were being dragged and piled under street lamps for pickup the following morning. A string of white lights twinkled in the tall tree in front of our building. I looked over the billboards and buildings on the opposite side of the street and stared at Stevie's former high-rise.

One month after moving into the International Village, we held a memorial for Stevie. It had been exactly a year since his suicide. Time and space had allowed most of us to look back on things with a little more perspective; a little more acceptance.

I took a day off work in late November and invited a group of friends over for a homemade breakfast buffet. Ciara had already left for work when I woke up. Half-a-dozen friends from our old crew soon gathered in the living room around our glass dinette table as Tom poured coffee from a French press into matching brown ceramic cups.

EVENINGS & WEEKENDS

In the kitchen, bacon and eggs crackled on a large frying pan coated with a thick layer of butter. Mike ran a spatula around a separate pan full of spicy hash browns, flipping and mixing the potatoes on high heat until they were crispy and golden brown. I sat down at the dinette table and peeled the skin from a clementine as friends told jokes and shared updates from work. Someone placed a record on the turntable. The mood was light as we reminisced about long, sweaty nights on the dance floor at Che and in the basement of Club Absinthe.

In the year since Stevie's death, I had slowly come to accept that he was gone. The first six months had been more surreal; thoughts were more fluid. I'd struggled to accept a world without him. I had made a habit of pulling his old skateboard from my closet and cruising around the quiet streets in Westdale Village at dusk. It was the only memento I'd taken from Stevie's apartment in the week following his death. I'd carve through long, deserted stretches of sun-bleached pavement near Cootes Paradise and Coronation Park – breathing in as I lifted my right leg in front of my body, exhaling as my sneaker connected with the pavement, launching the board forward. It had been an easy way to relax and unwind after a long day at the *Spectator*. But it was also a way to stay connected with Stevie.

• • •

While Ciara and I were settling into life in the International Village, a group of teenage alt-country devotees from the west side of the city were preparing to release their debut record, *Young and Old*. Harlan Pepper, named after the hilarious Christopher Guest character from the film *Best in Show*, was comprised of lead singer Dan Edmonds, guitarist Jimmy Hayes, drummer Marlon Nicolle and bassist Thompson Wilson – son

228

of former Junkhouse lead singer and noted Hamilton rocker Tom Wilson.

Originally known as the Goodie Two-Shoes while learning their chops during middle school, the band played a handful of shaky shows on Nicolle's street to a tiny crowd of sympathetic neighbours. When the four members entered Westdale Secondary School a few years later, they quickly shed their pop-punk repertoire in favour of a more refined, roots rock-oriented sound that complimented the players' natural affinity for twangin' Telecasters, rollin' snare drums and warbling vocals. Using Nicolle's father's home as an rehearsal space, the band fumbled their way through CCR, the Grateful Dead and Neil Young covers while experimenting with their own original compositions.

"At first, we were really into the Ramones. That was the band we wanted to be at the start," says Edmonds, relaxing in his parents' backyard not far from Chedoke Golf Club, a dark brown acoustic guitar on his lap. It's late August 2013. The night is cool and a light breeze rustles the thick greenery surrounding our dinette table and chairs. The band's frontman speaks in a low, measured drawl. His resemblance to a young Bob Dylan is uncanny, right down to the loose shrub of curly brown hair piled high over tired eyes.

"But listening to Neil Young's *Harvest Moon*, that whole album, I had never really heard that kind of music before. It just opened our eyes to what an acoustic guitar could do, or what a banjo could do. I'm not sure what exactly prompted us, but we soon decided that we really liked this style of music."

Well underage and lacking even one member with a driver's licence, the band was often forced to turn down shows at the Dakota Tavern and other famed Toronto venues – especially those that fell on a school night. Still, the group was eager to expand their reach beyond Westdale and wasted no time booking a string of shows outside Southern Ontario, once the opportunity to hit the road finally came up. Hayes's father, "Big Jim," was recruited as the band's driver and part-time tour manager, and the boys tested his patience on more than one occasion.

"We did a few shows in Wakefield, Québec, at the Black Sheep Inn," Edmonds begins. "Jimmy's dad did all the driving for us, and he's a trooper. He would drive us there, and we'd load in and soundcheck and play the show, and then we'd sleep over at this hotel room and just get drunk and have a wild time. We're actually banned at that hotel now, which is too bad.

"We were too loud in the hotel room, and this was like two or three in the morning," he continues. "This German lady knocks on the door really loud and was like, 'what's going on?' We had the shower on, because we were going to hotbox the bathroom. She was like, 'why do you have the shower on?' And we said, 'oh someone's taking a shower,' but she wasn't buying it at all. So the next time we went there the venue told us we weren't allowed in the hotel anymore."

Even as passengers, the band loved hitting the open road. Roaring down a deserted country lane en route to a rural show in some backwater town, Edmonds and co. would occasionally spin a thin joint in the back seat of a parental minivan and crack open a rear window while covertly puffing and passing. The sets were quick and the band was never allowed to drink, but the crowds were warm and receptive, and the songs grew tighter. It wasn't long before the band wanted to put their stamp on Hamilton's proud alt-country scene with a full-length offering of their own.

Young and Old is a fun record. It's refreshingly free and full of youthful zeal. From the opening banjo plucks of "Great Lakes" to Hayes's final wailing electric guitar solo on "Burnout," Harlan Pepper showcase a wide range of chops and licks that honestly and faithfully pay tribute to the legendary artists they grew up idolizing. Standout tracks include the slow and creepy saloon-shuffler "Reefer," as well as the album's second-last song, "Yeah" – a loud, loose and overtly psychedelic jam that offers a subtle tip of the hat to the Grateful Dead and Jefferson Airplane.

Huron guitarist and frequent Tom Wilson collaborator Aaron Goldstein, whom the band had greatly admired from afar, was tapped to produce their debut record at Vibe Wrangler Recording Studio on Cumberland Avenue. For Edmonds, it was an easy choice.

"We just knew he was passionate about music, and he was this local guy making good music," he explains. "We were like, 'hey, Tom, do you think Aaron can produce the record?' Aaron said he would really like to, and then we began showing him the songs and he came out to a few jams. We just became fast friends. I remember he brought a briefcase, which was just full of guitar strings and paper and picks and stuff. It was really funny."

"Aaron shares the same heart for music that Harlan Pepper does," says Thompson's older sister Madeline Wilson, director of Front Room Entertainment. "I think that he was a friend and mentor to the group. He was able to connect with them on a level that was not that of an adult, but guided them in a positive direction. He was learning to produce as much as they were learning to record. There is a great deal of trust between Aaron and Harlan Pepper. He let them explore and experiment, find their own sound and groove."

The accolades came quickly. Goldstein was nominated for Producer of the Year at the 2010 Hamilton Music Industry Awards on the strength of *Young and Old*. The band took home the award for Musical Event of the Year by People's Choice for their raucous hometown album-release show. Madeline Wilson was also nominated for Road Manager of the Year.

"Harlan Pepper was caught between two worlds," the elder Wilson sibling explains. "They were sixteen when they recorded *Young and Old* and, hence the title, they were old souls in sixteen-year-old, super-talented bodies. They grew up listening to the Grateful Dead, the Band and Bob Dylan – a rarity for most teens. They wanted to play music that they liked. They weren't walking around pretending to be hip-hop kids; they were true to what they knew. It surprised people."

Young and Old was followed by the February 2014 release of *Take Out a $20 and Live Life to the Fullest* on Toronto-based Six Shooter Records. To celebrate the album's release, the band famously played seven pop-up shows in one day at various sites throughout downtown Toronto, ending at popular Queen Street West venue the Cameron House. "We played a show in Toronto one night and after the show we were all sitting there – I think we had just turned nineteen," Edmonds told *CBC Hamilton*. "We were all broke. And Marlon had twenty dollars to his name in his bank account and he said, 'boys, I think I'm going to take out a twenty and live life to the fullest.' And that's sort of our philosophy."

Although noticeably more mature, and well received by fans and critics, the new album proved to be Harlan Pepper's last. The band parted ways in 2015, with Edmonds issuing a final statement on the group's Facebook page in August.

"After 8 years of fun filled rock n' roll, we've decide to call it a day as Harlan Pepper," he wrote. "To celebrate the bodacious times we've shared over the last few years we're gonna throw down one more time for all the fine folks in the hammer. Keep your eyes and ears peeled for information regarding our farewell show. Love, Peace and Chicken Grease, Harlan T. Pepper."

2011

I ARRIVED AT CAM MALCOLM'S rented home in Westdale Village with my semi-acoustic guitar in tow. We set up in the rear bedroom on the main floor of the house, floorboards creaking under our socks. The central air conditioner was whirring in the backyard. I sat down on a grey folding chair and plugged into an old Fender amp, twisting the gold tuning pegs until the chords rang true.

I had been recruited to play a one-off show as a member of Malcolm's solo project, the Owls. The band was a loose collective built for the sole purpose for performing and recording all of Malcolm's material that fell outside of Huron. It had been in operation in one form or another for several years. The next Owls gig was taking place at the Ship on Augusta Street – the final show at the cramped but inviting downtown pub that was a favourite among local musicians and McMaster alumni. The

Owls were sharing a bill with B.A. Johnston, a wacky and wickedly funny local performer Malcolm refers to as "Uncle B.A." It had been a long time since the two of us shared the stage as members of the Langston Heights, but I was eager to give live music another shot.

Malcolm and I ran through a handful of original tunes and jammed on a raw cover of the Creation's signature garage rock banger "Making Time," which eventually made the setlist. In the years since we'd first played together, Malcolm had developed a powerful and confident style. No hesitation between chords. Accents placed with careful precision and the perfect amount of restraint. I struggled to keep up, but soon fell into a comfortable pocket. During a break in the rehearsal, Malcolm swivelled toward his desk and opened a laptop.

"Want to hear something? I have the new Arkells record."

I leaned my guitar against the amplifier, strings resting on its silver face, and switched off the tubes. Malcolm left his red Epiphone Casino on his lap and rolled down the volume.

"Max just gave this to me. It's fucking incredible. This is going to be the one that takes them to another level."

He opened a folder on iTunes and double-clicked the top file. For the first time since witnessing the band's soundcheck in Washington, I heard the beautiful, intricate opening guitar line from "Book Club," a song that warmed the room and filled gaps in the hardwood. This time around, the composition was wide open, light and full of air, a by-product of endlessly road-testing new material. I knew Malcolm was right.

• • •

Five months earlier, Arkells had retreated to a picturesque and secluded plot of land on the northern shore of Lake Ontario to begin work on their much-anticipated sophomore record, *Michigan Left*. The sessions took place at the legendary Bathouse Recording Studio near Kingston, Ontario – a sprawling country estate and former coach house originally built during the early 1840s, and the de facto home base for the Tragically Hip for the better part of a decade. Complete with a swimming pool, hockey pond, billiards room and other amenities, the site was a far cry from the band's previous recording experiences in the suburbs and strip malls circling downtown Toronto.

This time around, there was no need to book overnight studio time or transport gear back and forth from Hamilton. Songs could be polished, melodies and harmonies expanded, arrangements perfected. With major label interest and a Juno Award to their name, this was the record that could put Arkells on the map in a much more permanent way. All they had to do was get it right.

"Looking back, it was a very hectic time," Kerman recalls. "We had originally planned to record in Mississippi with a producer named Dennis Herring. At the eleventh hour we changed our minds because Dan [Griffin] was very keen to produce the record, and we wanted to accommodate him. We had also changed managers and started working with Eggplant, who also manage the Hip. Since Gord Sinclair from the Hip was always inviting us to work at their space in Bath, it was an easy choice."

The band loaded their gear into the trailer on a cold winter morning, sorting and stacking in silence as sunlight broke over the horizon. They departed from Hamilton not long after first light, four hundred kilometres of flat black pavement and pristine white farmland separating them from the studio in Bath.

Once firmly installed in the rural studio, the group moved their personal effects into what Kerman describes as "a big old country house" next to the frozen shoreline. Arkells immediately got down to tracking the ten songs that would comprise *Michigan Left*, with Griffin alternating between playing keyboard and producing the album. Finding time to work was never a challenge. Surrounded by farmland, and isolated from the temptations and distractions that come with recording in a major city, work was often the only way to pass the time. Trips to nearby Kingston were only necessary when supplies ran low.

Midway through the sessions, Kerman was forced into solitary confinement for a number of days, contending with a bout of scarlet fever – "not as bad as it sounds," he says. Otherwise, the sessions were relatively uneventful, save producing the record. Regardless, the Bathouse trip had paid off. Everyone left feeling confident. Even as the group's frontman and leader, Kerman says he never felt any real pressure to deliver a hit. If the record flopped, so be it. More than anything, Arkells wanted to make a record they were proud to stamp their name on.

"The success of *Jackson Square* has never been a burden to me – in fact, it's been the opposite. I've always thought we have been extremely lucky to be validated early on based on work that was honest and authentic to us. I think young artists can get stuck in a bad place mentally if what they're doing isn't received. You start questioning everything you do and whether or not people will like it. We're lucky that we've had an audience that just likes us for being us."

The finished product was released October 18 via Universal Music Canada. More than anything, it sounds like a band trading in their denim vests and Marshall stacks for teal jackets and skinny jeans. It's light, melodic and full of anthemic choruses designed to fill the largest arenas in Canada. If *Jackson Square* got them noticed, *Michigan Left* made them stars. The band kicked off a massive promotional tour with an appearance at the 2011 Grey Cup in Vancouver, opening the live television broadcast with a rousing rendition of "Whistleblower" from the middle of the field at the colossal BC Place Stadium. Kerman wore a black and yellow Hamilton Tiger-Cats scarf around his collar, and the band's performance was viewed by millions.

"Maybe it'll be a hit; maybe it won't," music critic Brad Wheeler wrote in the *Globe and Mail* on the eve of *Michigan Left*'s release. "But you can bet Arkells' eyes are surely on the charts. It shows in the band's material, inspired with commercial success in mind. It's a tough road to take, though, with many of the old maps being outdated."

"Like the Juno-winning rockers' debut, *Jackson Square*, these are ten straight-ahead pop-rock tracks you could imagine blaring in any wing joint, dorm room or corner bar," Leah Collins wrote in the *National Post* on October 21 "– although this time they're less 'meaty' than the Springsteen-indebted 2008 disc. (A new-found interest in poppier sounds led to a little extra sweetness and softening – plus keyboard touches and vocal effects)."

Spurred on by the massive popularity of singles "Whistleblower," "Kiss Cam" and "Where U Goin," the band had a legitimate hit on their hands. Within six months of releasing their sophomore record, Arkells received their second Juno Award – this time besting Nickelback, Sam Roberts Band, Down With Webster and Hedley for Group of the Year – and confidently stepped into the spotlight alongside Canada's rock elite.

• • •

The closing show at the Ship was a huge success. I burned through a messy six-song set with Malcolm and the Owls, playing bass instead of guitar. Malcolm's younger brother Fraser held down the backbeat, his drum kit jammed into a bay window at the front of the pub – a century-old building that had once served as an elegant family home, like most of the bars on Augusta Street. At the end of the gig, Malcolm smiled as we hammered the final four chords in unison, feedback echoing throughout the bar.

Before walking on stage to cap the evening's festivities, headliner B.A. Johnston passed around a plastic shopping bag filled with squirt guns to the now-roaring crowd, packed shoulder to shoulder into the tiny main room. Hardcore fans and drunken university students blasted water all over the pub as Johnston peeled off his T-shirt and climbed on top of the bar. He wrapped a cable around his sweaty neck and howled into the microphone, rolling across the wet countertop. Digital bleeps and bloops blasted from his keyboard and through the club's overworked PA. Johnston worked through a string of cult classics from his 2010 record, *Thank You For Being a Friend,* as well as his extensive back catalogue. By the end of the night, everyone was soaked in sweat, beer and foul plastic-smelling water. It was a chaotic, fitting end to the Ship's reign as the coolest spot to catch a downtown DIY show.

After loading the Owls's gear into his parents' minivan, Malcolm ordered a final round of pints from the bar and invited me to join him.

"I don't ever want to stop playing music," he whispered, taking a long pull from an overflowing glass of Alexander Keith's beer. "It's just too much fun."

• • •

"When it comes to volume, for the audience there's something immersive about it. You can't ignore it," says Dave Nardi. The Dirty Nil's bassist is seated across from me at a large, wooden table on the second floor of the Ship in late 2013. "We've played with a lot of quiet bands, and to their credit those bands are very in control of their sound. But if people can talk over a band, they usually will. People are just not as attentive as they used to be, and sheer volume is just such an attention-grabbing thing. When you can't do anything but listen or leave."

Nardi pauses, takes a sip from his pint and continues. "The social climate of everything has changed. It's less about the real experience of what you're doing, as opposed to being there and being seen by the right people. Being there, seeing the band and being able to say what songs they played doesn't matter anymore. If you tweet a good photo of the lead singer, that's good enough."

Dirty Nil guitarist and singer Luke Bentham and drummer Kyle Fisher are nodding in agreement. Volume is everything for the three-piece power-punk band formed on the rural outskirts of Dundas, Ontario. It's their raison d'être. Their claim to fame. If they can't plug in, shotgun a beer and pin the audience to the back wall of a club with the very first chord, is it even worth showing up?

For Bentham, that fusion of punishing volume and gnarly tone has been a staple of the Nil's sound since their inception in a quiet suburban basement near Highland Secondary School. Originally a two-piece – Nardi was the last to join – the band began playing raucous sets at the Underground and other down-town clubs while still in high school. Although they often favoured cranking their speaker cabinets to the point of loosening screws, the band soon earned a reputation for balancing punishing vol-ume with a keen ear for melody and catchy hooks. Weezer is an easy comparison, but the Nil lean much further into their own shadows than Rivers Cuomo ever did. They effortlessly blend Black Flag and Black Sabbath; Descendents and Deep Purple; the Who and the Weakerthans. It's loud, but it's three-dimensional; you can touch and feel it on all sides.

"The furthest we'll go is to say we're a rock and roll band," Bentham explained to *Vice* in 2015. "The notion of calling yourself a punk band is a bit loaded for me. To me, it carries with it a certain badge of distinction that, unless you're an unmistakably punk band, it's a little bit of a pat on the back to be like, 'yeah we're a punk band. We don't give a fuck.' It's not really for me to say."

The group's very first tour outside Southern Ontario was an unmitigated disaster. It was an east coast run, which took place not long after Fisher and Bentham graduated from Highland Secondary, while they were still performing as a two-piece. The Dirty Nil and another band of friends shared a rental cargo van for the two-week Maritime adventure, which inexplicably only included only four shows, touching down in Ottawa, Montréal, Charlottetown and Halifax.

To make matters worse, the van only had two seats. Throughout the entire four-thousand-kilometre journey out east and back, the remaining passengers had to rotate through a shift on the stiff metal floor in the unfurnished cargo van, which was also loaded with gigantic speaker cabinets, guitar cases, drums, clothes, food, drinks and other amenities – none of which was strapped in place.

"It was literally the most illegal road trip," laughs Fisher. "We just put a whole bunch of sleeping bags and pillows in the back. We had an Ampeg cabinet there, and someone was always sleeping on top of it. The whole tour, someone was making a joke that the amp was going to come at us like a garbage compactor. The very last day, we're going down the 401 in Oshawa, which is always a shit-show. I had to stop, and because of all the weight it wasn't stopping fast enough, so I had to slam on the brakes. That thing just slid forward finally, and everyone in the back was like, 'ahhhhhhhhh!'"

As the tours improved, so too did the recordings. In 2011, the Dirty Nil retreated to a tiny cottage on the shores of Stewart Lake, just east of the Trans-Canada Highway. It was here, nestled in a lakeside village known as MacTier, that the band got to work on what would become their career-defining track, "Fuckin' Up Young," along with a handful of other rough songs for a planned independent album.

The band was joined by friend David Disher, who brought his recording equipment up north to capture the sessions. Up in MacTier, the band ran through their repertoire between three p.m. and three a.m. each day, with numerous beer-and-television breaks between takes. "It was really fun," recalls Bentham, smiling brightly. "We cut eight tunes, and we were all really stoked on what we had done."

The sessions were productive, but the results were less than adequate. When the band and Disher returned to Dundas and brought the tracks to local producer Michael Keire of Threshold Recording Studio, he was more impressed with the composition of the songs than their initial mixes. Eager to produce the best recordings possible, the band worked with Keire to rip apart and remix the tracks. The goal, as usual, was to make things as loud as possible without compromising the songs.

"I think it was super fresh and super novel for [Mike] to work with something so heavy and unhinged," says Nardi. "He kind of just went off on it, and gleefully pushed everything into the red. He loved it."

"My thought process was, well, the tracks don't sound great. Drums are out of tune, everything sounds really digital, no real tone aside from the amps themselves," Keire tells me.

"I just started thinking about bands like Minor Threat and Black Flag, and how those recordings sound completely fucked up, but in the perfect way – a way that served the music. So, I decided to do the exact same thing to my console that the guys were doing to their amps. I just started pinning all the metres into the red and driving the console like crazy. Everything was crapping out. I took every sensibility I had learned engineering and threw that book out of the window. And I just ran with the way it was making me feel until I couldn't squeeze any more out of the music. It was finding the sweet spot – how to make it sound as big and ruthless as possible without it collapsing. Because eventually, when you push things too far, they start to get small again. The trick was all energy and no finesse, balls to the wall and absolutely no brains. It was fun."

"Fuckin' Up Young" – arguably the best song from the MacTier sessions and the band's most well-known single – was released in June 2011 with B-side "Verona Lung." The former had an immediate impact on the local punk scene, bridging a stylistic divide between followers of Vatican Chainsaw Massacre and Cursed, and those who favoured the decidedly more garage rock and pop sounds of bands such as Young Rival, San Sebastian and TV Freaks. It was an instant classic, destined to become as influential and timeless as Teenage Head's "Picture My Face."

The accompanying music video was shot at a wild Hamilton house party, and featured members of New Hands, Chore and other friends of the band. For years afterward, it ensured their reputation as the city's premier pop-punk-grunge-hardcore three-headed monster.

The Dirty Nil released follow-up single "Little Metal Baby Fist" in November of 2012, before focusing their efforts on the completion of a proper five-song EP, *Smite*. Fabled west coast punk label Fat Wreck Chords – home to NOFX, Sick Of It All, Lagwagon, Anti-Flag and Propagandhi – released the group's next seven-inch single, "Cinnamon," in August 2014. One month later, the band opened for Arkells on the main stage at Supercrawl. They followed that milestone by touring America from coast to coast on the 2015 Vans Warped Tour and signing to Dine

Alone Records for the release of their debut full-length record, *Higher Power*. Released in early 2016, the buzz surrounding the album allowed the Dirty Nil to gain a foothold across the Atlantic for the first time, as tour dates quickly piled up in England and Germany.

"Everything that I've seen has been overwhelmingly positive," an enthusiastic Bentham told *Exclaim!* not long after the album's release. "I personally had modest expectations about what [*Higher Power*] would do for us, and they've already been broken, so everything from here on out is gravy."

. . .

There's an OB O'Brien who exists in a world of gold chains and private jets. A world of beautiful women and luxury cars, of expensive champagne and designer clothing and Instagram posts from five-star resorts around the globe. At the centre of this decadent universe is the Once and Future King of Canadian hip-hop. The Boy. The 6 God. Aubrey Graham, better known to his millions of loyal disciples as Drake.

This is the OB O'Brien who so expertly plays the comic foil in Drake's immensely popular "Started From the Bottom" and "HYFR" music videos. The flamboyantly dressed, ginger-bearded, tattooed, scene-stealing ham who serves as a perfect counterpoint to Drake's smooth-talking, nouveau-playboy, larger-than-life celebrity persona. He's as fun to watch as he is to listen to.

Then there's the OB O'Brien who still goes by Matty when he's rolling through his childhood neighbourhood in Hamilton's west end, which is often. The version who attended Humber College to study in the school's renowned Comedy: Writing and Performance program. The one who adores his mother, idolizes his older brother and still counts neighbourhood friends from grade school among his closest allies. This is the version of the city's most well-known rapper-producer I know best. It's the very same Matt O'Brien I grew up with.

In a cool and quiet basement studio, a few blocks from Westdale Village and McMaster University, O'Brien is carefully rolling a fat joint. It's another long, hot evening in the middle of July 2013. Young children are laughing and playing on the street, spraying each other with a hose and licking banana popsicles.

"Do you smoke?" asks the twenty-nine-year-old. "I've also got some water, pop, Hennessy…whatever you want."

Within ten minutes, everyone in the room is lifted – including a friend of O'Brien's browsing Versace underwear on a MacBook Pro. The clean, comfortable studio is isolated from the rest of the basement by a pair of double glass doors with the blinds closed. Next to the entrance sits a futon, and beyond that a simple but efficient recording set-up mounted on a sleek white desk – complete with a pair of high-end studio monitors, a keyboard, and various samplers and other recording gear. The only splash of colour in the slate-coloured room is an oversized coffee-table book featuring the work of New York painting prodigy Jean-Michel Basquiat, a recent gift from lifelong friend and frequent collaborator Ori Haripko.

On the surface, O'Brien's public persona is all about flash and bravado. Tall, muscular, covered in tattoos, with an unmistakable red beard and thick glasses, he commands the room with a natural swagger and witty, off-colour quips. Outside of the limelight, he's quiet and surprisingly introspective as he looks back on his ten-year foray into the music business. During the late 1980s and early 1990s, Hamilton rock and blues mainstays such as Tim Gibbons, Brian Griffith and Junkhouse vocalist Tom Wilson were regulars in the O'Brien family household. They would frequently jam with teenage piano prodigy Jesse – a full decade older than his basketball-obsessed kid brother Matt. The boys' father, the late Michael O'Brien, was also a well-respected blues musician who encouraged musical education for his children from the time they were old enough to plunk a piano key.

"As I get older, I kind of, like, step out of it and think about it more. But when I was young, the biggest influence was just how natural and normal it was to be involved in music and stuff," he recalls. "I would always want to go to Grant Avenue (Daniel Lanois's famed east-end recording studio). Whenever my brother or my dad had a session there, I would always go check out Grant just to, like, take in vibes. I always just thought it was a cool place."

"To me, rap is today's form of blues," O'Brien explained to the *Hamilton Spectator* in 2012, reflecting on his unique musical upbringing. "I would say less melodic, but it shares some of the same themes as old blues, a lot of the same rhythms and chords."

By the time O'Brien had graduated from Westdale Secondary School in 2003, his dreams of becoming an NBA point guard were replaced with a new desire to break into the Southern Ontario hip-hop communities centred in Hamilton and Toronto. Fuelled by a love of California gangster rap – Westside Connection's "Bow Down" remains a favourite to this day – and with a natural technical flair for recording and engineering music, he began experimenting with friends and local writers before linking up with more prominent Hamilton MCs Tommy Knox and Arcane during the mid-2000s. Both would elevate the would-be producer to new levels, and expose him to a much wider audience.

"I recorded my album with OB in his studio in the west end," says Arcane, a two-time King of the Dot freestyle champion and two-time Grand Prix champion who released a well-received full-length offering, *Arcane*, in the summer of 2010. "We put in countless hours, you know what I mean? I've got nothing but respect for OB. He really helped me get through the experience of recording my first solo project. I was working a full-time job from, like, four or five in the morning until two in the afternoon. I'd get off work, and I'd have maybe an hour to eat, shower and get ready. Then it would be off to the studio to try to get some tracks recorded."

"OB's focus on production and songwriting has seen results," James Tennant wrote in *Hamilton Magazine*, as part of an extensive feature on the Westdale hitmaker. "OB has pulled in heavyweight co-writers like Ajax-born T-Minus, who worked with Drake, Nicki Minaj and Kendrick Lamar. He got rave reviews for his guest rhyme on 'Say I' by Toronto's Saukrates. He produced an album for local battle rap champion Arcane, all the while writing and producing his own tracks."

Toward the end of the decade, O'Brien began working on a song that would officially serve as his formal introduction to the city's music community. After years of toiling behind the scenes with the occasional local gig, O'Brien and a team of peers and collaborators launched the Funny Colour Money music label to help bolster their brand. It was through this vehicle for independent creative expression that the budding MC debuted his most popular track to date – "Hamilton." Recorded at home and featuring a smooth, looping piano sample from older brother Jesse, also known as "J-Beans," the hypnotic single elevated O'Brien to an entirely new plateau. But it was the accompanying music video – filmed in various iconic locales throughout the city, including Ivor Wynne Stadium, and released with a gritty black and white treatment – that truly set the tone.

"At that moment in time, I was just really Hamilton'd out," he begins. "I was working on shit, and I wasn't really out of town that much. I was just [in Hamilton] for a long time, starting the groundwork and the foundation for everything I was working on. I was at a point where I just started completely over, just started again ... I remember J-Beans brought over a piano riff, just an instrumental piece of music or whatever. I chopped it up and we found a loop of it and I just put drums to it and shit like that."

Lyrically, the song is an unmistakable love letter to the Steel City – with a subtle hint of melancholy and longing that is so often a stylistic trait of homegrown songwriters. The track's principal hook, "Hamilton/I'm goin' Hamilton/all the smog, all the fraud, all the gambling," is a nod to the conflicting emotions local residents so often grapple with. We love the city and despise it at the same time. We struggle to get clean and struggle with our demons. We long to return home after travelling abroad, but soon feel the walls closing in. Regardless, it's still home. And it always will be.

"A lot of people from Hamilton, it's like, they're either really proud to be from here or they're really, overly negative," offers O'Brien. "But Hamilton's always been cool to me. It's not that big of a deal either way. [The song] is just where I'm from and what I was doing. I just came up with the line and that ended up being the hook. It's just nine-oh-five 'til I fucking die."

"OB is definitely a very talented guy in his own right. This guy is potentially the biggest success of all [Hamilton rappers], and that's fabulous. It's well deserved. He's worked hard for it," says local producer and ex–Canadian Winter bassist Scott Peacock. "Drake is pretty solidified, but all that stuff, especially modern hip-hop, can just vanish overnight...I think being humble about [success] is always an excellent trait to see in an artist. That's usually the sign of a successful artist."

• • •

I stepped onto our wooden patio in the International Village, barefoot, and stared at the rear wall of Theatre Aquarius. It was a little after ten a.m. I placed my elbows on the chipped railing and balanced a mug of steaming coffee on the ledge. The sky was bright blue and cloudless, save two white jet streams running north and south. The air was still clean from the previous night's thunderstorm.

I was due to meet Mike and Tom at the Mulberry Coffeehouse in less than an hour. Ciara was visiting her family in St. Catharines for the weekend. I finished the last sip of coffee, poured the remaining drops over the railing and walked back inside to make breakfast and read the paper until it was time to go.

I arrived ten minutes late at the café. Mike was already at a table on the side patio, facing Mulberry Street. Tom was also running behind. I entered the shop and ordered an Americano and a glass of ice water. I glanced out the door and saw Tom whip around the front of the building on his bicycle, making a reckless turn onto Mulberry from James Street North. He barely avoided a speeding car, its horn echoing down the block. A group of loud teenagers entered the building, laughing as they settled into a booth. I could hear Tom chaining his bike to the wrought iron fence surrounding the patio. Within moments he was beside me, damp with sweat and peeling off a pair of white riding gloves.

"Drew, what's happening?" he asked, slapping my back. He was dripping.

"Not much, man. How are things?"

"Good, good."

"Did you see Mike out back?"

"No, I missed him. Is he out there?"

"I think I saw him on my way over, but he hadn't ordered anything. Let's get him a coffee."

Outside, Mike was unfurling a thin strip of plastic from a new box of cigarettes. He was wearing dark sunglasses with a pair of brown deck shoes dangling from his toes. I placed Mike's drink on the metal table and watched it wobble back and forth, spilling over the lip of the cup, dripping through the grate and onto the sidewalk.

"Fucking yes," he said, tipping his head back. "You read my mind." Mike tapped the cardboard box against his thigh and removed two cigarettes. "What's good?" he muttered, lighting up and tossing the packet of matches on the table. "How are you guys?"

We chatted and swapped stories, and let the morning slip away. Soon we were quiet, watching the traffic lurch along James Street, smoking and sipping, content to just be there with each other.

• • •

Ciara returned from St. Catharines and we spent the next few days preparing for a much-needed vacation. The morning of our trip, the air was thick and warm in our white, windowless bedroom. Our thin sheets had been pushed onto the floor during the night, along with my T-shirt. I rolled over toward Ciara but she was already awake and bouncing around the apartment, clothes and books and hair products piled at the foot of the bed. In the next room, I could hear water begin to splash against the tiles in the shower.

I walked into the living room in my boxer shorts and peered out at King Street East, still quiet in the pre-dawn haze. A lone taxi was parked near the front of Club Absinthe. The driver was sipping coffee, waiting for a fare. I checked my watch – it was 5:10 a.m. In less than an hour, we'd be hauling a pair of suitcases down three flights of dusty, carpeted stairs. Pearson Airport was our first stop.

I heard the water stop and walked back toward the bathroom.

"All set?" Ciara was peering from behind the shower curtain, smiling.

"Our bags are at the back door. Do you have anything else to pack?"

"We just need to bring the garbage down before we leave. Can you do that, babe?"

Later that morning, I peered out of the tiny oval window next to my seat and watched a heat wave rise from the simmering tarmac. I clicked the two sides of my metal seatbelt together and Ciara placed her head on my shoulder. I took a deep breath and unbuttoned the middle of my shirt, running my fingers over Stevie's initials on the left side of my chest. The plane taxied toward takeoff position as sunlight shifted across the inside of the cabin. Two gigantic engines began to roar as the plane charged down the runway. Wind rushed underneath the wings. The cabin rumbled and luggage bounced in the overhead compartments. I held my breath and squeezed both armrests.

Then the white nose of the plane tore into the pink morning sky and we took off toward the Pacific, San Francisco on the horizon. I watched as the houses and highways and buses and cars began to blur and fade out of sight as we entered the clouds.

EPILOGUE

As popular and successful as Hamilton's music scene became during the mid to late 2000s, the best and most intense movements always burn out as quickly as they were ignited. Hamilton's diverse community of punks, rockers, DJs and hip-hop heads was no exception. Some groups pushed forward, while others simply fizzled out. But there was no mistaking the fact that 2011 was a year of great transition for those at the centre of the Hamilton music scene.

Toronto Star music critic Ben Rayner wrote a long and detailed feature on the perpetually struggling Young Rival, which ran in the paper on April 13, 2011. He opened with a remarkably well-balanced assessment of their career to date: "Young Rival will have its day, no question, and Young Rival – aware of the strengths that it has worked exceedingly hard to develop – is itself quietly confident that it will have its day," Rayner wrote. "The stumbling block, however, is how long it's going to take to turn the cool kids on to a classicist power-pop trio that plays such a pure and timeless breed of rock 'n' roll that, perversely, it finds itself perpetually unfashionable." Young Rival never became superstars, but they still tour the globe with passion and vigour. They released a self-described "psych-croon" record *Interior Light* in 2015 via Toronto's Paper Bag Records, which received strong reviews, followed by an uptempo companion EP titled *Strange Light* the following year.

In August of 2011, Alexisonfire called it a career. "After ten years, Alexisonfire has decided to part ways," frontman George Pettit wrote in a heartfelt and candid open letter to fans, posted to the group's website. "Was the breakup amicable? Not really. Was it necessary? Probably. Regardless, the members of this band are my family and I wish them nothing but good fortune." Alexis would re-form for a string of international shows in 2012 and 2015, including a sold-out performance at Hamilton's Copps Coliseum on December 29, 2012. They're scheduled to play a number of festival dates in Australia in 2017, but no permanent reunion is on the horizon.

One month later, Dan Griffin – whose natural musicality and technical flare had guided Arkells from basement jam rooms in Westdale Village to the country's most famous concert halls – left the group prior to the release of *Michigan Left* to pursue a law degree at the University of Windsor. Griffin was replaced by Toronto-based pianist and musical virtuoso Anthony Carone, who soon became a full-time member. "Dan's still part of the gang, that's how we look at it," Kerman told me not long after Griffin's departure. "He'll always be a friend." Arkells released their third record, *High Noon*, in 2014, with Carone now fully involved, and earned two more Juno Awards the following year in the city that launched their career. During the March 20, 2015, awards ceremony, the band performed the song "Come to Light" in front of a full house at Hamilton's FirstOntario Centre, accompanied by the National Academy Orchestra of Canada. The band's fourth record – the decidedly poppier *Morning Report* – was released August 5, 2016.

Nearly a decade after launching one of the most successful club nights in Hamilton's history, Club Absinthe was also

EPILOGUE

preparing to embark on a whole new adventure – only long-time Motown DJs Owen Smith and Ashish Sharma were no longer along for the ride. "At some point I felt like the hassle of this was outweighing the enjoyment, and it totally was," says Smith, before letting out a big sigh. "I don't regret it and [Club Absinthe] is doing well still, so good for them. I don't ever think anything bad about those guys, because they gave me an opportunity."

Smith officially pulled the plug in November 2011, ending his long-time relationship with the establishment that made him a local star. The club's transition to its new digs at 38 King William Street also prompted the closure of another legendary downtown club, the Pepper Jack Café. On New Year's Eve 2011, the original Club Absinthe held its final party in its hallowed and notorious location at 233 King Street East. A few days later, Lubarda, long-time business partner Billy Pozeg and other staffers quietly packed up their remaining supplies and souvenirs, and prepared to host their first Motown Wednesdays event at the club's new digs on King William Street – in the former home of Inouye's Pepper Jack Café, and just around the corner from the bourgeoning music and art scene on James Street North.

"The Pepper Jack closing marked sort of an end of an era for me," says Terra Lightfoot. "That was the place I grew up in musically and where I learned to play solo. Ken [Inouye] hired me for all sorts of things there, and in a way he sort of took a chance on me by letting me open bigger and bigger shows...I still have pieces of that place with me, I have a bunch of their wine glasses and a giant yucca plant that Ken gave me when the place closed down."

On the other side of the downtown core, McNamee and Gurman continue to soldier on as Rockstars for Hire, maintaining their traditional Friday residency at Che. However, their closest musical peers and allies in the city's wild club DJ scene have all but called it a career. For Simon Toye, the original Disco/Punk series began its slow death as soon as routine became a factor. By 2011, the twenty-nine-year-old had quietly walked away from the revolutionary nightclub empire he had built with a handful of friends from McMaster, and resigned himself to the odd club gig in Hess Village and other venues throughout the city.

"The greatest thing for me, initially, with doing that night, was the challenge of just doing something totally unproven and untested and making it work," says Toye. "And then when it did, you know, you can't reinvent the wheel every week. At that point you just have a thing, and you have to stick to it...once I had lost that hunger, I just kind of got turned off."

By the end of 2011, Sailboats Are White, Cities in Dust, Pantychrist, Cursed, Vatican Chainsaw Massacre, the Reason, Canadian Winter, Huron and several other groups had either imploded or exhausted their original runs. They were soon replaced by a new wave of local bands, including the likes of synth-rock innovators New Hands and Illitry; punk iconoclasts Born Wrong and Flesh Rag; and garage rock street rats Pet Sun and Billy Moon, among many others. Young, hungry rappers and producers such as Emay, Aaron Hutchinson and Mother Tareka ushered in a new era of Hamilton hip-hop, building an underground scene around the Hamilton Audio Visual Node (HAVN) on Barton Street East. Still, many in the old guard maintained a quiet optimism. Looking back, it was easy to see just how much the scene had grown and evolved during such a short period of time.

"I think Hamilton has always had this magnetic thing where artists are drawn to the city," says local hip-hop producer SUPA 83. "There are a lot of artistic people out here. A lot of people just go to work, come home and they're just doing music. That's really how it is. If you were to have X-ray vision and look into people's houses, there's a big chance that they'll probably be musicians. I feel like it's a real diamond in the rough for all types of music. That's the one thing I love about this city."

"I think there definitely was something special happening during this time in Hamilton," adds Harlan Pepper's Dan Edmonds, reflecting on the subtle transitions in the scene around 2011. "Maybe pop music at the time wasn't the greatest, and it was sort of a do-it-yourself ideology that was going around Hamilton, in the high schools and the universities, to form your own bands and write your own songs…people were getting together and recording songs and writing songs, and that's good for any sort of artist community."

"There were a lot of bands who were pushing through the odds, or pushing against them, which was very commendable," adds San Sebastian guitarist Brodie Dawson. "There were a lot of venues opening up and new spaces all over the place, and then there was all of the art stuff we had involved in that, too…it's kind of interesting that the indie scene, with all of the genres mixed together, is kind of holding its own now. The past five years were the build up, and it's only going to keep getting better."

ACKNOWLEDGEMENTS

I owe this book's completion to my wife, Ciara McCann. Your patience, kindness and good humour keep me centred and motivated. I would also like to thank my parents, Patricia and David; my sister, Allison; and the extended Baulcomb, Baird, Beale, Kaye, McCann and Turnbull families for your ongoing love and support. Noelle Allen, my editor at Wolsak & Wynn, took a chance on this project and helped transform a loose collection of transcripts and anecdotes into something I'm incredibly proud of. I owe a great deal of thanks to the rest of the team at W&W – Ashley Hisson, Paul Vermeersch and Joe Stacey – for championing this book. Andrew Wilmot, surely one of the best copy editors in Canada, was instrumental in bringing the final draft home. Liz Worth and Sam Sutherland, whose work I admire greatly, were more kind and accommodating than necessary as I peppered them with questions during the book's early stages. Krista Foss, my confidant and sounding board while writing the first two drafts of *Evenings & Weekends*, was invaluable as a mentor and a friend. Max Kerman, who invited me on the road with Arkells while I was working for the *Hamilton Spectator*, unknowingly sparked this entire project and never turned down an interview request – even at the eleventh hour. To all of the innovative, passionate, generous musicians who appear in these pages, I can't thank you enough for inviting me into your homes and lives. I would be remiss if I didn't acknowledge the impact of Dave Bidini, Michael Barclay, Ian A.D. Jack, and Jason Schneider, whose salient observations about underground music and Canadian culture left a big impression on me during my teenage years. To all of the independent bookshops and record stores around the world, keep fighting the good fight. To all of my friends – those who are still here and those who departed far too soon – thank you for simply being you.

SELECTED BANDS AND MUSICIANS:

...And You Will
    Know Us By The
    Trail of Dead
Alexisonfire
Arcane
Arctic Monkeys
Arkells
Attack in Black
Bedouin Soundclash
Born Wrong
Broken Social Scene
Brown, Dex
Bruce Peninsula
Burning Love
By Divine Right
Canadian Winter
Caribou
Change of Heart
Charlemagne
Cheese Shop Paddy
Chokehold
Chore
Cities in Dust

City and Colour
Constantines
Cowlick
Crowbar
Crux of Aux
Cuff the Duke
Cursed
Daft Punk
Death From Above
    1979
Dell'Unto, Robyn
Dinner Belles, The
Diodes, The
Don Vail
Doucet, Luke
    (Whitehorse)
Drake
Edwards, Kathleen
Electroluminescent
Elkas, Peter
Elliott Brood
Ellison, John
Emay

En Francais
Flesh Rag
Flux AD
Forgotten Rebels
Gunnar, Hansen
Harlan Pepper
Hawkins, Ronnie
Hayden
Haymaker
Henderson, Rachael
Hoosier Poet
HUREN
Huron
Hutchinson, Aaron
Hypodust
Illitry
Johnston, B. A.
Jones, Miles
June & July
Junior Boys
Junkhouse
Justice
Killjoys, The

EVENINGS & WEEKENDS

Knox, Tommy
Lanza, Jessy
LeE HARVeY OsMOND
Left for Dead
Lightfoot, Terra
Lighthouse
London, Sara
Long John Baldry
Marble Index, The
McClelland, Melissa (Whitehorse)
Miramichi
Monster Truck
Moon, Billy
Motëm
Mother Tareka
Neighbourhood Noise
Newell, Richard (King Biscuit Boy)
New Hands
New Slang
Northern Chorus, A
O'Brien, OB
Owls, The
Pantychrist
Pet Sun
Phoenix
Plaskett, Joel
Pumps
Racket, The
Realistic
Reason, The

Red Echo
Reed, Lee
Rest, The
Ride Theory, The
Riotstar
Roberts, Sam
Rockstars for Hire
Sailboats Are White
Saint Alvia
San Sebastian
SebastiAn
Secret Heights
Shallow North Dakota
SIANspheric
Simply Saucer
Sloan
Snake Charmer
Social Divorce
Stills, The
Strokes, The
SUPA 83
Surly Young Bucks, The
Swarm, The
Teenage Head
Tegan and Sara
Tell the Divers
Threat Signal
Thrush Hermit
Tokyo Police Club
Tragically Hip, The
Treble Charger
Tristan Psionic

TV Freaks
Uncut
Vatican Chainsaw Massacre
Viletones, The
warsawpack
Weakerthans, The
WTCHS
Young Rival

MUSICIANS AND INDUSTRY PROFESSIONALS INTERVIEWED:

Andrew, Jamie
(Valleyview Studios)

Annobil, Kobi
(Canadian
Winter)

Bentham, Luke
(The Dirty Nil)

Bentley, Adam
(The Rest)

Bourassa, Matt
(Sailboats Are
White)

Colohan, Chris
(Cursed)

Damptey, Kojo
"Easy"

Dawson, Brodie
(Pumps, San Sebastian)

DeAngelis, Mike
(Charlemagne,
Arkells)

Delottinville, Danielle
(Pantychrist)

Dika, Nick
(Charlemagne,
Arkells)

Douglas, Kevin
(Sailboats Are
White)

Drake, Alex (Arcane)

Eberhard, Gregory
(Motëm)

Edmonds, Dan
(Harlan Pepper)

Fisher, Kyle
(The Dirty Nil)

Fralick, Noah
(The Ride Theory,
Young Rival)

Goldstein, Aaron
(Huron)

Greenspan, Jeremy
(Junior Boys)

Griffin, Dan
(Charlemagne,
Arkells)

Gurman, Aaron
(Rockstars for
Hire)

Harvey, Jon
(Monster Truck)

Hawley, Brett
(Gunnar Hansen)

Henderson, Rachael
(DJ Donna
Lovejoy)

Inouye, Ken
(Pepper Jack
Café)

Katz, Becky

Kerman, Max
(Charlemagne,
Arkells)

Kiely, Steve
(Monster Truck)

Keire, Mike (Threshold Recording Studio)
Kuchmey, Kyle (The Ride Theory, Young Rival)
Lightfoot, Terra (The Dinner Belles)
Lubarda, Marko (Club Absinthe)
Malcolm, Cam (Huron)
McDonald, Scott (Che Burrito & Lounge)
McNamee, Christopher (Rockstars for Hire)
Nardi, Dave (The Dirty Nil)
Nelan, James "Cubby" (The Reason)
Nicolson, Nicole
O'Brien, Matt (OB O'Brien)
O'Connor, David (Vatican Chainsaw Massacre, TV Freaks)

Peacock, Scott (Canadian Winter)
Pearson, Sean (Boxcar Sound Recording)
Pettit, George (Alexisonfire)
Potocic, Tim (Sonic Unyon Records, Supercrawl)
Pozeg, Billy (Club Absinthe)
Raback, Lee (Lee Reed, warsawpack, Peoples Republic)
Robinson, Leon (Crown A Thornz)
Rockingham, Graham (*Hamilton Spectator*)
Sakala, Aaron (Realistic, warsawpack, Peoples Republic)
Schwendiman, William "Brodie" (The Underground, The Casbah)

Sheeler, Kevin (Vatican Chainsaw Massacre, Social Divorce,)
Smith, Jamie "Gunner"
Smith, Owen (Motown Wednesdays)
Tennant, James (McMaster University's 93.3 CFMU)
Toye, Simon (Cities in Dust)
Troup, Daniel (Snake Charmer, Social Divorce)
Veerman, Greg (Pumps, San Sebastian)
White, Adam (The Reason)
Wilson, Madeline (Front Room Entertainment)
Wright, Graham (Tokyo Police Club)

ANDREW BAULCOMB is a freelance writer and former reporter based in Hamilton, Ontario, Canada. His interviews and music features have appeared in *Vice*, the *Hamilton Spectator, I Heart Hamilton, Zink Magazine, Niagara This Week, View Magazine* and several other publications. In 2008, he graduated from McMaster University with a combined honours degree in Cultural Studies & Critical Theory and Art History. For more than a decade, his fascination with Hamilton's thriving arts scene and shifting cultural identity has informed much of his work.